BOLIVAR

A Continent and its Destiny

Simón Bolívar.

BOLIVAR

A Continent and its Destiny

by

J. L. Salcedo-Bastardo

Edited and Translated
by
Annella McDermott
Lecturer in the Department of Hispanic and
Latin-American Studies of the University
of Bristol

The Richmond Publishing Co. Ltd.
1978

English Edition first published 1977 by
The Richmond Publishing Co. Ltd.

2nd English impression (eighth overall impression)
published 1978 by
The Richmond Publishing Co. Ltd.,
Orchard Road, Richmond, Surrey, England.

ISBN 0 85546 201 9

Typeset by Computacomp (UK) Ltd.,
Fort William, Scotland
and printed in Great Britain by
Kingprint Limited, Richmond, Surrey

CONTENTS

Author's note

I am delighted that this work, in Miss McDermott's excellent translation, is being made available to English-speaking readers. It is my sincere hope that it will contribute to knowledge and understanding of the Latin American continent and its future, through one of its great historical figures.

It is worth pointing out that Bolívar knew and admired Great Britain, which he visited in 1810, and that he always had British officers in his immediate circle. He helped to promote understanding between the two peoples, and expressed the desire that the New World should find inspiration in the British virtues of common sense, stability and respect for others, and would achieve true freedom and democracy without sacrificing its identity.

He also admired those sons of Great Britain, the North Americans, whom he visited in 1807 and amongst whom he first saw in operation 'rational liberty'. He called them a 'model people, which has combined the greatest sum of social happiness with the power which produces order and liberty'. One hardly needs to add that his admiration for the Anglo-Saxon peoples in no way compromised his political beliefs nor the direction of his revolutionary, republican and anti-imperialist aims.

I should like to dedicate this book to the friendship which I formed on a number of occasions with the students of the Universities of London, Oxford, Cambridge, Liverpool, Edinburgh, Manchester, Bristol, Columbia, Chicago, Harvard, Stanford and Berkeley.

J. L. Salcedo-Bastardo
Paris, 13 October, 1976.

EDITOR'S NOTE

In the interests of clarity for the English-speaking reader I have, with the agreement of the author, abbreviated some sections and added explanatory comments. This work was originally written in Spanish and in view of the specialized nature of many of the terms used, I have written a version rather than a direct translation of the original. In some cases, I have retained the Spanish terms, defining them when necessary in the select glossary. For advice on the translation of specialized terms and for general assistance and advice I am indebted to Dr. M. P. Costeloe and Dr. G. Carl of the University of Bristol.

A. McD.

Select glossary

adelantado : In Spain, an official who acted in the name of the King. In colonial Spanish America, an official possessed of a combination of executive, legislative and judicial powers, similar to a military governor.

audiencia : high court of justice.

ayuntamiento : town council.

cabildo : town council.

cacique : Indian chief.

caudillo : 'leader'. In the early 19th century, the term was used of military leaders, especially in the Independence Wars. Later, political boss, a person of influence in the political affairs of a province or even a nation; the term was often applied to dictators.

Colombia : in Bolívar's period this referred to the union of present-day Colombia, Venezuela, Ecuador, and Panamá. The name *Gran* (Greater) *Colombia* was introduced later to distinguish this union from present-day Colombia.

consulado : merchant guild and its court.

criollo : person of Spanish descent born in America.

encomienda : grant of Indians. The Indians performed services and paid tribute to the *encomendero*.

hacienda : large landed estate.

latifundio : large estates, of thousands of acres, often absentee-owned and inefficiently worked.

llanos : grassy plains in Venezuela, used for cattle-raising. The inhabitants are the *llaneros*.

mantuanos : term used in Venezuela for the local white aristocracy.

mestizo : person of mixed race, strictly speaking one of mixed white and Indian ancestry.

pardo : general term for person of mixed racial ancestry.

zambo : person of mixed Indian and negro ancestry.

Select guide to persons and places mentioned

Angostura: former name of Ciudad Bolívar, Venezuela, site of the Congress (1819) at which Bolívar attempted to create an institutional basis for the independence movement.

Antioquia: department of north-western Colombia.

Apure: state in south-western Venezuela: also a tributary of the Orinoco.

Aragua: state in Venezuela, close to Caracas.

Arequipa: town and department of Peru, on the Pacific coast.

Aroa: town now in the state of Yaracuy, Venezuela.

Asunción: present-day capital of Paraguay.

Ayacucho: city and province of south central Peru, site of the battle (1824) which ended Spanish domination of Latin America.

Barinas: state of Venezuela in the *llanos* region.

Bello, Andrés (1781-1865): Venezuelan educationalist, legal expert, grammarian and man of letters.

Bogotá: capital of Colombia, known in the colonial period as *Santa Fe de Bogotá.*

Bolivia: named in honour of Bolívar, formerly known as *Alto Perú.*

Bombóna: near Pasto, site of an indecisive battle (1822).

Boves, José Tomás (1782-1814): Spanish-born leader of royalist guerrillas in Venezuela.

Boyacá: south-west of Tunja, Colombia, site of the battle (1819) which freed New Granada (Colombia) from Spanish domination.

Briceño Méndez, Pedro: one of the leaders of the Venezuelan independence movement.

Bucaramanga: town in Colombia in which Bolívar lived for a time.

Buria: town in the state of Yaracuy, Venezuela, famous in the colonial period for its gold mines.

Callao: principal port of Peru.

Carabobo: province of Venezuela, site of the battle (1821) which freed the greater part of Venezuela and New Granada from Spanish domination.

Caracas: capital of Venezuela, known in the colonial period as *Santiago de León de Caracas.*

Cariaco: village on the eastern coast of Venezuela, site of a Congress (1817).

Carora: city in western-central Venezuela.

Cartagena: port in Colombia.

Carúpano: city and port on the eastern coast of Venezuela.

Casanare: city in the *llanos* of Venezuela: also a tributary of the Orinoco.

Cajamarca: department of Peru.

Chacachacare: Venezuelan island between Trinidad and the Paria Peninsula.

Charallave: town in the state of Miranda, Venezuela.

Chavín: important archaeoligical site on the shores of Lake Titicaca, Bolivia.

Chayonta: town in Bolivia.

Chichén Itzá: archaeological site in northeastern Yucatán Peninsula, formerly an important Mayan ceremonial centre.

Chillán: city and department of Chile.

Chimborazo: one of the highest Andean peaks, in Ecuador.

Choco: province of Colombia.

Chumbivilcas: town in Peru.

Chuquisaca: department of what is now Bolivia.

Cochabamba: city and department of Bolivia.

Conchucos: former province of Peru.

Copán: Mayan archaeological site in Western Honduras.

Coro: city and region on the western coast of Venezuela.

Cúcuta: city in Colombia, near the border with Venezuela. The Congress of Cúcuta (1821) made Bolívar the first Constitutional President of *Gran Colombia*.

Cumaná: city and (formerly) province of Venezuela.

Cundinamarca: province of Colombia: also an earlier name for *New Granada*.

Cuzco: city in Peru, formerly the capital of the Inca Empire.

El Tocuyo: city in the state of Lara, Venezuela.

Flores, Juan José (1801-1864): cavalry officer in Bolívar's army, later President of Ecuador.

Gran Colombia (Greater Colombia): political union of present-day Colombia, Venezuela, Ecuador and Panama, established in 1819, broke up in 1830.

Gual, Manuel: leader of a revolutionary movement to free Venezuela from Spanish domination.

Gual, Pedro: Venezuelan politician of the independence period.

Guárico: province in central Venezuela.

Guayana (or Guaiana): a province of Venezuela (now Estado Bolívar) south of the Orinoco.

Guayaquil: principal port and city of Ecuador.

Guayas: river in Ecuador.

Güigüe: town in the state of Carabobo, Venezuela.

Güiria: Venezuelan port on the Paria Peninsula.

Guyana: formerly British Guiana, now an independent republic in north-eastern South America.

Junín: in the Peruvian central highlands, site of the battle (1824) which was a notable victory for the patriot forces.

La Paz: capital of present-day Bolivia.

La Victoria: town in Venezuela.

León: city of Nicaragua. During the colonial period, it was the capital of the province of Nicaragua, which was under the *Audiencia* of Guatemala.

Los Cayos (Les Cayes or *Aux Cayes):* town in south-western Haiti.

Magdalena: river in Colombia.

Maracaibo: city and province of Venezuela.

Margarita: large island off the coast of Venezuela.

Mariño, Santiago (1788-1854): one of the leaders of the Venezuelan independence movement.

Miranda, Francisco de (1750-1816): Venezuelan precursor of independence and the leader of the First Venezuelan Republic. In 1812, he was granted full dictatorial authority, to meet the royalist offensive led by Domingo Monteverde. Having capitulated to Monteverde, he was prevented from leaving Venezuela by the patriots and arrested by the Spaniards in violation of the terms of the capitulation. He was taken to Spain where he died in prison in 1816.

Monay: small town and region in the state of Trujillo, Venezuela.

Monte Albán: archaeological site a few miles south of Oaxaca, southern Mexico, formerly a ceremonial centre of the Zapotec Indians.

Monteverde, Domingo: leader of a royalist insurrection in Coro, Venezuela, in 1812.

Morillo, Pablo: Spanish commander of the expeditionary forces sent to America by Napoleon.

New Granada, Viceroyalty of: created in 1717. An older name for the area, now the Republic of Colombia, was Cundinamarca.

New Spain, Viceroyalty of: in the colonial period, this viceroyalty included present-day Mexico, Central America, the southern half of the United States, the Antilles and the Phillipine Islands.

Nirgua: a small town in the state of Yaracuy, Venezuela.

Ocaña: city in the state of Santander, Colombia, site of a Convention (1828) at which Bolívar tried unsuccessfully to avert the break-up of *Gran Colombia* by constitutional reform.

Ocumare: port in the state of Carabobo, Venezuela.

O'Higgins, Bernardo (1778-1824): principal hero of Chilean independence and Supreme Dictator of Chile (1817-1823).

O'Leary, Daniel F. (1800?-1854): Born in Cork, Ireland, O'Leary went to South America in 1818 as a member of a cavalry corps recruited in Great Britain. He fought in the independence wars and acted as Bolívar's personal envoy during and after the wars. He compiled a thirty-two volume work *Memorias del General O'Leary* which published by his son in Caracas between 1879 and 1881. Only the three volumes of the *Narración* can properly be called memoirs, the other twenty-nine volumes consisting of documents and letters to or by Bolívar.

Orinoco: river which rises in the border region between Brazil and Venezuela and crosses the southern edge of the Venezuelan *llanos*.

Oriente: a general name for several provinces in north-eastern Venezuela.

Oruro: a department of Bolivia.

Páez, José Antonio (1790-1873): hero of the Venezuelan independence movement. In 1826, Páez launched a revolt in favour of greater local autonomy within *Gran Colombia*, which he ended in January 1827 in return for an amnesty from Bolívar. Late in 1829, he led a successful movement to make Venezuela entirely separate from Gran Colombia. He was President of Venezuela for three terms and Dictator from 1861 to 1863, after which he was exiled and spent the last ten years of his life in New York.

Palacio Fajardo, Manuel: Venezuelan patriot and writer of the independence period.

Palacios, Esteban: uncle and godfather to Bolívar, he lived for a time in Madrid.

Palenque: ruined ancient Maya city in the state of Chiapas, Mexico.

Pasto: Andean town and region of Colombia.

Pernambuco: state of Brazil, site of an unsuccessful republican revolt in 1817.

Peru, Viceroyalty of: created in 1542, it originally included all of present-day Spanish South America, except the coast of Venezuela. The territories of present-day Colombia, Ecuador and Panamá were detached from its jurisdiction in 1739, as were those of present-day Argentina, Uruguay, Paraguay and eastern Bolivia in 1776.

Perú de Lacroix, Louis Gabriel: French soldier who emigrated to the West Indies and offered his services to Bolívar. On his death, he left some historical writings and his *Diario de Bucaramanga* which describes Bolívar's daily life during his stay in that city.

Pétion, Alexandre Sabès (1770-1818): one of the heroes of Haitian independence and President of Haiti 1807-1818.

Piar, Manuel (1782-1817): one of the heroes of Venezuelan independence, a mulatto from Curaçao.

Pichincha: to the west of Quito, Ecuador, site of the last major battle of the independence struggle in Ecuador (1822).

Picornell, Juan Bautista: Spanish intellectual who together with Manuel Gual and Jose María España fomented a movement to free Venezuela from Spanish domination.

Puerto Cabello: city and port of Venezuela.

Quito: present-day capital of Ecuador. In the colonial period, what is now Ecuador was known as the Province of Quito.

Recife: city in Pernambuco, Brazil.

Revenga, José Rafael: Venezuelan patriot and politician of the independence period.

Rivadavia, Bernardino (1780-1845): President of Argentina 1826-27, regarded as one of the founders of the Argentine Republic.

Rodríguez, Simón (1771-1851): Bolívar's private tutor.

Rodríguez Francia, José Gaspar (1776-1840): Supreme Dictator of Paraguay.

Roscio, Juan Germán (1769-1821): Venezuelan patriot and politician of the independence period.

San Martín, José de (1778-1850): principal leader of the independence movement in Argentina and southern South America. After Peruvian independence, he assumed full military and political command with the title of Protector of Peru. After an interview with Bolívar at Guayaquil in 1822, he resigned as Protector of Peru. In 1824 he left South America.

Santander, Francisco de Paula (1792-1840): Colombian general and political leader in the independence period, Vicepresident of *Gran Colombia* 1821-1827. When Bolívar replaced him in 1827, Santander became the rallying-point for Bolívar's opponents, and after an attempt was made on Bolívar's life in 1828, Santander was exiled. He returned to become President of Colombia, 1832-1836.

Sucre, Antonio José de (1795-1830): Venezuelan general, victor at the battles of Pichincha and Ayacucho. He became the first Constitutional President of Bolivia, 1826-1828, and was assassinated in 1830.

Tacubaya: town in Mexico to which the Panamá Congress of 1826 moved.

Teotihuacán: Archaeological site about twenty miles north of Mexico City.

Tiahuanaco: archaeological site on the south shore of Lake Titicaca.

Tikal: Mayan archaeological site in Guatemala.

Tucumán: province of present-day Argentina.

Tumbes: river which flows through Peru and Ecuador.

Tunja: city in Colombia.

Tuy: Fertile region in the state of Miranda, Venezuela.

Unanué, José Hipólito de (1755-1833): Peruvian writer, naturalist and political leader of the independence period. He was a minister during the first independence governments.

Urdaneta, Rafael (1789-1845): Venezuelan patriot, one of Bolívar's close military collaborators.

Urubamba: city and province of Peru.

Uxmal: archaeological site in Mexico.

ILLUSTRATIONS

I The Background

An intermediate Society

Bolívar's political career spanned an area of approximately 5,000,000 square kilometres in the north and west of South America, from the southern border of Central America to the northern frontiers of Chile and Argentina, and from the Pacific over the Andes to the Amazonian borders of Brazil and up to the Atlantic and Caribbean coastlines.

Within this extensive territory can be found a greater variety of natural phenomena than anywhere else on earth. There are marked differences of landscape, climate and especially topography; mountains, valleys, plains, rivers like the Orinoco, the Magdalena, the Guayas and the Tumbes, impenetrable jungles and inhospitable deserts. It contains all the rich variety of flora and fauna to be found in the Latin American continent.

At the time of the Discovery, America's most characteristic feature was the diversity of peoples and cultures. Three different types of society can be distinguished; in fact, one could talk of three different Americas: (i) the most highly advanced, with the largest population, (ii) less advanced, fairly densely inhabited, with an inferior cultural level to (i) but superior to that of (iii) the scattered communities which correspond to the vast expanses of sparsely-populated land.

The first, highly developed type of society was to be found in the area which extends from Mexico to the north of Chile. There were two important zones within this area: the first, in the north, stretched from Mexico to Nicaragua, and the second, in the south, embraced Ecuador, Peru, Bolivia and the north of Argentina. In the first of these zones, the Aztecs developed a civilization which, despite the ruthless destruction of its remains by the Spaniards, continues to astonish the world. One thousand years before Christ, the Mayas had dominated this area and created a brilliant civilization. They had a relatively sophisticated system of writing and an advanced knowledge of Mathematics and Astronomy. Traces of their highly developed culture are to be seen in the remains of cities such as Copán, Palenque, Chichén Itzá, Tulum, Uxmal and Mayapán. Subsequently, different groups achieved supremacy, such as the Toltecs, the Zapotecs and the Chichimecs. Finally, it was the turn of the Aztecs, who in 1325 founded Tenochtitlán, the original site of the modern capital, Mexico City.

Similarly in the southern zone, the area of influence of the Incas, there was a succession of different civilizations. And there, too, the ruins of towns like Cuzco continue to astonish modern man. There were two important centres around Lake Titicaca: Tiahuanaco and Chavín. The Quechua Indians created an important empire, ruled over by the Incas, who gave their name to the most significant culture of South America, technologically inferior to those of the Mayas and the Aztecs, but socially more advanced. It, too, was ravaged by the attacks of the Spaniards.

Acting as a sort of bridge between the two most advanced areas, centred on Mexico and Peru, was the area of the Indians loosely called Chibcha, which corresponds to (ii) in the schema outlined above. It was fairly densely inhabited, and its population well fed thanks to a system of agriculture that was at an interesting stage of development. It was famous for the Quimbaya Indian potters and goldsmiths, and surviving goldwork testifies to the perfection of their art. They did not leave spectacular architectural monuments. Within this second or intermediate group, endeavouring to simplify the very complex pre-Columbian situation, one could perhaps include the Caribbean Tainos and the Araucanians of Chile, both groups somewhat inferior to the Chibchas. The third America, at the bottom of the scale, was characterised by poverty, primitivism and endless war, by very simple cultural manifestations, an elementary political and social structure and a sparse population. Its people were nomads, scattered and utterly diverse in their languages, beliefs and customs.

Concentrating on socio-political aspects of the continent during the long pre-Columbian period, we find amongst the Aztecs a theocratic and military structure, and a social hierarchy, tending to the creation of an aristocracy. The Incas were ruled by a centralised, absolute régime. The Chibchas, Tainos, Araucanians, Timoto-Cuicas, Tupis, Guaranis and Caribs, as well as many groups belonging to the third category, had one belief in common with the Aztecs and Incas: that of the insignificance of the individual. Compared with the majesty and power of the state, in the case of the advanced, complex societies, or with the simple tyrannical authority of the *cacique* or chief, in the case of the primitive tribal societies, the individual was nothing. He belonged to the chief or sovereign and passed as booty to the conqueror. There was slavery in pre-Columbian South America and cannibalism and human sacrifice were practised in various places.

Within Bolívar's sphere of activity, which included the present-day Republics of Panamá, Colombia, Venezuela, Ecuador, Peru and Bolivia, there were representatives of the three Americas. In this sense, it occupies a central or intermediate position in the hemisphere.

The Venezuela of the colonial period into which Bolívar was born was racially mixed, though the Indian element was slight. There was not the overwhelming native Indian population that there was in Mexico and Peru, nor the complete absence one observes in areas where the Indians were exterminated, and only the negro and white races were left to mingle with each other. Careful investigation has revealed that there were not more than 350,000 inhabitants in the 1,000,000 square kilometres of the region at the beginning of the Conquest. For various reasons, there was a long and bloody confrontation between this Indian population and the Spaniards.

In the first place, there did not exist the unity which would have enabled the Spaniards to capture the capital or nerve centre and so gain control of the entire area and its inhabitants. The Indians were divided into numerous groups; no fewer than fifteen language families, apart from many dialects, have been found in this area, within which modern anthropology discerns about ten 'cultural areas' in the pre-Columbian period. Dominating the Indians meant overcoming them group by group, or annihilating them. The Conquest, in Venezuela, could not, therefore, be rapid and bloodless. It was not so much a war as a massacre. A considerable number of the Indians were Caribs, known to be brave warriors. The cultural level of the majority of the Indians, however, with the possible exception of the Timoto-Cuicas in the Andean region, was one of the lowest in the hemisphere. Nevertheless, the Indian population, though decimated by the Spaniards, did not disappear completely in the confrontation, and it served as a base for the racial mixture that gave rise to the Venezuelan people. The cultural, spiritual and psychic characteristics of the Indian, however we define these qualitatively and quantitatively, were passed on to the races which emerged from their mingling with the white and black populations.

It is worthwhile to emphasise this factor of the diversity of Indian cultures in Bolívar's native land. There was no such thing as 'the Venezuelan Indian'. There were Indians, not very many, with striking differences between them, in physical and genetic characteristics, in culture and in geographical distribution. There were notable variations in colour or shade of skin, in size, in shape of skull, in eyes and lips. It can be deduced that such diversity was the result of earlier racial mixtures, previous to the Discovery.

The Spaniards who arrived in Venezuela, the so-called 'white element', carried within themselves traces of many of the people of Asia Minor and Europe, as well as of many African races, brought to the Iberian Peninsula by the Arab conquerors. About sixteen different races were combined in the Spaniards. Moreover, people came not only from Castile, but also from Aragon, Andalusia, Extremadura and Leon, followed by others from the Basque Country and Catalonia. The Spaniards came without women and interbreeding was frequent. The number of Spanish *conquistadores* in Venezuela was very small; it is estimated that not more than 5,000 arrived in the first 100 years after Columbus. This group, tiny in relation to the number of Indians, had the advantages of cultural unity, in politics, language and religion, and technological superiority, especially in weapons. The product of the combination of Indians and Spaniards took its tone from Spain and western civilisation. 'Its symbols' as one author points out, 'were not the African fetish nor the Indian totem-pole. Its symbols were universalised versions of Spanish symbols. In historical terms, we represent the evolution of the Spanish world.'[1]

The African was brought to the melting-pot of Latin America by force. The number of negroes brought to Venezuela was also relatively small: approximately 10,000 in the first 100 years. There were no economic or other motives to justify importing a larger mass of slaves. Anthropologists insist, in relation to the controversial question of 'race' that the black races are those which show the greatest variation, and this diversity was evident in the forced migration to America. Again, it is worth insisting that there were not only physical and genetic differences, but even greater cultural differences.

In the Venezuelan, this mixed background is seen perhaps more clearly than in any other people of America, and we should keep it in mind when examining Bolívar's actions. There were the Indians, with strong traces of their Asian inheritance, and possibly a Polynesian influence, through contacts across the Pacific, as suggested recently by expeditions like that of the Kon-Tiki. The Spaniards brought traces of the European peoples, Iberians, Ligurians, Celts, Romans, Basques, Greeks, the Germanic peoples, Visigoths, Swabians and Vandals. Asia Minor also arrived, with traces of the Phoenicians, Jews, Arabian Muslims: and Africa, with the inheritance from the peoples of Carthage, Egypt, Lybia, Tunisia, Algeria, Morocco, the Congo and Niger, who had poured in waves over the Iberian Peninsula. Africa also appeared in her own right in the Bantu, Sudanese and Yorubas, torn from their native cultures and thrust into humiliating slavery.

All these races and cultures flowed together onto the soil of Venezuela, which had once been also the cross-roads of internal migration, for this area saw the passage of many groups, moving from the Caribbean to the south or viceversa, or from east to west or west to east all along its coastline. After the Discovery, the mingling of races came about, resulting in a highly diversified and completely mixed race. This open and favourable attitude to the mixture of races can be verified in the highly significant testimony of Humboldt. Around 1800, that is, 300 years after the beginning of the process which was to create a new human type out of 350,000 native Indians, 5,000 Spaniards and 10,000 Africans, Venezuela had 800,000 inhabitants. Humboldt states that half of these, not less than 400,000, were of mixed race, neither Spaniards nor Indians nor Africans. A similar phenomenon occurred in other parts of Latin America, where the mixture of the races was also the rule, but in a number of cases the result was the predominance of the Indian element in the mixture, or else it happened that because of the annihilation of the Indians, and because of economic factors, the large negro population predominated. In Venezuela there was a balanced mixture, so that Bolívar's country represented an intermediate state in the question of population as well as cultural characteristics.

The early years

As I have stated, unlike the huge societies of Mexico and Peru which epitomised as few societies on earth have done the imperial ideal, the situation in Venezuela was one of primitive tribalism. Probably none of the tribes consisted of more than 40,000 or 50,000 Indians, and it must be remembered that from the point of view of language alone, no less than fifteen different language families could be distinguished. Social and political fragmentation was the norm in pre-Columbian America, including that part of it that would later be Portuguese. The tribe was fairly primitive and ruled in an absolute or near-absolute fashion, by a chieftan whose powers were only slightly restricted, if at all. This system could not serve the aims of the Spanish *conquistador*, who in any case had not come to take lessons from social insititutions he had left behind, nor to accept a descent to ways of life and structures different from, and inferior to his own. On the contrary he had come with the idea of imposing his ideas and achieving complete domination. From the very beginning, the Spanish conqueror was determined to import the Peninsular system into Latin America. The decision was in his hands and his behaviour was dictated by the powerful psychological forces of imitation and habit. In short, it was simpler for him to transplant what he already knew and was familiar with from Spain.

The system, then, was the Spanish system with, of course, the modifications imposed by the very different circumstances operating in the two continents and also, naturally, by the differences of scale between the old, established world of the Peninsula and the new world that was being born in America. There could not be an absolutely identical system for a city like Madrid or Seville and new ones like Cumaná, Coro or Santiago de León de Caracas. In the early years, let us say, the sixteenth century, a primitive social structure came into being, the structure demanded by the circumstances. Spain's aim was to achieve complete domination, to superimpose her own structures on American society.

The first and principal objective, that of dominating the whole territory and all it contained by overcoming the troublesome resistance of the native Indians, was achieved by the creation of the conquering expeditions. The Spanish Crown, despite its immense power, illustrated in the recently established but flourishing absolutism in the fields of politics, the economy and religion, was not in a position to finance the American adventure wholly out of the public purse. The collaboration of private individuals was required, and the Crown had to reach a compromise with them in the form of the *capitulaciones*, the basis of law for the American territories, which established the duties and rewards for participants in the risky ventures of conquest and colonisation.

At the head of each expedition, a motley crew of mercenaries recruited from all walks of life, was the *adelantado*. By the terms of the *capitulación*, the monarch conferred on him political, administrative, military and judicial powers. He had the right to make gifts of land and of Indians to his troops, he was entitled to dictate regulations, impose taxes and even mint his own coin. The tremendous shortage of people, as well as the nature of the Conquest, which demanded strong decisive leadership, explain this early concentration of power in one individual and a corresponding weakness in the law, all of which combined to make the *adelantado* the centre of a small-scale absolute system. This was how the dangerous task of exploration and settlement was carried out.

The next objective was spiritual domination, a vital consideration for an idealistic race like the Spaniards, steeped in religion for centuries. It implied cultural domination, especially in religion, language and customs, and this gave rise to the abortive plan of Pure Evangelisation which the Dominican friars destined for Venezuela. They aimed, like Jesus and the Apostles, to proselytise without the use of firearms or force. Despite the failure of this initiative, it fell to the Dominicans and Franciscans to begin the work of converting this part of America to Roman Catholicism. Other religious orders joined in later, so that between the second half of the seventeenth century and the first half of the eighteenth, a network of missions covered the territory that would later be Venezuela.

Institutions like the *encomienda* and the *reparto de tierras* were set up in response to social and economic needs. The first was intended to achieve a number of aims; it was a reward and an incentive to the *conquistador*, and it imposed discipline on the Indian by incorporating him into a system that involved the loss of his freedom, and which in effect involved a sort of slavery. The *encomienda* reduced the massacre of the Indians, it facilitated the propagation of Christianity by bringing the population together, under control, and it hastened the integration of the Indian into Hispanic culture.

Complementary to the *encomienda* was the *reparto de tierras*, which was a cover for theft. It was the final, practical outcome of a series of doctrines and beliefs which enjoyed immense prestige at the time: the doctrine that temporal power over the whole earth was vested in the person of the Pope, as the successor of Christ, so that he had the right to dispose of the continents; the rights of the Spanish Crown, derived from the Papal Bulls *Inter Caetera*; and the right of the *adelantado* to make gifts of land by the provisions of the *capitulaciones*. Thanks to the *encomienda* and the gifts of land, the Spaniards began to farm and raise cattle. This represented a significant advance in productivity, in place of the scattered, individualistic agricultural system of the Indians. The latter, however, in the last analysis, were deprived of what belonged to them, and from being their own masters or subject to their own local authority became the servants of a dominant foreign power. As for the African, he was not even treated as a human being. He was an object, or an extra animal, and was bought and sold like any other commodity. Thus an offensive lack of equality, and tangible injustice stood side by side at the bases of Latin American society at its formation in the sixteenth century.

Development of colonial society
But if this was the situation in what I have called intermediate America, there were differences in more extreme cases, though not very important ones. Wherever there was a mixture of only two races, Spanish and African, whether due to the extermination of the Indian, or because he had never inhabited the area, the Spaniard found it easier to dominate. He created or copied a system of open slavery, and it was up to the African to adapt and submit to his betters. It must be said that the latter also had to make certain concessions, which are necessary when men live together in a state of inequality, but the negro's sacrifice was greater. In Venezuela, and in general throughout Latin America, the first thing the African immigrant lost was his native language.

So far as the relatively more advanced, organised and densely-populated part of America was concerned, the Conquest meant primarily a change of master and language and a few superficial changes. The Aztec and Inca masses identified the conqueror with a humiliating contempt for their traditional creeds and a forced and rapid assimilation of a series of new and foreign beliefs. Yet Spain took every advantage of local systems of injustice, oppression and inequality which existed amongst the Indians and continued to use them, the only difference being that they substituted a Spanish ruler for the native one, and made a few other trifling alterations. There is a good example of this in Peru, where Spain confirmed the authority of the Indian *caciques* or chiefs, using them as a means of dominating and exploiting the native society. No doubt from the point of view of the conquerors, this was an ingenious method; to corrupt a tiny, select group of the vanquished and use them in the administration and control of the majority. Bolívar, in 1825, was to abolish, hopefully for ever, this sort of shameful collaboration.

The seventeenth and eighteenth centuries were not quiet times, despite the false image of the colonial period as a time of peace and tranquility, an idyllic backwater. There were continuous internal struggles, due to inequalities in the incipient societies, and repeated attacks by pirates, this latter a problem which had important consequences for the new society, for in facing an outside aggressor the Venezuelans became conscious of their own identity, since the common danger brought them together and overcame local rivalries. For the first time they thought of themselves as one nation, when faced with an enemy whose beliefs, language and customs were foreign to them.

Moreover, all over Latin America, the two hundred years from 1600 to 1800 saw the crystallisation of the colonial system. Major and minor boundaries were drawn up, the centres of population grew with the influx from Spain, and slaves were imported as demanded by the expansion of the economy. Culture flowered in many different fields; architecture in Mexico, Lima and Córdoba, painting in Quito, music in Caracas. Colonial absolutism reached its peak, cut off from outside influences. The viceroy of Mexico could confidently remind the Latin Americans that it was not their place to express an opinion on the government, that this was a task reserved for the great monarch who sat on the Spanish throne, and theirs was to keep quiet and obey. The power of the Church increased. Religious orders like the Jesuits secured an influential position for themselves through their role in education.

Despite Spain's pretension, the Latin American environment did not permit the wholesale transplantation of all the characteristic institutions of the Peninsula, and in the long term the result was rather different from what had been intended. Co-existence demands certain compromises and each of the active elements in the process was modified by contact with the others. There was one stage and many actors, but they shared a common duty and a common destiny.

The mature colonial system

Venezuela at the beginning of the nineteenth century was very different from the land that Columbus, Juan de la Cosa and Alonso de Ojeda had seen. In the delightful territory Columbus christened 'Land of Grace' there had been practically nothing but a few, scattered Indian communities with their precarious culture. Now there was a race of people with three hundred years of history behind them. In the first hundred years, thirty towns were created, six of which had a province attached. These six provinces had no ranking-order amongst themselves, and they were dependent on various centres. The case of Cumaná is a good illustration: policy-decisions were made in Madrid, matters of day-to-day government and judicial matters were decided in Santo Domingo and Santa Fe, economically it was dependent on Mexico, in religious questions on San Juan de Puerto Rico and in University matters it fell within the jurisdiction of Caracas.

The unification of what we now call Venezuela (the province of Caracas was sometimes known as Venezuela) was initiated by the Royal Guipuzcoana (Basque) Company. It obtained from the King a sort of preview of independence during the colonial period, when the Sovereign agreed to detach the Venezuelan provinces from Santa Fe and place them under the control of Caracas. This was in 1739 and the decision was ratified in 1742. The King stated that the Basque company's representations had been an important factor in the decision. Originally, only the province of Caracas had been assigned to the company, though with permission to supply also the provinces of Cumaná, Trinidad and Margarita, which were later included in their empire, as well as Guayana where they led the war against contraband trade. Finally in 1739 Maracaibo came within their radius, which in the end covered the whole of Venezuela.

Venezuela was further unified by the creation of a number of institutions in the decade 1776–86: the intendancy, which centralised fiscal matters; a captaincy-general, superior in military and administrative matters to the captaincies-general and *gobernaciones* of Cumaná, Guayana, Margarita, Trinidad and Maracaibo (1777); the *consulado*, a commercial court of justice also charged with fomenting economic growth (1785); and the *audiencia* or supreme court, which also discharged the functions of government and even of a legislative body (1786). In 1804, it fell to Monsignor Francisco de Ibarra to be the first Metropolitan Archbishop of Caracas, in accordance with the bull of the previous year. This meant that the united territory of Venezuela was released from the triple ecclesiastical jurisdiction of Puerto Rico, Santo Domingo and Santa Fe, since the prelate of Caracas was raised up as stated and the bishops of Mérida, Maracaibo and Guayana were subject to him. The creation of the archdiocese confirmed Caracas as the real capital of the nation. The establishment of the University in 1721 had already given her the undisputed lead in cultural matters. Bolívar happened to be born in the middle of this decade. When he reached the age of reason, to be a native of Caracas, Guayana, Cumaná, Trinidad, Margarita, Maracaibo or Mérida was not important. It was more important to be a Venezuelan.

Developments did not run exactly parallel during these significant two hundred years in the rest of Latin America. Venezuela was always behind. In the more densely populated areas of Latin America, thanks to the larger scale, one can see right from the sixteenth century the same phenomenon that appeared later in Venezuela, which was the improvement and invigoration of the colonial system. At first the Spanish Crown had been dazzled by the discovery of America: but soon it realized it was in business and abandoned its passive attitude. Charles V created the viceroyalties of New Spain and Peru. In the eighteenth century, those of New Granada and the River Plate were created. The captaincies-general of Guatemala, Chile, Cuba and Florida and the presidency of Quito also came into being. A series of *audiencias* appeared, first in Santa Domingo in 1511, then Mexico in 1527, Panamá or Tierra Firme in 1535, Lima in 1542, Gautemala in 1543, Guadalajara in 1548, Santa Fe in 1549, Charcas in 1551, Quito in 1563, Chile in 1609, Buenos Aires in 1661 and Caracas and Cuzco in 1786.

The Bourbons established a number of Intendancies in Latin America. It was a step forward in fiscal administration, far removed from the primitive bureaucracy of the early period. As for *consulados*, there were eleven in the whole continent. Moreover, the number of *cabildos* or municipal councils had multiplied, these being the only form of deliberative assembly, and that at a very local level, that the absolute monarchy permitted. The *cabildos* fluctuated in importance, but they nevertheless played a vital role. They did represent the will of the community. The Caracas *cabildo* in 1676 won the right to have their *alcaldes* or magistrates rule, should they ever be left without a Governor. These bodies were jealous of their prerogatives and by their nature tended to represent, almost exclusively, the interests of the *criollos*, that is, people of Spanish descent born in America.

The body of law by which Latin America was governed was originally that of Castile, a collection of laws of mainly Roman extraction. By the end of the seventeenth century, in 1680, the task of drawing up a body of laws expressly designed for the New World was completed. These were the *Leyes de Indias*, in nine volumes, with 218 headings and 6,377 statutes. This body of legislation is admirable from many points of view. Besides being a reflection of the social and political order from which it sprang, and serving the interests of the Crown, it was also animated by a spirit of idealism which is the outstanding feature of the Spanish character. In many aspects of the *Leyes de Indias* there is a clear leaning towards lofty aims. However, everyday practicalities, as well as the Latin American situation and the clash of interests involved, destroyed that high aspiration, with its markedly humanitarian stance in favour of the Indians which, even if it did not quite get off the ground, is still a credit to its inventors.

In this remarkable body of law, one can see the origins of a social phenomenon that was to be highly significant in Latin America, the gap between the law and reality. In contrast to Anglo-Saxon societies, in Latin America the law has been abstract and theoretical, a model of perfection rather than a practical, efficient, functional rule of conduct. The legislation relating to America was characterised by its idealism and by the fact that it never worked and ever since those early days the law in Latin America has been a sort of luxury item, far removed from everyday realities.

During the three hundred years of the colonial period, Spain's imperial domination remained unaltered, characterised throughout by its stern and intransigent attitude. The monarch changed, but the system, which relied on laws and legal processes, was passed down from one to the other with no waning of its authoritarian structure. Yet one can see differences in character and style between the two dynasties that occupied the throne of Spain. The reign of the Hapsburgs was severe, obsessively Catholic and closed to innovation except in the arts, and even they were overshadowed by the political and theological philosphy of the régime. This dynasty, which encouraged national unity, and was representative of Spain's incipient nationhood, was an efficient instrument of the old concepts. Its absolutism was based on theocratic and selfishly centralist notions, with more than a trace of mediaeval attitudes.

The Bourbons marked a change. In France they had presided over a daring policy of reform and innovation. They were moderate Catholics and encouraged the arts, philosophical inquiry and scientific research and progress, though they remained absolute monarchs. In the Peninsula, their policy was one of legal uniformity and increased centralism. Among his first actions, Philip V took away the ancient rights of Aragon, Catalonia, Valencia and Majorca. Thus, from the beginning, he reinforced his personal power. The Intendancy system was incorporated into the machinery of government and soon became more or less the linchpin of the new administration. As a result, the *Cortes* and the *cabildos* decreased in power. America also felt the impact of Bourbon policies in social matters. The dynasty prided itself on being liberal and made no secret of its intention to bring to heel the Peninsular and Latin American aristocracies. Its policies in Venezuela were clearly directed to the people, and while the original, innate inequalities did not disappear, nevertheless it is undeniable that by 1800 new possibilities could be glimpsed in Latin America. Population growth and the mingling of the three main races (despite laws to the contrary) showed up inequalities even more clearly, and how absurd it was to maintain them.

Slavery, of course, was now more important than ever. From modest beginnings in the sixteenth century, as a sort of experiment, it had grown remarkably, thanks to the enormous profits that could be made: 20,000% according to some estimates. The trade was now shared between England, Holland, Portugal and France. It has been calculated that between 12,000,000 and 30,000,000 people were taken out of Africa during the colonial period. About 120,000 negroes were taken to Venezuela. There were large settlements in the West Indies, in Brazil, on the north coast of the Gulf of Mexico and along the Caribbean coast of the mainland.

By the beginning of the nineteenth century, slavery had increased on the sub-continent. In pre-Hispanic America, it had been common practice amongst some Indian groups to trade in prisoners, they being part of the victor's booty. The trade was so lucrative that many Indian chiefs devoted themselves to taking captives from amongst their enemies and selling them to the Spaniards. Even in the more advanced societies, slavery was not unknown. Despite the fact that the Spanish Crown declared the Indians 'free vassals', the permission granted by Isabel in 1503 to reduce the Caribs and Araucanians to captivity on the grounds that they were cannibals and rebellious amounted to royal approval of the incipient slave system.

Even apart from the existence of slaves, which is sufficient to show the blatant inequalities of the society, it was also an undeniable fact that not all free men were equal. In Venezuela there were at least eight different social strata. The whites, who were a privileged group were divided into three categories. There were the Peninsular Spaniards at the top of the social pyramid, then the proud *criollos* and *mantuanos*, as the local aristocrats were known, then the inferior Canary Islanders. Then in descending order came the enormous numbers of *pardos* or 'coloured' people, people of mixed race, no less than half the population of Venezuela in 1800: *mestizos*, strictly speaking, were of mixed white and Indian blood, mulattoes of mixed white and negro and *zambos* of mixed Indian and negro, and there was a rich variety of terms to describe all the possible combinations[2]. Finally, near the base of the pyramid were the free Indians, below them Indian slaves, then the free negroes and finally negro slaves.

Blood, or race, was not the only determinant of social class. There were legal criteria, and education, wealth and cultural factors also played an important part. The rules went so far as to take into account whether or not an individual wore a cloak, jewels, pearls, silk, velvet, and whether he used cushions, an umbrella and a prie-Dieu in Church. Even in worship, negroes were segregated from whites, and for a long time only the latter could aspire to the priesthood. In Caracas the churches corresponded to certain social classes; Candelaria was for people from the Canary Islands, San Mauricio for people of mixed race and San Francisco for the *criollos*.

The same could be said of trades and professions. Education reinforced the the established order and gave additional support to social distinctions. The type of education open to an individual trained him for certain professions which in turn correspond to precise points on the social scale. The same thing happened with apprenticeships and access to particular trades. Not surprisingly, the most advanced training was reserved for influential people, that is the Peninsular Spaniards and the *criollos* or *mantuanos*. The University charged high fees. Schools were systematically denied to people of mixed race. No-one bothered to educate the negroes, in fact, there was a case recorded in Catamarca of a negro who taught himself to read and was publicly whipped when this was discovered. As for the Indians, under the *encomienda* they were taught just enough to understand the Catholic religion.

There were other distinctions relating to occupation, for example whether a man was a soldier, or had a university degree, or holy orders, the type of occupation or the branch of it in which he worked, his length of service and experience. These all served to draw distinctions between the inhabitants of the colony. To aspire to a university degree, a man had to prove that he was a legitimate child, of pure blood and known parentage. Foundlings, even if they were white, could not graduate without a dispensation from the King.

For a long time, any kind of manual work disqualified an individual from the class of *hidalgos*. Philip II in 1562 had defined the 'low, mean and mechanical' trades unworthy of social dignitaries. A number of *pardos*, by carrying out tasks essential to the community, including minor surgery, increased their financial standing, an important factor in their rise in social status. The hardest, most demanding and dirtiest work was left for the negroes and they were subject to intolerable restrictions. For example, they could not go about at night, nor go from one town to another. In Caracas, they were not allowed to go to the quays 'except to fetch water' for domestic use. After 1545, they were forbidden to ride on horseback. Around 1620 they were reminded that they could not bear firearms. It was forbidden to do business with a slave and there was a presumption of guilt against them, in the sense that it was always assumed that they had stolen or got by ill means any money in their possession.

The majority of the *pardos* were the victims of contempt and exploitation. They were confined to minor posts, they could not attend courses in the University, far less hope to gain a degree or diploma, nor could they enter a seminary, nor take holy orders. They were not admitted into the College of Lawyers nor to the *audiencia* even as porters. There was a special, segregated militia, but even there they could not aspire to a higher rank than captain. They were forbidden to marry whites, the Cathedral Chapter could not be present at their burial, they could not sit on the benches in church nor carry a mat on which to kneel. Even in 1805, the *ayuntamiento* or municipal council was still refusing them any kind of education. In 1796 this body had voted to deny them education 'which they have not hitherto received, nor should receive in the future'.

Economy and ideology

In drawing a picture of colonial Latin America, the Inquisition should be mentioned, as an institution that was highly effective in the service of the absolute monarchy, against freedom. In contrast to the mediaeval Inquisition, which was primarily religious and in the hands of the clergy, the Inquisition in Spain was political and economic, though still disguised, of course, as the protector of the faith. In the Holy Office the King was the dominant influence. In 1478, Pope Sextus IV had granted the monarch authority to appoint the judges of the Inquisition. Four years later, the Pontiff took back this power, but he left the Crown the right to present the candidates. Either way, the guardians of dogma were always instruments of the political power.

The initial aim of the Inquisition was to destroy Judaism, but then it turned its attention to Islam and finally to Protestantism. Its effectiveness in America is open to debate; but in any case it did frighten even the religious authorities and it naturally served as a discreet threat in favour of the Spanish monarchy's designs. The legend as it has been passed down no doubt exaggerates the diabolical and terrifying effects of the Inquisition, but its disappearance freed men's minds of an additional worry on top of the general atmosphere of suspicion, inhibition and fear that reigned in the colony.

Economically, Latin America's development was based on injustice. According to the teaching of León Marsicano,[3] the Pope had the right to distribute portions of the globe as he saw fit. The Catholic Kings received the New World as a gift from the hands of the Pope and they in turn disposed of it in the *capitulaciones*, whereupon the *adelantados* made a further distribution. In any case, the Spanish possession of America, based on conquest, meant the theft of their lands from the Indians. With their labour, and that of the negro slaves, great fortunes were founded. The *haciendas* or great estates were a direct result of the conquest and the existence of slavery. In all the countries of Latin America there are remnants of these immense colonial *latifundios*: the Church was also a large landowner. Whether a man owned a piece of land, its size, whether he had good harvests or bad, the number of slaves he had, or the number of head of cattle, in short, his wealth, influenced his social status. On the one hand were the powerful *mantuanos, grandes cacaos* who could buy a title with the profits from cocoa-production, high-level officials, assured of a rapid fortune, and people of private means who lived off the considerable income from their accumulated capital: and on the other were small landowners and tradesmen, condemned to inferiority by their poverty, and even lower down the social scale, those who owned absolutely nothing, not even their own freedom. Many aristocrats in Venezuela had no scruples about engaging in trade: in Latin America, generally speaking, to be in mining, agriculture or cattle-raising, with Indians held under the *encomienda* system or African slaves, was no shame for a gentleman.

As for culture and the spread of knowledge, it must be pointed out that Bourbon absolutism, which in the Peninsula presided over the period of the Enlightenment, with somewhat uncertain results, when it came to the colonies always insisted that the King was supreme arbiter and that only a limited freedom was possible. The Crown, not by any deliberate decision, but spontaneously, as part of its policy of controlling every aspect of society, did not encourage education. So far as religious or private education was concerned, these were controlled with an eye to the all-important designs of the monarchy.

The Venezuela into which Simón Bolívar was to be born was one of the most backward and neglected areas of the Empire in cultural matters. Its University was founded in 1725, whereas that of Santo Domingo was established in 1538 and that of Mexico of 1551. The same was true of the printing press: it was introduced into Mexico in 1536; mention is made of its earlier arrival in Gautemala; it was in existence in Peru by 1581 and it was introduced into Paraguay and Cuba in 1705 and 1707 respectively; by 1747 it was to be found in Brazil and by 1750 in Haiti; it had previously been introduced into New Granada (1738) and subsequently into Quito (1775) and the River Plate (1776). Venezuela, on the other hand, did not have a printing press until 1808.

The Venezuelans' intellectual curiosity had to fight against tremendous odds. Latin America was a closed world, thanks to the absolute régime, and was treated with severity and suspicion. The *Leyes de Indias* laid down the death-penalty for trading with foreigners, whatever the reason. There were innumerable restrictions on the publishing and sale of books, and it was the job of the inflexible agents of the Holy Inquisition to give the permit for the entry, distribution and use of books, no matter where they came from or the language in which they were written. The King ordered his lay and ecclesiastical officials in the New World to confiscate heretical texts and any printed matter the Protestant pirates might leave behind in their barbarous attacks. So great, indeed, was the imperial vigilance that it descended to minute details, like forbidding profane and fantastical books, which narrated fictitious events. This appears in the legislation relating to Latin America and was ratified by royal decree of Charles V on 29 September, 1534. The Crown, moreover, was especially careful with books about the New World. The Council of the

Indies had to approve such publications before they could enter Latin America; no publisher or book-seller could print or stock them unless they had been examined by the Council, on pain of a heavy fine and confiscation. Even so, books did arrive in Latin America, through legal channels, and often very quickly. However, it was really smuggling that made possible the formation of important libraries in Caracas and elsewhere. The Guipuzcoana Company was relatively protected and brought over the latest, most outspoken publications in its ships.

This was Latin America as it developed over the first three hundred years: a series of political and administrative entities, dependent on the Crown — viceroyalties, intendancies, captaincies-general, *consulados* and *audiencias*; more or less elegant cities, palaces, mansions, cathedrals, churches, convents, cattle-ranches, plantations, slaves, universities, roads, forts, mines, sugar-plantations, and refineries. In short, a material, cultural and institutional structure which, objectively speaking, is astonishing. If we reflect that before Columbus's arrival there was in effect no such entity as America or the Americans, and that three hundred years later there was a New World, and within it many different nations, we shall have an idea of the scope of the achievement of this continent, and of the particular part of it which gave birth to Bolívar.

A sense of identity

The achievements of the colonial period were considerable. Just as the Latin America and Venezuela of 1800 were very different from those of 1500, so all the different races had flowed together to make one Latin American, who was neither Indian, Spanish nor negro, but a universal type, representative of all the continents of the world. The very name America was new, and so were those of Venezuela, New Granada, New Spain, Hispaniola, Puerto Rico, Santo Domingo, Santa Fe, Florida, the River Plate, Asunción and many others. A certain spirit, a certain sense of identity came into being and it was mature and self-confident, though still recent, by 1800.

300 years was a long time in some ways, but in others it was short. There is no example anywhere else on earth of a civilisation of such magnitude being created in such a short space of time. In Spain, the Roman period lasted 600 years, and the Arab domination 800. Similarly, in England, the Normans maintained their dominance for more than 400 years. Yet these periods, though any one of them is considerably longer than the whole colonial reign in Latin America, are considered mere phases or incidents in the historical process of those two countries. For Latin America, 300 years constituted her entire history, and it was during that period that a spirit was born and culture formed. Spain transferred her absolute system to America. It was basically no different from the

régime that other colonial powers established in their dominions. However, Spanish absolutism was the strongest that has ever existed. It was unique, unequalled even in France, where at the high point of the *ancien régime*, Louis XIV could say 'I am the State'. He was right, for he held the political system in the palm of his hand, but the Spanish monarchs could say more. They claimed that the monarch had personal rights over the empire and all it contained.

Spanish absolutism was manifest not only in the political sphere, but also in economic and religious matters. The mercantilist system gave the sovereign complete control over production and the whole economic process, including consumption, was subject to him. Particular importance was given to mining, for the Crown's principal aims were to accumulate gold and precious metals and to prevent riches falling into the hands of rivals. A whole series of extremely severe regulations shaped this highly interventionist system. Ecclesiastical patronage and the Inquisition increased the King's power by giving him an authority in matters of conscience and all religious matters such as only a Vicar of Christ could normally exercise. The Kings were effectively head of the Church within their kingdoms: not only were they protectors of holy dogma and ecclesiastical administrators, but on the basis of the *Pase Regio* they also controlled the dissemination of the Pope's word amongst their Catholic subjects. The Holy Office, moreover, besides establishing one unified faith, brought the Kings considerable riches, confiscated from heretics.

Only the personal honour of his subjects was not within the absolute jurisdiction of the king. Queen Isabel stated that kings owned their kingdoms. Within this framework of unrestricted power, it was stressed that the individual's right to property was based on the sovereign's grace or favour. Liberty was also a grace, conferred by the sovereign, who also had the right to give or take away life. There were no individual rights or guarantees under the absolute régime. The individual, in effect, did not exist in the face of the omnipotence of the state.

This absolutism was taken to its logical conclusion in the American colonies. There was neither freedom of thought nor of expression, these being restricted by two institutions emanating from the king: lay or governmental censorship and religious censorship. There was no freedom of movement or residence, for in theory the king had expressly to permit every single journey or move, even from one province to another. Nor was there freedom of work, since there were wide and detailed restrictions on access to professional training, and on the right to practise. There was not even freedom of worship, since this was viewed as a threat to Spanish unity. The expulsion of the Jews from Spain was decreed in 1492. Ten years later, that of Muslims still unconverted to Christianity, including the old *mudéjares* of Castile, and in 1608 that of the *moriscos*.

Protestants were not tolerated, either, and it was mainly they, and some people of Jewish tendencies, who attracted the attention of the Inquisition in Latin America. Nor was there, given the absolute régime's monopoly, freedom of trade or navigation, though Charles III would decree freedom of trade and in 1797 Charles IV would allow non-Spanish ships to reach the ports of Latin America. The absolute system, in short, was a totalitarian régime, under which the Crown, through its officials, did not hesitate to levy excessive taxes, to cover the escalating cost of its army and administration.

The basis of absolutism, it must be remembered, was that while it was undoubtedly legalistic and conformed to its own rules, it was based on the complete absence of political rights. Those who governed had not been elected to do so; they were simply the people the monarch saw fit to appoint. The only deliberative assemblies that existed in Latin America were the *cabildos*, which were relatively autonomous, but only operated at municipal level, and the *consulados*, which dealt with trade and production. These were the only bodies to which the *criollos* had unrestricted access. The Latin Americans were excluded from the higher spheres of government in their own country. Manuel Palacio Fajardo, after original and detailed research, stated that 'from the first years of the colonial period until 1810, of the 166 viceroys and 588 captains-general, governors and presidents, [that is, out of 754 holders of high office in Spanish America,] only 18 were *criollos*'.[4] The Latin Americans were second-class citizens in their own country. Preferment, as we have seen, always went to *peninsulares*. Simón Bolívar had the following to say on this point: 'The situation of the inhabitants of the South American hemisphere has for centuries been one of sheer passivity ... We were in a state lower than serfdom ... America was deprived, not only of liberty, but even of active and native tyranny ... We were humiliated by this treatment, which not only took away all our rights, but also left us in a state of permanent childhood in relation to public affairs ... The role of South Americans in this society is that of serfs, fit only to labour, or at best to provide a market, though even this is hedged-about with intolerable restrictions ... We were estranged and cut off from reality, so far as the science of government and administration was concerned. We had never been viceroys nor governors, except in very unusual cases; very seldom archbishops or bishops; never diplomats; soldiers, only in the lower ranks; aristocrats without any real privileges. We were not magistrates, financiers, nor hardly even merchants.'[5]

The history of resistance

Latin America showed signs of rebellion against the state of affairs outlined above, perhaps from the time of the Discovery. The mingling of races and the growth of the spirit of rebellion went hand in hand, and slavery and revolt co-existed. At different times, the Latin Americans' self-respect forced them to rise up in action, even at the cost of life itself. It was not from fashionable English, French and Yankee writings that the Latin Americans obtained their ideas on freedom. Nor was it the French example of the storming of the Bastille and the execution of the Capetian Kings that inspired them and persuaded them to fight. They did not need any foreign thinker or inspired Jacobin to teach them about liberty.

The Latin American people learned to love liberty, they were determined to achieve it and did no stop to count the cost. Bolívar would later point to a powerful argument in favour of liberty and independence in the annals of the very nation that was attempting to deny these to its colonies. Thus he spoke of independence and liberty 'which Spanish law, and the examples from her history, encourage us to achieve by force of arms.'[6] Miranda, another famous representative of the same country, could say: 'I devoted myself to the service of liberty long before France had even begun to think of it.'[7]

As early as 1501, there was a black slave rebellion on the island of Hispaniola and between 1519 and 1533 there were the rebellions of the Indian Enriquillo in Santo Domingo. In the end, the native Indians were almost totally wiped out in the Caribbean. Around 1534, there was intense Indian resistence in the Araucanian Wars in Chile. In relative terms, the massacre there was a great as that of the Caribs in the West Indian islands and along the Caribbean coast. In Peru, in 1536, Manco II led a revolt of about 100,000 Indians: and yet they could not overcome the Spaniards' technical superiority.

In Venezuela, according to early documents, there was a slave uprising in 1532 in the recently founded Villa de Santa Ana de Coro. The next significant uprising was that of the negro Miguel in the Buría mines in the state of Yaracuy. There were also disturbances in the Inca area. There was a serious attempt at rebellion in Quito, which spread right down into Chile. Feelings ran so high in this area that in 1577, when the pirate Drake approached Callao in Peru the negroes of the zone attempted to reach him to offer their help. And, in Topia in the north of Mexico, an insurrection sprang up in 1589.

In the course of the seventeenth century, there were more and more frequent signs of the rejection of the system, even while it was still only in embryonic state in a number of places. The Pijao Indians rose up between Huila and Tolima in Columbia in 1601. Panamá suffered a similar shock in 1608 and Mexico in 1612. The continuous warfare waged by the Indians of Peru against their Spanish masters reached a particularly intense phase in 1625. Lima and the north of Peru suffered disturbances between 1629 and 1630. Tucumán in Argentina was the stage for a tremendous conflict in 1645 and again ten years later. The threat, and the reality, of internal revolt, hung over Lima in 1666, 1675 and 1676. Mexico experienced the same problem in 1692.

There were a number of uprisings in Venezuela in the seventeenth century. A brief summary will show the variety of episodes. In 1603, the negroes engaged in pearl-fishing in Margarita revolted against the inhuman treatment they were receiving and the revolt spread to the coast of Cumaná. In Nirgua a revolution was averted in 1628. But the Crown authorities could not impose their will by force on the 'coloured' majority, who in the end won special recognition and the right to organise themselves into what was sarcastically called 'the mulatto and *zambo* Republic'. Numerous bands of runaway slaves were at large in 1650 in the Tuy valleys and around Charallave, Yare, Pariaguán, Paracotos and La Guaira. The authorities ordered summary execution of the leaders, and severe measures against any free man who helped the rebels. Depleted by a more or less systematic campaign of annihilation, groups of Caribs and Otomacs led by Chief Chiparara conducted the last great assault on the Spaniards on the savannas of Guárico. Disturbance was rife around Carora and Monay in the years 1671 and 1677.

What did all these movements have in common? Firstly, the decisive role played by the lower ranks of society, especially the most oppressed groups, that is the Indians, who were determined to shake off the foreign yoke, so much more detestable than the ancestral tyranny of their own kind, the negroes and the people of mixed race, mulattoes, *mestizos* and *zambos*. The conflict, which took many different shapes and forms, always had as its main object the revindication of the social, economic, cultural and political rights of a people who refused to accept their inferior position, filled with that spirit of rebellion which is a source of inner strength.

In the eighteenth century, subversive movements gained in maturity. Besides economic and social motives, there was now a political dimension to the struggle. In 1721 there erupted in Paraguay a *criollo* rebellion which triumphed in its aims. It was directed by the magistrate Antequera against the authority of the viceroy. A government was formed, which lasted ten years, supported by the *comuneros*, but the movement was crushed in 1735. Five years previously, in Cochabamba in Bolivia the silversmith Alejo Calatayud had led an uprising against the system of taxation. This was the period of protest against fiscal charges and administrative regulations. The cry arose: A New King and New Laws! These were *criollo* movements. Later, according to Carlos Pereyra, 'each country glorified its remote Indian past, as a point of departure for its nationalist aspirations'.[8] There arose an 'ism' for each area: Aztecism, Incaism, Araucanianism, Caribism, Nativism (in Brazil) and Siboneyism.

MIRANDA.

ANVERS.

Francisco de Miranda.

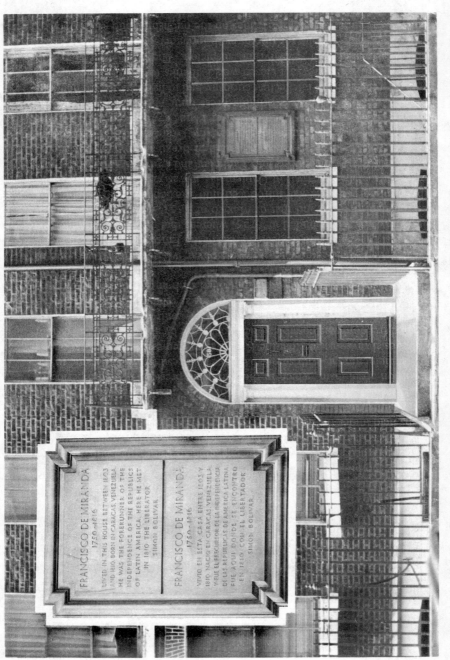

FRANCISCO DE MIRANDA
1750–1816

LIVED IN THIS HOUSE BETWEEN 1803
AND 1810 BORN IN CARACAS, VENEZUELA.
HE WAS THE FORERUNNER OF THE
INDEPENDENCE OF THE REPUBLICS
OF LATIN AMERICA. HERE HE MET
IN 1810 THE LIBERATOR
SIMON BOLIVAR.

FRANCISCO DE MIRANDA
1750–1816

VIVIO EN ESTA CASA ENTRE 1803 Y
1810 NACIO EN CARACAS, VENEZUELA
Y FUE EL PRECURSOR DE LA INDEPENDENCIA
DE LAS REPUBLICAS DE AMERICA LATINA
FUE AQUI DONDE SE ENCONTRO
EN 1810 CON EL LIBERTADOR
SIMON BOLIVAR.

58 Grafton Way, Miranda's London House

The Royal Guipuzcoana Company in Venezuela, with its tr monopoly which hurt the rich and its indiscriminate persecution of contraband trade, which hurt everyone, provoked the first united action of the different social groups in the Venezuelan provinces. A *zambo* from Valencia, Andrés López del Rosario, better known as *Andresote*, began the war against the Basque company in 1732. The action took place in the Yaracuy valleys and on the coastal belt at Puerto Cabello and Ticacas, a smuggling area where Dutch influence was strong. In 1741, the San Felipe mutiny occurred. Although the immediate pretext was a jurisdictional dispute, the mutiny was really directed against the whole colonial order, under which the *criollos* were obliged to follow the orders of the Guipuzcoana Company.

El Tocuyo was the scene of an important uprising against the Provincial Government and its local representatives. In the course of this episode a concept came into being, and for the first time a precise term was used, which recognised the existence of a new entity. This word stands out in the report drawn up by a number of gentlemen in El Tocuyo, a report in which they offered three reasons to the masses why they should act: 'the defense of our Catholic religion, of our king, who is our natural ruler and of our *patria*.'⁹ Six years later, the rebellion of the negro Miguel Luengo in the haciendas of Yare was put down. There was talk of a royal decree freeing the slaves, said to have been kept secret by the slave-owners. In 1749 the disturbances continued, with conspiracies in the Indian *cumbes* and on the *haciendas* of Tuy and the negro Manuel Espinosa, the presumed instigator of these events, was executed.

The most notable incident in these fifty years of struggle was the rebellion of Juan Francisco de León in 1749 and 1751, when incipient patriotism once more rose to the surface. The term *patria* was used by Nicolás de León, the Caracas-born son of the leader from the Canary Islands. 'It is our duty to defend our *patria*, for if we do not defend it we shall be slaves to others.'¹⁰ Over and over again, the wild countryside of Tuy was the seed-bed for subversion. From 1771 till 1774, the negro Guillermo, slave of Marcos Riba, kept the colonial authorities in check.

While *Andresote* was fighting in Venezuela, Juan Vélez de Córdova in Oruro was struggling against the tribute and in favour of the restoration of the Inca régime. Castrovirreina and Catabamba also rose up in revolt. From 1742 till 1761 the Peruvian guerilla leader Juan Santos Atahualpa kept alive the flame of rebellion. In 1750 the viceroy crushed an attempt at rebellion in Lima. By this time, the whole of America was tense. In 1775 insurrection broke out in Cuba. In Chile there was a renewal of the Araucanian War. Jesuit sympathisers provoked disturbances in Mexico in 1767 and 1768. In these same years, there were frequent revolts in Quito, Chile, New Granada and Peru, against customs-duties and the state monopoly in *aguardiente*, or native brandy, against taxes, against officials. In 1778 and 1784 there were movements in Buenos Aires. The malcontents also shook up Puebla, Guanajuato, San Luis de la Paz, San Luis Potosí and Patzcuaro in Mexico. Later, the same phenomenon spread to the Peruvian towns of Chumbivilcas, Llata, Urubamba, Lambayeque, Conchuces, Huaras, Yungay, Huancavelica, Pasco, Arequipa and Cuzco.

Special mention should be made of the notable rebellion led by José Gabriel Condorcanqui or Túpac Amaru, as he called himself in honour of the Inca chieftan put to death some two hundred years before by the viceroy Toledo. He mobilised 60,000 men behind the ideas of abolishing the *mitas*, the system of forced Indian wage-labour, closing the textile workshops and prohibiting the distribution of Indians as slaves. This Indian multitude over-reached itself in its desire for vengeance. Despite the apparent extension of its power, which at one time spread over a large part of Peru, as far as Tucumán, its lack of organisation and military discipline reduced it to helplessness even when faced with a much smaller army. The leader was executed and quartered in 1781. A cousin of his, Túpac Inca, managed to prolong the struggle for another couple of years. Carlos Nina Catari laid siege to La Paz and Sorata. Another Catari attacked Chayonta. There were many followers of Túpac Amaru who took the law into their own hands. Jacinto Rodríguez in Oruro, Diego Cristóbal, the brother of Condorcanqui, Mariano, the son of Diego Cristóbal, Luis Lasso de la Vega, Julian Apasa (Túpac Catari), Alejandro Calisaya, Pedro Vilcapasa and various others.

Through an affinity of ideas, and because of the similar circumstances, events in Peru had immense repercussions throughout Latin America. In New Granada, discontent exploded in the *comuneros* movement in Socorro. In this area, the population, commanded by José Antonio Galán and Juan Francisco Berbeo, adopted a united stance against the taxes and obtained the *Capitulaciones de Zipaquirá*, though, in fact, these were never put into effect. Galán died on the scaffold with three of his faithful companions.

The fever of insurrection was contagious. In July and August of 1781, the regions of Táchira, Mérida, Maracaibo and Trujillo in Venezuela were convulsed by a wave of genuine popular insurrection which it was hoped would spread to the whole of the recently created captaincy-general. At the head of this massive insurrection, chosen by the people as their commander-in-chief, stood Juan José García de Hevia, from La Grita. His slogan was: Long Live the King, Down With the Government, and his goal was the abolition of the crippling dues levied by the tax inspectors. The skirmish ended in Trujillo when the *cabildo* decided to deny their support to the Mérida *communeros*; at this point the movement was advancing towards Barinas and Zulia.

The Caracas *mantuanos* also showed their dislike of some measures which harmed their economic interests. In July 1781, Don Juan Vicente de Bolívar y Ponte wrote to Miranda about the political tyranny exercised in the opinion of the local aristocracy by the intendant, José de Abalos. The following year, exactly eighteen months before the birth of Bolívar, the same man, Don Juan Vicente, along with Martín de Tovar and the Marquis of Mijares, went to Miranda and again evoked before his eyes the spectacle of liberty. All three of them offered to follow their young fellow-countryman as *caudillo* and to shed 'even the last drop of our blood, in a great and noble cause'.[11]

From an account of these various episodes in the vast Latin American continent, we can see that the struggle for liberty, justice and equality, ideals dear to the heart of the new Latin American man, was a long sustained battle. Every single one of these episodes displays to a greater or lesser degree the same indomitable will to oppose subjection, to endure sacrifices, to refuse to accept the colonial system, with its weight of injustice. They acted as a inspiration and showed that the colonial system, with its slavery, injustice and despotism, had not crushed the American spirit.

Beginnings of the independence movement

The last decades of the eighteenth century were the period of the precursors, the most outstanding amongst them being Francisco de Miranda, José Joaquim da Silva Xavier, Juan Pablo Viscardo de Guzmán, Francisco Eugenio de Santa Cruz y Espejo and Antonio Nariño.

Miranda (1750–1816) was a key figure in the shaping of the Latin-American nationality. He was the first *criollo* of international importance, for none before him had won such an exalted position amongst the most advanced powers of the time. His dedication to the cause of Latin-American Independence had a precise moment or origin, as he himself explained. When he was fighting in the Independence Wars in the United States, he said, 'the first thought that came into my mind was a fervent desire for the independence of the land of my birth, for at that time I did not dare to call South America my *patria*'.[12]

Miranda was the centre of the revolutionary movement for the whole of the Latin-American continent. Around him were men from many different places, united by their beliefs. Thus O'Higgins would say, in 1828: 'To Miranda I owe the inspiration that set me on the road to revolution for the sake of my country.'[13] There were also the Peruvian, José del Pozo y Sucre, Antonio Nariño and Pedro Fermín de Vargas from New Granada, Pablo de Olavide, Manuel José Salas and the Cuban, Pedro José Caro. Many of these had been initiated into the Masonic

Lodge of the *Gran Reunión Americana* which Miranda founded in London. Bello and Bolívar were also among the members. The Mexican Fray Servando Teresa de Mier, Carlos Montúfar from Quito, Vicente Rocafuerte from Guayaquil, and José de San Martín, Bernardo Monteagudo and Mariano Moreno from the River Plate were members, and it had branches in Mexico, Caracas, Guatemala, Rio de Janeiro and Buenos Aires. These men felt they were citizens of a single country.

When he came to liberate Venezuela, Miranda thought of the whole of Latin America. His troops were known as the 'Colombian Army at the service of the free peoples of America' and he swore and made them swear in Jacmel 'to be faithful in the service of the free peoples of America, independent from Spain, and loyally to serve them against their foes and enemies'.[14] 'America' meant Hispanic America. At that time, Texas and California were Spanish, Canada was a frozen, whitish-green desert, the United States a group of colonies which were experimenting with federal union. Miranda, like the other precursors, did not consider it necessary to specify which America he meant. At that time there was only one: Hispanic America. Miranda had carefully-laid plans for the new America. Many of his ideas were further elaborated by contemporaries of his such as Picornell, Gual and España. Many were adopted by Bolívar and put into effect by him; an example is the formation of Gran Colombia.

In the immense territory of Brazil an outstanding figure was José Joaquim da Javier, (1784–1792) known as *Tiradentes*. The 'revolution' originated, as in the rest of Latin America, in the Portuguese Crown's excesses in relation to taxation. This discontent grew until a complete programme was drawn up which included the creation of an independent republic in Brazil. The flag was to be white, with a line from Virgil: *Libertas quae sera tamen*. Back-debts for taxation would be wiped out. Slavery would be abolished (as an experiment), there would be free trade, schools would be created for the people and factories in which to manufacture goods at present imported from the Peninsula, and the state would aid families of more than five children. The cry of the conspirators would be: Long Live Liberty. This conspiracy collapsed, the ring-leader was imprisoned and tried along with his comrades, he was condemned to death and his was the only sentence that was not commuted. He was executed on the 21 April, 1772, with the utmost ostentation, in accordance with the viceroy's instructions. He lives on in the hearts of the Brazilian people as an example of commitment to a cause and as an inspiration.

Francisco Eugenio de Santa Cruz y Espejo (1747–1795) represents the first step towards independence in Ecuador. He was of mixed racial ancestry, white, Indian and black, and an exceptional individual; doctor,

Andrés Bello.

jurist, philosopher, theologist, journalist and well-known writer. He, too, saw South America as one unit, and his revolutionary plan embraced the whole continent without distinction. He advocated autonomy and self-determination for the South Americans, without the extermination or persecution of the Spaniards, whom he wished merely to remove from the pre-eminent positions they occupied in political life. He proposed the nationalization of the clergy and the expropriation of the Church's enormous wealth for the benefit of the general population. This *mestizo* was the most outstanding figure in the three hundred years of Ecuador's colonial history. His followers and disciples, who suffered dreadful persecution, prepared and carried out the glorious action of 10 August, 1809. On that day, the inhabitants of Quito decided to exercise the sovereign will of the people and change the government by deposing the Spanish authorities and setting up a Supreme Junta which would exercise power completely independently of the Peninsula. The sufferings of Espejo and the martyrdom of the patriots, who were cruelly assassinated, immortalized the memory of this extraordinary struggle on behalf of his country.

In Peru, an important precursor was Juan Pablo Viscardo de Guzmán (1748–98), born in the zone of Arequipa. He was a Jesuit as a young man, but was later estranged from the Order. He was a fierce critic of the colonial régime, and was vividly impressed by the anti-Spanish uprisings in America and the attempt at British penetration into Argentina. He first of all conceived the idea of independence for Peru, then later, in his famous *Letter to the American Spaniards* he extended his plans for emancipation to the whole of the Spanish American continents. He expressed the *criollo* resentments against the *peninsulares*. His letter was widely divulged, having been published initially in French, to enable the Americans' arguments to circulate more widely in Europe. It contains a bitter indictment of the injustices of the colonial situation, in terms it would be difficult to refute. His criticism of slavery, isolation and the exploitation of America for the benefit of a selfish metropolis, were calculated to move the most indifferent spirits.

Don Antonio Nariño (1765–1823) in the viceroyalty of Santa Fe also carried out at this time a task that was the precursor of the changes Bolívar was to bring about. Nariño was a friend of Miranda's and, like the latter and Espejo, a man of great culture and refinement. In August 1749, he acquired a copy of the French text of the *Rights of Man*, which he translated and printed on his own press. His house was the meeting-place of the Bogotá *criollo* intelligentsia which was discussing the future political transformation. The colonial authorities treated Nariño with their usual severity. His possessions were confiscated and he was sentenced to ten years' imprisonment in Africa. Of all the precursors, he was the only one who survived to witness the triumph of the independence movement he had nursed into being. In 1782, Antonio de Prado was working towards the emancipation of the River Plate and Peru. The Mexican Francisco de Mendiola was also active on behalf of his country, as was the Chilean priest Juan José Godoy y del Pozo.

By the beginning of the nineteenth century, when Bolívar was not yet twenty, Venezuela had already a wide experience of the struggle for justice and liberty, through a number of recent activities. José Leonardo Chirinos had led an important uprising in Coro. The intolerable behaviour of a tax-official was the cause of the bloody events. Echoes of the French Revolution and inspiring news of the epic Jacobin struggle in Haiti reached the ears of Chirinos' negroes in Coro and they advocated not only the abolition of slavery and the hated taxes, but also the adoption of the French political principles of liberty, fraternity and equality and the establishment of a Republic.

While Chirinos was still awaiting the verdict of his captors and judges, the mail-ship *La Golondrina* put into La Guaira, carrying on board a wanted man accused of crimes against the state; Picornell, who was to be the architect of the revolutionary movement in Venezuela, a movement that was to be clearly pro-independence. Subversive activity had been taking place in this port since 1794. Picornell immediately took up with Manuel Gual and José María España. He had arrived at the right place and at the right time to create a revolution. The basic ideas of this group of conspirators were contained in the *Ordenanzas-Constituciones* written by Picornell. There one finds the complete ideological basis of the movement, with a clear analysis of the situation and a call for independence. Venezuela was to be organized as a federal, democratic republic, based on the principles of legality, justice and liberty. There would be absolute equality, including racial equality: 'Natural equality between all the inhabitants of the province and districts is decreed, and whites, Indians, negroes and those of mixed race shall live in harmony, considering each other as brothers in Christ, equal in the sight of God, the only distinctions being those of merit and virtue, which are the only real distinctions existing between men, and the only ones which will exist in our Republic.' In line with this disposition, 'slavery is, of course, abolished, being contrary to humanity'.[15]

Although it was a Venezuelan project, centred on La Guaira, and with ramifications in Caracas, Carúpano, Valencia, Puerto Cabello, Barlovento and so on, the plan was meant for the whole of Latin America. So the central principle of unity was constantly emphasised. The idea suggested by Miranda in 1782 was here developed to its logical conclusion. Never before had there been such an explicit and determined affirmation of Latin America unity and brotherhood. All the documents, slogans, songs and pamphlets, without exception, were addressed to the 'American people'. From this point onwards, the concept of the unity of Latin America was central to the Venezuelan ideology. It was the common link between Miranda, Bolívar and Bello, and Venezuela thereafter was in the vanguard of the movement in favour of continental integration and understanding.

The failure of this conspiracy in July 1797 did not restore calm to the Spanish territory of Venezuela. After Picornell, Gual and España, came the abortive uprising of Pirela in Maracaibo and some unsuccessful attempts in Oriente. In 1806, Don Francisco de Miranda in person was off the coast of Venezuela, resolved to liberate his country. It was another step forward in a mature and resolute plan, which included foreign help and was based on a solid appreciation of the vast enterprise that would reach fruition in the crucial years of 1810 and 1811.

In Venezuela, from the first slave uprising in Coro (1532) to the occupation of the same city by Miranda (1806) there had been more than 250 years of self-sacrifice and constantly renewed faith in ideals which signified unmistakeably the existence of a sense of nationhood. In the final episodes, the long line of leaders who existed simultaneously or succeeded one another can be seen as a historical relay, in which the torch was passed from hand to hand, from Chirinos to Picornell, to Gual, to España, to Pirela and Miranda. All over the Latin American continent there had been a succession of rebellions and uprisings, full of bravery and self-sacrifice. Blood had been shed generously in the cause of justice, independence, liberty and equality, that is, for a new and better order.

At this point, when the colonial system had reached a state of crisis and the revolutionary movement had attained maturity, when Francisco de Miranda was already a veteran of the struggle for liberty, Bolívar appeared. He inherited three centuries of conscious struggle by a world in rebellion. The burden of hopes and desire fell on the shoulders of this hero from Caracas, later known as the Liberator.

Chapter I References

(1) M. Briceño Iragorry, *Introducción y defensa de nuestra historia* (Caracas, 1952), p.78.

(2) *tercerones, cuarterones, quinterones, moriscos, coyotes, chamisos, ahí te estás, salto atrás, gíbaros, sambaigos, tente en el aire, no te entiendo, cholos, cuadralbos, tresalbos, castizos* etc.

(3) Cardinal-Archibishop of Ostia, learned in Holy Scripture, d. ca. 1118.

(4) *Bosquejo de la revolución en la América española* (Caracas, 1953), p.16

(5) *Obras completas*, (2 vols. Havana, 1947), I, 164–166.

(6) *Obras completas*, II, 1130.

(7) C. Parra-Pérez, *Historia de la Primera República de Venezuela* (2 vols. Caracas, 1959), I, 121.

(8) *Breve historia de América* (Chile, 1938), p.367.

(9) C. Felice Cardot, 'Rebeliones, motines y movimientos de masas en el siglo XVIII venezolano: 1750–1781,' *El Movimiento Emancipador de Hispanoamérica*, (Caracas, 1961), II, 204.

(10) *Documentos relativos a la insurrección de Juan Francisco de León* (Instituto Panamericano de Geografía e Historia, Caracas, 1949), p.88.

(11) F. de Miranda, *Archivo* (15 vols. Caracas, 1929–38), XV, 68.

(12) J. Mancini, *Bolívar y la emancipación de las colonias españolas*, (Paris-Mexico, 1914), p.160.

(13) P. Ugalde, 'Presencia y magisterio de Miranda en la revolución chilena,' *Cultura Universitaria*, Universidad Central de Venezuela, Caracas, XVII–XVIII (1950), 47.

(14) J. Biggs, *Historia del intento de don Francisco de Miranda para efectuar una revolución en Sur América* (Caracas, 1950), pp.37, 38.

(15) C. F. López, *Juan Bautista Picornell y la conspiración de Gaul y España* (Caracas-Madrid, 1955), p.354.

Simón Rodríguez.

II The Man

Origins and early education

The first member of the Bolívar family, also named, coincidentally, Simón, arrived in Venezuela in 1589 and over the next 200 years this original Spanish ancestry was modified by contact with the American environment. It appears that Bolívar had no Indian blood.[1] Amongst his ancestors on the paternal side, however, was doña María Josefa Marín de Narváez, an illegitimate daughter of Francisco Marín de Narváez, born in Caracas in 1668, of unknown mother, and this fact, taken with Bolívar's appearance and his dark skin, has given rise to speculation that he may have had some negro blood (over and above that which came to him through his Spanish forebears).

Simón Bolívar was born in Caracas on 24 July 1783, the fourth son of the marriage of don Juan Vicente Bolívar and doña María de la Concepción Palacios y Blanco. Caracas at this time was a modest city of some 20,000 inhabitants, recently inaugurated as capital of the Venezuelan provinces. When the boy was two and a half years old his father died and his education was entrusted thereafter to the best masters and tutors that the city could provide. His mother spared no expense for his education, which was the normal one for the son of rich parents in the Spanish colony. His first teachers were José Antonio Negrete, Carrasco, Guillermo Pelgrón, Fernando Vides and other notable educators, including the distinguished poet and grammarian Andrés Bello, his tutor in literature and geography. He had lessons in mathematics from the renowned Capuchin friar Francisco de Andújar, who established a private academy in Bolívar's home. The most influential of his teachers however, was undoubtedly Simón Rodríguez, for it was he who awakened the boy's intellectual and political curiosity and encouraged personal independence in this man who was later to free a whole continent. Rodríguez helped him to throw off the weight of tradition, to understand historical forces and to adopt new and creative ideas. He undermined the power of his environment and his friends, who would have encouraged him to think only of preserving or increasing his family's social position, and rising in the colonial hierarchy, which he might easily have done, assuring himself of wealth and influence without exposing himself to any kind of danger.

Rodríguez was the formative influence on Bolívar all during his adolescence, for Bolívar lived in his home as well as attending his school.

More importantly, when Bolívar was a young man, they travelled together in Europe, where the boy completed a second important stage in his education. His lessons in Caracas had been unsystematic, with many disturbances and interruptions caused by his own restlessness and the indulgence shown towards him. In Madrid he studied mathematics at the San Fernando Academy and he also attended for a short time the Royal Military School at Soreze in the south of France. According to one authority, the three years spent in Madrid was the most significant period of Bolívar's education: 'It seems that the passion for reading and study which remained with him for the rest of his life was definitively awakened in Madrid. [The unsystematic lessons received in Caracas] were transformed in Madrid, thanks to the change in environment and the influence of Esteban Palacios, into an ordered and methodical application to his studies, carried out with all the determination of which he was capable.'[2]

In Madrid, Bolívar also studied French and English with qualified masters, under the watchful eye of his guardian, the learned Marquis Jerónimo de Ustáriz y Tovar, a frank and amiable old gentleman with a wide knowledge of political and moral philosophy. 'In Madrid', the same authority continues, 'Bolívar received the education proper to young aristocrats of the time who were destined for a career in the army ... While applying himself energetically to his studies, he no doubt also frequented cafés and parties, went to the theatre and perhaps even to Court.' We must add that those responsible for Bolívar's education did not concentrate exclusively on theoretical studies. From early childhood he had lessons in fencing, riding and dancing and in later life he mentioned the advantages of a varied education. Intuitively, his masters had followed the concept of education in its widest sense, that is, a process which tends to develop the personality so that it can continue to grow and learn long after the end of formal instruction.

Travel was another significant formative influence on Bolívar, in that it taught him understanding and tolerance of other cultures. One observer wrote: 'His Excellency is electrified whenever he speaks of his trips to Europe: one can see that he has been observant and has profited by what he has seen. Besides the liveliness of his spirit and his active imagination, he has rapid and sound judgement: he knows how to evaluate and compare, having that rare talent of making his comparisons with due regard for time, place and circumstance: he realises that a thing may be good in itself, even excellent, yet not suitable at a particular moment, or suitable in one place but not in another.'[3]

In all, Bolívar went to Europe three times, on each occasion for a different reason, though in every case the underlying motive was the same: to gain experience. The first trip began when Bolívar was fifteen years old, and was intended as part of his education. He left Venezuela in February 1799 and travelled via Mexico and Cuba to Spain, from which he visited France. This trip culminated in his marriage in Madrid on 26 May, 1802, after which he returned to Caracas in August of the same year.

His second trip was to console him for the recent death of his wife. He sailed from Venezuela at the end of October 1803 and again he remained in Europe for about three years and eight months, in which time he dissipated a considerable fortune. The culmination of this trip was the visit to the Monte Sacro in Rome where he vowed he would free his country. It was on this trip also that he formed his close friendship with Simón Rodríguez and that his future destiny began to take shape. After visiting Spain, France, Italy, Austria, Belgium, Holland and Germany, he sailed from Hamburg to Charleston in the United States, arriving in January 1807 and remaining in the States for a few months before returning to Caracas in June. Incidentally, he said about this visit: 'During my short stay in the United States, for the first time in my life I saw rational liberty.'[4]

A moderate relativism was the outcome of these experiences. Bolívar's contact with the traditional societies of Europe made him weigh the differences between them and Latin America: on the one hand a continent with an identity forged over a thousand years, on the other a problematical mixture of cultures, with scarcely three hundred years of history behind it. From a distance Bolívar saw Latin America more clearly. He acquired a sense of proportion, a larger view of mankind and a recognition of certain defects in himself, though he remained convinced that his basic ideas were correct.

On his third trip to Europe, in 1810 he went as a diplomat, travelling to Great Britain at the head of the first important Venezuelan mission to that country. He thus had the opportunity to sample English life, and thereafter he professed enormous admiration for the British people who he felt had qualities that his fellow-citizens lacked: stability, respect for others, dignity, common-sense and a democratic system that had come into being without the use of violence. Their love of tradition he saw as an important stabilising force in society.

From adolescence onwards, and in particular after the period spent in Madrid, he was a voracious reader. In his own home he had access to a good library, for his father left a sizeable collection which was divided amongst his sons. Pérez Vila's research has shown the type of literature to which Bolívar had access at this time. Apart from numerous individual works, the library contained the fifteen volumes of the Abbé Pluche's famous *Espectáculo de la naturaleza*, eighteen volumes of the works of Padre Feijóo, thirteen volumes of *Ordenanzas militares* (Military

Regulations) thirteen volumes on ancient history and seven volumes of the plays of Calderón, as well as a number of recently published works.

While it has not been possible to draw up a complete list of the works read by Bolívar, one can infer from his writings that he was justified in claiming a knowledge of the Greek and Roman classics: Homer, Polybius, Plutarch, Caesar, Virgil. He was also familiar with a wide range of recent classics in Spanish, French, Italian and English: his letters contain many spontaneous references to the French Encyclopaedists, for example, and in general to the ideologues of the French Revolution, whose works he had read and thoroughly digested, as is obvious from a study of his ideas. He continued to read and study under the most adverse conditions: 'Although from April 1810 onwards, and more particularly after 1813, his time and energy were devoted almost exclusively to military and political action, nevertheless he remained eager to read newspapers, pamphlets and books which attempted to throw light on recent developments in other countries, or explained the latest thought and ideas. During the campaigns, whenever they camped or made a halt, Bolívar's officers and men saw him give any orders required, then settle down to read, while others rested, gambled or drank. In his house there is still to be seen a well-thumbed copy of Caesar's *Comentarios*. According to the historian José de Austria, an officer in the independence army, it was always to be seen "in the Liberator Simón Bolívar's hammock, where he always kept it and read it in the camps"'.[5]

Appearance and character

Bolívar's appearance has been described as follows: '[He] had a high forehead, not very wide, furrowed with lines from an early age, this being the sign of a deep thinker. His eyebrows were thick and shapely, his eyes black, lively and penetrating and his nose long and perfectly formed; though there was a small cyst on it, which troubled him until in 1820 it disappeared, leaving only a faint scar. He had prominent cheekbones and hollow cheeks, ever since I first met him in 1818. His mouth was ugly, with rather thick lips; the distance from nose to mouth was remarkable. His teeth were white, even and strong, for he took great care of them. His ears were large, but well placed and his hair was black, fine and curly: he wore it long from 1818 to 1821, when it began to turn grey and from then on he wore it short. His moustache and side whiskers were lighter in colour: he shaved them off for the first time in 1825, in Potosí. He was five feet six inches tall, narrow-chested and slim, especially in the legs. His skin was dark and rather rough, his hands and feet so small and shapely that a lady might have envied them.'[6]

For his spiritual side, another intelligent, and impartial, foreigner, the Canadian General John Robertson, offers a useful portrait. 'Amongst his fellow-citizens [Bolívar] has no equal, never mind a superior. Few men have a stronger sense of honour and delicacy. His generosity and unselfishness are infinite; his kindness is displayed on all occasions, when his sympathy is aroused. His greatest satisfaction, when in possession of the fortune he inherited, was to help the poor and unfortunate. He never failed to relieve their sufferings in a quiet and delicate fashion. His concentration never wanders, in which aspect he is exceptional. He can suffer privation and fatigue better than anyone. Few can rival his tranquility in the face of danger or adversity and his perseverance is without limits. These last two qualities have been amply demonstrated in incidents personally known to me.'[7]

Bolívar also made some interesting self-appraisals which tie in well with the views of impartial observers, and suggest a high degree of self-knowledge. He was clear about his temperament and aptitudes, stating that he detested the sedentary life, and was not cut out for administrative tasks. He found danger and adversity stimulating. Moreover, he did not need peace and quiet to think, for he could isolate himself in the midst of a crowd and calmly become absorbed in his thoughts.[8] In 1825 he remarked: 'I am not slow and deliberate, but impulsive, careless and impatient ... I like to express a multitude of ideas in a few words.'[9] At times, this latter trait could degenerate into thoughtlessness. Bolívar confessed that he was in the habit of signing letters without checking them, and also of dictating several simultaneously: 'I signed the letter without reading it, as I very often do when I am in a hurry.' One of his letters contains the following: 'Demarquet tells me that your wife has given birth to a fine boy, at the same time as you have sadly lost an older child. I believe you will soon make good this loss, and so I congratulate you and Dolorita on both events.' On another occasion, he sent condolences in the following manner: 'The gentleman's death was only to be expected, as life on this earth is not eternal.' However, it remains true that one of his principal virtues was his power of synthesis, even though this has meant that his writings have been subject to extremely varied interpretations and that politicians of every shade of opinion have used his ideas as slogans. Incidentally, this development would not have surprised him, for he himself said: 'My name is used in Colombia for good and evil and many people quote it in support of their stupidity.' For this reason, one must always consider his work as a whole, without laying undue stress on any one part.

Another of Bolívar's virtues was his ability to be objective. He declared on one occasion: 'The utmost severity is required towards our enemies, be they Spaniards or patriots: for the republic gains equally from the destruction of a good royalist or a bad patriot.' This objectivity extended even to the members of his family: in a message to Briceño Méndez

33

he said: 'Tell don Perucho I am glad he has quarrelled with my sister, since that was his duty, and that I should have despised him if he had done anything else.' He was a keen student of human nature, studying his friends' psychology and treating them accordingly. For example, his most affectionate letters went to Sucre, while the most careful and diplomatic letters were those to Santander. Yet another of Bolívar's characteristics was his moral integrity. He was convinced that the existence of the republic depended on men of virtue and that without morally sound leaders, society would go astray, for 'sometimes Governments are swayed by men, not by principles'. He had a will of iron, strengthened, not weakened, by adversity and was above pettiness.[10] Bolívar was above all practical and dynamic, eager to achieve his aims, especially that of justice, which he called 'the first law of Nature and the universal guarantee for all citizens'.[11] He followed the principles of justice in choosing men for posts of responsibility. 'I look only for ability and honesty', he stated. 'I have sought out hidden merit so that it should shine in the Courts of Law, amongst those people who worship at the altar of conscience the religion of the law ... All I asked of the candidates was moral integrity: I ignored certain aspirants for the post of magistrate and sought out shy, retiring virtue. My abiding principle has been one that is often preached but seldom practised: choose candidates who fear responsibility, who flee from public life.' It was his stated intention to 'employ men of honour even if they are enemies ... and reorganise the State on the basis of the honesty and abilities of its most distinguished citizens, without regard to other considerations.'

Bolívar's conduct as a public figure was irreproachable in such matters as his handling of public funds. As early as 1814, he enunciated his concept of fiscal honesty to the people of Caracas: 'National revenue is not the property of the Government. All your representatives are duty bound to disclose how they have used these funds.' In the proposals for a constitution which he presented to the Angostura Congress, he included amongst the duties of the citizen that of 'keeping watch on the use of public money, ensuring that it is used in the public good and denouncing any fraudulent practice to the representatives of the people, whether committed by the tax-payers, the tax-officials or the government itself.'[12] This declaration, by the way, illustrates Bolívar's desire to create a true, participatory democracy rather than simply a representative one. It was not enough that the laws were observed, each citizen was to become the jealous guardian of their observance. Honest administration is the touchstone by which a people judges its leaders. Bolívar emerges triumphant from this test, for he was completely uninterested in wealth. He was rich when he began his political career (his fortune in 1804 has been estimated at 4,000,000 *pesos*) but he spent this inheritance in the

Antonío José de Sucre.

independence campaigns. In the Colombian National Archive there are the originals of numerous communications from Bolívar to the Vicepresident of the Republic mentioning sums that are to be deducted from his salary.[13] After handling the revenues of Venezuela, Colombia and Peru for fifteen years, with no check except his moral principles, he died poor. His will reads: 'I have no property other than the lands and mines at Aroa in the province of Carabobo, and some jewels which are detailed in an inventory amongst my papers.'[14] These mines had been purchased by his ancestors 'at the time of the conquest, for 40,000 *pesos*'.[14a] It should be added that they had been mortgaged to bring Joseph Lancaster, the great English educationalist, to Venezuela.

Various other pieces of evidence testify to his implacable hatred of corruption. On 11 September 1813, he demonstrated the new principles of fiscal honesty, as well as defending the independence fighters' only source of revenue, when he declared: 'Any man convicted of evading the tax laws in relation to tobacco, whether by selling it illegally, stealing it, or by any other means, will be executed and his property confiscated to make good the loss.'[15] On 12 February 1824, in Lima, he was equally forthright: 'Any public official convicted by summary trial of misdirecting or appropriating from public funds a sum in excess of 10 *pesos* will be subject to the death penalty.'[16] On this occasion, as on the earlier one, it was stated that judges who did not act in accordance with the obligations of this decree would be subject to the same punishment. In Venezuela, these sanctions applied equally to public officials who connived with lawbreakers to mitigate the death sentence. A decree issued in Caracas on 8 March 1827 declared that any person who usurped the rights or monies of the state 'no matter how small the sum, will be subject to the death penalty and to the confiscation of all his wealth, if he has no children, or a third or fifth of it if he has, as well as being obliged to pay the legal costs and restitution of the original sum'. Any Treasury employee who stole 'any sum, no matter how small, simply on the word of three witnesses and any corroberating evidence, will also be subject to the death penalty'.

Another revealing episode concerns a proposal by General Santander that he and Bolívar should jointly place themselves at the head of a company formed to build the Panamá Canal, a proposal couched in flattering and tempting terms.[17] Bolívar replied firmly: 'I have read your letter, in which you propose I should be the patron of the company which aims to link the two oceans across the isthmus. Having thought about the matter, I think it right, not only to have no part in the business, but to urge you not to do so either. I am certain that no-one could look with favour on our participation in this purely business enterprise, when we have been and are leaders of the government: our enemies, particularly yours ... would put an evil interpretation on this plan, though it can only lead to prosperity and well-being for this country. Such is my opinion with regard to what you should do. For myself, I am resolved not to become involved in this or any other commercial enterprise.'[18]

Again, when the Peruvian Congress, amongst other acts of homage, voted on the award of 1,000,000 *pesos* to Bolívar, he twice rejected it. In his final refusal, he stated that there was 'no human power could force me to accept a gift my conscience abhors ... The Congress has named me the Father and the Saviour of Peru: it has honoured me with the title of Life President: it has engraved my likeness on a medallion: it has given me the name of Liberator and has obliged me to take charge of Peru: now it wishes to vote me an enormous fortune. I have accepted everything with joy, except the last, for the laws of my country and of my heart forbid it.'[19] Similarly, he wrote from Pativilca on 9 January 1824 to the President of the Colombian Congress: 'I renounce, of course, the annual pension of thirty thousand *pesos* which the generosity of the Congress has been kind enough to award me. I do not need it to live, while public funds are exhausted.' When he served Peru and Colombia jointly as Supreme Head, he received no salary whatsoever. He himself recognised that he was a rare case, as he explained to Santander: 'Incidentally, I am in a strange position at the moment, in that I have no means of support, though I am both President of Colombia and Dictator of Peru. Not wishing to be in the pay of the latter country, I declined the salary they offered me, and as I have no authority in Colombia I cannot ask for a salary there. So that I have had to borrow, and must live by borrowing, until I return to Guayaquil.'

Bolívar frequently insisted that his aims in life were to free his country and win glory for himself. The earliest mention of these goals dates from 1795, when he was twelve years old, and his last words, when he resigned from his post in 1830 and took leave of his compatriots, were a summary of his struggles against tyranny. If the two notions were ever in conflict, Bolívar did not hesitate: 'My greatest weakness is my love of liberty: this leads me to forget even my desire for glory. I will undergo anything, abandon all my hopes, rather than pass for a tyrant, or even be suspected of it. My ruling passion, my one aspiration, is to be known as a *lover of liberty*.' It was this obsession which influenced his destiny, according to his own words, by forcing him to be not merely strict but absolutely inflexible: 'The love of liberty', he declared to Santander, 'made me occupy a position contrary to all my feelings.' In 1829, he reiterated to Leandro Palacios: 'I fought for liberty and glory, therfore to be judged a tyrant and ignoble is a double grief.' His attitude to the liberation of Peru was also significant, as can be seen in the following declaration from 1823: 'Yes, Colombia will do her duty in Peru. She will take her soldiers to Potosí, and afterwards these brave men will return to their homes, their only reward that of having contributed to the destruction of the last tyrants of the New World. Colombia does not lay claim to a single inch of Peruvian territory, for her glory, her happiness and her security lie in preserving her own liberty and allowing her neighbours to retain their independence.'

For Bolívar, liberty and glory were not empty concepts; on the contrary, they formed part of rigorous and coherent ideology. Liberty he defined as 'the right of every man to do anything not forbidden by law',[20] and he also declared that it was 'the only goal worthy of the sacrifice of human life'.[21]

Glory was the stimulus that led men to face danger and to fight for the common good, forgetful of self. Bolívar's conception was far removed from the traditional notion of glory as being related to power, fame and riches. Towards the end of his life, in a memorable letter to the Marquis del Toro, he wrote: 'If I am sad, it is for you, for I have known such good fortune that it would be difficult for me to consider myself unfortunate. Even if I were to lose everything, I should still have the glory of having done my duty to the utmost, and this glory will be my eternal reward and happiness.'[22] 'Glory', he wrote on another occasion, 'lies in being great and being useful.' Greatness he defined as follows: 'The principal qualities of the great man are: courage to face danger, intelligence to win battles, love of his country and hatred of tyranny.' He laid great stress on the primacy of courage: 'Bravery and skill will more than compensate for lack of numbers. It would go ill with men if these moral virtues did not balance and even outweigh physical strength. The leader of the most densely populated country would soon be lord of the earth. Luckily, it has often happened that a handful of men have overcome vast empires.'

Intelligence, another of the attributes of the great man, he felt should always be accompanied by a strict moral sense; the first without the second was inappropriate to public service. 'Enlightened and honourable men should direct public opinion. Talent without morality is a scourge.' Similarly, patriotism and hatred of tyranny should go hand-in-hand, and he advocated unremitting struggle against despotism. 'It is always great, it is always noble, it is always just to conspire against tyranny, against a usurper, against a ravaging and unjust war.' He had faith in ultimate victory for men of resolution. 'All the peoples of the world who have fought for liberty have in the end destroyed their tyrants.'

As for the concept of usefulness, Bolívar gave practical examples of this for no task was too humble, or unworthy of him, if it was directed towards some lofty and positive aim. He did not consider it beneath his dignity, for example, to concern himself with day-to-day details of logistics. There are numerous references in his writings to food supplies, nails for the horses' shoes, paper, needles and cloth for making the soldiers' uniforms. No detail escaped his attention: 'Troops are to advance three or four leagues a day, the day's march to be divided into two parts: early in the morning, they are to march for two or three hours, and the same in the cooler part of the afternoon. They are to set up camp amongst trees or on slopes where there is water, and they are to take a *siesta* so that they do not become tired and worn out.'

Finally, we should note that when Bolívar made a promise he kept it. On 4 August 1826, he was awarded a medal by Bolivia and on receiving it he promised: 'I shall keep it all my life, as a mark of my profound gratitude to Bolivia, and on my death I shall return this gift to the nation through the Legislature.' On 10 December 1830, as he dictated his last will and testament, he remembered that promise: 'It is my wish that the medal presented to me by the Bolivian Congress on behalf of the people should be returned to them as I promised, as proof of the affection I feel for the Republic, even in my last moments.' As early as 1815, he had announced that his last breath would be for his country. At the end of his life he said: 'My last wishes are for the prosperity of my country.'

Chapter II References

(1) A distinguished Chilean historian mentions the wife of Luis de Bolívar y Rebolledo (1627–1702): 'María Martínez de Villegas was descended from Elena Fajardo and through her from the famous *mestizo* Francisco Fajardo, son of a Spaniard and an Indian princess ... [who] in the middle of the sixteenth century ... gained prominence in the political life of the mainland through his skill, boldness and resourcefulness. The few drops of Indian blood handed down to Bolívar from this remote ancestor were concealed as though they were a shameful stigma, yet they were so important psychologically that without them his career would perhaps have failed at the outset, due to his lack of affinity with the classic *mantuano*. In the event, this was balanced by his sympathy for the *criollo*, who was generally also a *mestizo*.' F. A. Encina, *Bolívar y la independencia de la América española* (Chile, 1958), p.302. However, this does not tally with the view of the Venezuelan genealogist Suárez, who agrees that María Martín de Villegas was descended from Elena Fajardo, but states that the latter was the daughter of Alonso Yañez Fajardo, grand-daughter of Juan Alonso Fajardo and great-grand-daughter of Alonso Yáñez Fajardo who in 1383 was rewarded by King John I of Castile with the post of *adelantado mayor* of the Kingdom of Murcia. R. Suárez, *Genealogía del Libertador* (Mérida, 1970), pp.75, 108, 109.

(2) M. Pérez Vila, *La formación intelectual del Libertador* (Caracas, 1971), pp.48–54.

(3) L. Perú de Lacroix, *Diario de Bucaramanga* (Caracas, 1935), p.230.

(4) W. R. Manning, *The Independence of the Latin American Nations* (2 vols. O.U.P. 1925), II, 1322.

(5) Pérez Vila, *La formación del Libertador*, p.81.

(6) D. F. O'Leary, *Narración* (3 vols. Caracas 1952), I, 491.

(7) C. Pi Sunyer, *El General Juan Robertson, un prócer de la Independencia* (Caracas, 1971), p.257.

(8) Perú de Lacroix, *Diario de Bucaramanga*, p.154.

(9) This quotation and those following occur in *Obras completas* in the following order: I, 1099; II, 725, 680; I, 758; II, 837; I, 417, 853; II, 1142.

(10) In May 1823 he wrote to General Santander: 'In your situation, you must show tolerance and a generous spirit. Rousseau declared that over-sensitive and rancorous temperaments were always weak and miserable and that nobility of spirit was shown in contempt for pettiness. I have made many friends through magnanimity, and this should be an example to you.' *Cartas del Libertador* (Caracas, 1959), XII, 280.

(11) This quotation and those following occur in *Obras completas* in the following order: II, 1266, 44, 1203–1205, 293, 1048.

(12) D. F. O'Leary, *Memorias* (33 vols. Caracas, 1879–87), XVI, 141.

(13) *Cartas del Libertador*, XII, 254–270.

(14) *Obras completas*, II, 988.

(14a) *Obras completas*, I, 1020.

(15) O'Leary, *Memorias*, XIII, 358.

(16) This quotation and the following one occur in *Decretos del Libertador* (3 vols. Caracas, 1961), I, 283; II, 146.

(17) Santander's letter read: Bogotá, 22 September 1825. To His Excellency General Bolívar: Sir: I resolved to send this letter, in the hope that it will overtake the mail, which left yesterday, to inform you about a splendid plan drawn up by a group of Colombians. We intend to link the two oceans, either by joining up the rivers, as in the old plans, or by building a railway across the isthmus. It has been estimated that the work will cost some 10,000,000 *pesos*, and we can rely on some foreign capital. Don Jerónimo Torres, Domingo Caicedo, Mosquera and Baralt will head the company, and many friends of yours are involved. We are anxious to see a Colombian company, not a foreign one, in charge of this affair. In order to obtain sole rights, we must make a request to the Congress and we are confident that it will prefer native capital to foreign. As you have shown an interest in the construction of a canal, or at least in the linking of the two oceans, I felt that this project might find favour with you. I am taking the liberty of asking for two favours, which I hope to see granted, if you think it possible to do so without in any way compromising yourself: (i) that you should advise the government to support the plan of linking the two oceans, if carried out by a group of Colombian businessmen who inspire confidence and guarantee to finish the job: (ii) that you agree to be the patron of the company. I feel, and the Secretaries agree, that your name at the head of this company would enhance its reputation and facilitate its task. Engineers from the United States are on their way to survey the terrain and various other important preliminary steps have been taken. The Guatemalans are trying to link the seas by using the Lake of Nicaragua, and it is a matter of national pride and national interest not to be beaten to the goal. I believe that both these ends can be served very easily, and that your participation, far from

compromising you, would add to your glory. However, I submit, as I must, to your judgement and will be guided by what you say. If you are in agreement, may I ask you to expedite matters by arranging for your reply to arrive immediately, with no loss of time, as the petition must come before Congress in January. Nothing of note has occurred. I remain your loyal and grateful servant, F. de P. Santander.' V. Lecuna (Ed.) *Cartas de Santander* (3 vols. Caracas, 1942), II, 96.

(18) *Obras completas*, I, 1276. Santander's reply was contained in a long letter relating to other matters and read as follows: 'Bogotá, 6 May 1826. To His Excellency General Bolívar etc. etc. Sir: I have received your two letters, dated 21 and 27 February. The plan for linking the two oceans has been postponed, as I had certain doubts. I see that you are not in agreement [with the plan] through excessive, though commendable scruples, and I bow, of course, to your judgement. Illingrot cannot be Intendant of Guayaquil yet, as the Constitution requires ... ' *Cartas de Santander*, II, 202.

(19) This quotation and those following occur in the *Obras completas* in the following order: I, 1052, 866, 1021; II, 124; I, 1417; II, 719, 1189.

(20) O'Leary, *Memorias*, XVI, 138.

(21) *Obras completas*, II, 1078.

(22) This quotation and those following occur in *Obras completas* in the following order: I, 1000, 986, 287, 356; II, 479; I, 492; II, 1036, 558; I, 1406; II, 988, 1282.

III Active Service

The decision

There exists a document, signed by Bolívar when he was twelve years old, that is the oldest surviving testimony to his love of freedom. The death of the boy's father, the appointment of his uncle as guardian, and his fleeing from the uncle's house to seek asylum with his sister, had been a subject of gossip in *criollo* circles in Caracas. He was called to the Chamber of the *Real Audiencia* and made a bold statement, which the clerk heard but did not dare to note, this being left to the uncle: Bolívar declared on that occasion that 'the courts might take possession of his wealth and do as they wished with it, but not with his person. For if slaves had the right to choose the masters they preferred, surely he had the right to decide in whose house he wished to live?'[1]

At the beginning of 1797, when Bolívar was not yet fourteen, he entered the White Militia Batallion of the Aragua Valleys, in which his father had been a colonel. There are numerous indications that his guardians had destined him for a distinguished career in the army. He was promoted to second-lieutenant in July 1798, not without reason, for his record states: 'Courage: cannot be doubted. Application: excellent. Ability: good. Conduct: good.'[2] Thus far, he was merely following the normal route taken by boys from good families. In 1799, however, he went to Spain and certain experiences he had there and in other parts of Europe were decisive for his future. His first trip was the fulfilment of a dream he had had to postpone for five years due to family circumstances: he was going to meet his beloved uncle and god-father, Esteban Palacios. In the Spanish capital, Bolívar was attracted to a beautiful young lady, a distant relation. At the request of the future father-in-law, who felt that the bridegroom was too young, the wedding did not take place immediately. Finally, in 1802, with a permit granted by King Charles IV in Aranjuez, the young Venezuelan officer was married. He returned to Venezuela, but within eight months his wife died. He felt that this catastrophe played a decisive role in his choice of destiny, as he showed in some remarks to Perú de Lacroix in May 1828: 'If I had not been left a widower, perhaps my life would have been different: I should not be General Bolívar, nor the Liberator, though I agree it was not in my temperament to be the mayor of San Mateo ... Had it not been for the death of my wife, I should not have made my second trip to Europe ... My wife's death made me turn early to politics: later, it made me follow Mars' carriage instead of Ceres' plough: so you can see that it had a decisive influence on my destiny.'[3]

He returned to Europe in 1804, a year in which two decisive encounters took place. The first was in Fanny Du Villar's house in Paris, where he met Humboldt, recently returned from his long journey around the New World. Exchanging ideas about the future of Latin America, they spoke of independence and Humboldt declared: 'I think your country is ready for it, but I do not see the man who can bring it about.'[4]

The second event was the coronation of Napoleon, as Bolívar himself has recounted: 'I was beginning at that time to take a certain interest in public affairs and politics and I was trying to keep abreast of current developments. In the last month of 1804, I saw the coronation of Napoleon in Paris. I was impressed by this magnificent occasion, less for the ceremonial than for the feelings of affection which the immense crowd showed towards their hero. The universal love, the free and spontaneous movement of the people, excited by the glory and heroic deeds of Napoleon, cheered on that occasion by more than a million Frenchmen, all this seemed to me the utmost to which one could aspire, the ultimate desire or ambition of man. The Crown which was placed on Napoleon's head I consider a poor thing, a Gothic trifle: what seemed wonderful was the universal interest and acclamation he aroused. This, I must confess, made me think of my country's enslavement and the glory that would accrue to the man who set it free.'[5] Several months later, on 15 August 1805, while walking in the outskirts of Rome with Simón Rodríguez and Fernando Toro, Bolívar stood on the Monte Sacro and vowed: 'I swear before you: by the god of my fathers: by my parents: by my honour and by my country, that I shall not rest in body or soul till I have broken the chains that bind us to the will of Spain.'[6] We should remember that when Bolívar referred to his country, he meant not only Venezuela, but the whole of Latin America. The situation was substantially the same all over the continent, though with visible differences of degree. Life was lived under a colonial and absolutist régime of complete dependency, without freedom of any kind. All the societies were characterised by inequality, injustice, the existence of slavery and underdevelopment.

Another influence on Bolívar's choice of destiny was his background. His father had taken part, shortly before Simón's birth, in a conspiracy against the tyranny of the Intendant Abalos, who was harming the *mantuanos'* trade. The execution of José Leonardo Chirinos in December 1796, for his resistance to oppression and for exacting payment in blood for numerous insults, no doubt impressed the boy who a year before had demanded freedom to choose where he would live. There seems little doubt that his teacher Simón Rodríguez was implicated in the conspiracy of Picornell, Gual and España. Although his name does not appear on the records, his participation is accepted by a reputable historian, Alfonso Rumazo González, in his excellent biography of Bolívar. Rodríguez was apparently imprisoned for a short time and was visited in prison by his young pupil. This must have made a strong impression on the adolescent boy, for whom the sudden disappearance of his tutor would be like a third bereavement.

For all these reasons, one can understand why, when Bolívar stopped in Mexico on his first journey to Europe, and the viceroy Azanza questioned him about events in Caracas, the boy was not taken aback but replied with a spirited defence of the conspirators and harsh criticism of the régime that made martyrs of them. The historian Felipe Larrazábal mentions that Bolívar recalled the occasion with the words: 'I defended unflinchingly the rights of Latin America to independence.'[7] When he returned to Caracas in June 1807, though still a minor under Spanish law, he was already a prominent figure. His country house was to become a centre where political matters were discussed with total frankness. A conspiracy was hatched here in 1808, which envisaged the possibility of a *criollo* Supreme Junta or Congress and a 'youth party' which included the Bolívar brothers amongst its most enthusiastic adherents. These subversive activities were discovered and the ailing governor sentenced some of the plotters to be confined outside the capital. Bolívar had to leave Caracas, where the political situation continued to evolve, in response to events in Spain, toward the successful coup of 19 April 1810.

Caracas takes the lead

During the years 1808–9, the *criollos* adopted the idea of forming a Junta like that of Seville to replace the deposed King. However, the officers in the *pardo* militias and the lower classes of society supported the Spanish authorities against this attack by the aristocracy, and one of the ring-leaders was captured and sent to Spain. The *mantuanos'* case failed to find support amongst the people, because they were the group mainly responsible for the discrimination against the *mestizo* majority of the population. They had recently opposed the *Cédula de Gracias al Sacar*, which permitted the purchase of certain privileges, that is, it permitted *mestizos* to rise in society by means of a payment. They had also opposed the opening of the universities and seminaries to *pardos*, and the latter had even been unable to find in the whole of Caracas premises in which to set up a school for their children; indeed, they had been forbidden by the *cabildo* to do so in 1805. The *mantuanos* had the dominant voice in the *consulado* and in the Church — they even had an Archbishop, Monsignor Francisco de Ibarra. The only thing they required was political power, for they were already supreme in the economic, social, cultural and religious spheres. King Ferdinand aroused more sympathy amongst the people, because in previous instances of social conflict he and the other members of the Bourbon dynasty had generally come out in favour of the poorer classes. If the *pardo* militias were firm supporters of the Crown, this was only logical, for it would have been too much to ask that they even passively approve, far less actively intervene to bring about, a social change that was not in their interest. There had been a great deal of comment in the colony about the liberal decisions and decrees promulgated by the king, with no regard for the complaints of the *mantuanos*. In fact, it was precisely this tendency to favour what they considered the mob that deprived the monarch of the support of certain powerful and influential sectors in the colony. So far as the *pardos* were concerned, however, a distant monarch, if he was understanding, was preferable to a proud and arrogant local aristocracy, determined to maintain social distinctions.

In May 1809, a new Governor and Captain-General, Vicente de Emparán, took up residence. In an effort to win over the unruly *criollos*, he named Bolívar to the post of *Teniente Justicia Mayor* of the town of Yare on 24 July. Bolívar wished to take up this post by proxy, but the *ayuntamiento* demanded his presence, which provoked his protest. On 19 April 1810, having cleverly avoided the difficulties of the previous year, he was on his estate in the valleys of Aragua when the *mantuanos* engineered the coup which deposed the Spanish authorities. This time they did not speak in terms of a break with the Crown. On the contrary, they contrived to give the appearance of being more royalist than the king's representatives, declaring that the purpose behind their actions was to safeguard the monarch's rights. They thus made it appear that the Captain-General and the Intendent were less zealous and less trustworthy in their loyalty to the king than themselves. That day, Holy Thursday, there was a confused special session of the *cabildo*. Seven gentlemen burst into the chamber, describing themselves variously as 'representatives of the clergy and the people', 'representatives of the people' and 'representatives elected by the *pardo* guilds'. They and the whole *cabildo* proceeded to a *pronunciamiento* or insurrection. Roscio was the brains behind this coup and Cortés Madariaga the main activist. The Supreme Junta was formed that day: on 24 May, Bolívar was promoted from lieutenant of the 5th Company, White Militia Batallion of the Aragua Valleys to captain of the 4th Company.

While this was taking place in Venezuela, important events were taking place in Europe and the rest of Latin America. Napoleon helped the New World by shaking up the Old, especially Spain and Portugal. Godoy, the favourite of Queen Maria Luisa, obtained permission for the French troops to march through Spain to Portugal, but on the way they changed their mind and decided to seize Spain, not counting on Spanish resistance. The decadent King Charles IV was forced by the population to abdicate in favour of the young and popular Ferdinand, but Napoleon, with his curious insistence on legality, reversed this decision and made the son restore the throne to his disgraced father, so that it was the latter who handed the sceptre of Spain to Napoleon's brother, Joseph Bonaparte.

The Spanish reaction to the French occupation, the formation of the Central Junta and the Regent Council and the heroic struggle of the Spanish people in defense of their nation, had obvious repercussions in the New World. Emissaries were sent by Napoleon to inform the Latin Americans of the new situation and to propose a peaceful transfer of the Spanish colonies from the decadent rule of the Bourbons to the flourishing rule of the Bonapartes, but the suggestion was not well received. In fact the revolution in Venezuela began over the question of Ferdinand. Since he had been deposed, the Captain-General, the Intendent, the gentlemen of the *audiencia*, the *Auditor de Guerra*, the *Asesor General* of the Government and the Lieutenant-Governor were also deposed. The *consulado* was retained, being a *criollo* stronghold. In the name of the Supreme Junta, certain key posts were confided to trustworthy supporters of the new régime. A new military structure was quickly established, and a government which represented the *criollos*, with twenty-three members, two Presidents and two Juntas, one of War and Defense and one of Finance, with seven members each.

The Supreme Junta immediately invited the other provinces to follow the example of Caracas, sending people to the interior to explain the measures taken. The influential regional oligarchies took advantage of this opportunity to stress their dissatisfaction with the confederation set up by Charles III, which had reduced their traditional autonomy by making them subordinate to Caracas. Guayana hesitated at first, then came out in favour of the Spanish Regency Council. Maracaibo was also firm in its opposition to the Caracas Junta. The town of Coro took advantage of the confusion to free itself from Caracas, declaring that with the deposition of the federal authorities there was now no capital city and that since Coro was the oldest city in the country, it should become the capital. In the other provinces, there was a provisional acceptance of the measures taken in Caracas, on condition that provincial autonomy was re-instated. From this one can see that the recently formed links between the different provinces were weak and easily broken.

The Junta was extremely cautious in matters of foreign relations, which they considered especially important. The concern for the rest of Latin America, already visible in Miranda and in the writings of Picornell, Gual and España, re-appeared in the statements and writings of this time. Within a week of 19 April, the Caracas Junta had issued an invitation to all the *cabildos* of Latin America to follow Venezuela's example. Under Roscio's direction, diplomatic missions were set up to try to elicit support for the new régime. The most important of these was that entrusted to Bolívar, now promoted to colonel, at the age of twenty-six. He was sent with Luis López Méndez and Andrés Bello to London, where between July and September they revealed the true intention of the Caracas Junta, which was not to 'safeguard' Ferdinand's rights, but to prepare the way for independence.

Bolívar's contact in London with Miranda was crucial. On the younger man's insistence, Miranda returned to Caracas after an absence of nearly forty years. When he presented himself at La Guaira, the government hesitated over whether to admit him, since it did not seem logical to admit the sworn enemy of the King in whose name they were exercising authority. Finally, however, a cleverly arranged mass demonstration accompanied Miranda in triumph to Caracas.

On 29 May 1811, Venezuela took another important step in foreign relations when she signed the first treaty with the neighbouring country of Cundinamarca, a Treaty of Alliance and Federation, the foundation of Gran Colombia, so dear to the hearts of Bolívar and Miranda. The treaty was ratified by the Venezuelan Congress, with no opposition, on 22 October 1811. In the list of articles, besides the usual political statements, there was one that shows the extraordinary interest taken at that time in cultural matters: 'Schools, colleges and universities in either country will be open to citizens of the other.'[8]

The documents produced by the Junta are of an extremely high standard, and the arguments in defense of the measures taken are brilliant and convincing. The patricians of 19 April and the parliamentarians of 1811, as well as the journalists and members of the Patriotic Society who guided public opinion, were well informed. There is evidence of a solid intellectual basis, a knowledge of men and politics and a gift for argument in the documents and declarations of this period. If the polemic with Spain could have been carried out at international level, before a body of impartial experts in civil law, there is no doubt that the verdict would have gone to Venezuela, for the correctness of her arguments.

After his return to Caracas at the end of his mission to London, Bolívar was busy as a speaker and activist in the cause of independence, especially in the Patriotic Society. On the anniversary of the revolution, 19 April 1811, his speech was one of the most vehement, with those of Antonio Muñoz Tébar and José Félix Ribas. The first Congress, convened by the Supreme Junta with the aim of stabilising the situation, had met on 2 March, with delegates from Cumaná, Margarita, Barcelona, Barinas, Caracas, Mérida and Trujillo. By 4 July, pressure on Congress reached its height and independence became the main subject of debate. It was a polemic on law and politics that recalled the debates in the French Constituent Assembly in 1789. On 5 July, independence was solemnly declared, with only one deputy, Maya, from La Grita, refusing to sign the Act. The provinces of Guayana and Maracaibo were not represented, nor was Coro.

In the 'first free and representative constitution in Latin America', that is, in the constitution accepted in Caracas on 21 December 1811, there was a novel epilogue, in which the Venezuelans declared: 'Since the Supreme Legislator of the Universe has inspired in our hearts friendship and sincere love for each other and for all the other inhabitants of Latin America who are willing to join us in defending our Religion, our natural Sovereignty and our Independence ... we promise to observe ... each and every article of this Constitution ... promising also to change them at any time, according to the will of the majority of the peoples of America, if they are willing to form a single national body to defend and preserve freedom and political independence; we will modify, change and correct them by collective agreement, so that they correspond more closely to the interests of those peoples, as expressed by a body composed of all their representatives, the General American Congress ... ' This was a clear commitment to Latin American unity, as was the article relating to those eligible for membership of the Triumvirate, Venezuela's Executive Power at this time: the only condition laid down was that they should be 'born on the American continent or adjacent islands (previously known as Spanish America)'.[9]

Under the First Venezuelan Republic Bolívar had no responsibilities other than the military functions with which he was charged between July 1811 and July 1812. Even Miranda was ignored when the time came to form a government, and instead Cristóbal Mendoza, Juan Escalona and Baltasar Padrón were the men chosen. They were honest and upright citizens, aristocrats, with solid reputations, chosen for their integrity. While this kind of man is ideal in easy times, in the crisis that was fast approaching for Venezuela they were to prove useless. Then the old generation were swept away, Miranda amongst them, and the new generation took its place, led by Bolívar.

War

The most unexpected allies conspired together against the new Venezuelan Republic. Nature herself, with a devastating earthquake on 26 March 1812, seemed to be supporting the insurrection led by Domingo Monteverde which arose in Coro and soon spread to the interior. Although the victory of independence had been won by all the social classes in Peru, as soon as the *mantuanos* had achieved their aims, they hastened to rid themselves of people who had hitherto been necessary to them. The Canary Islanders, still smarting from long years of humiliation followed by the frustration of their hopes that with independence they also could throw off their chains, joined Monteverde.

The First Republic was thus faced with a serious crisis and, as in crises of Ancient Rome, the triumvirate gave way to a dictatorship. This time Miranda was chosen, perhaps deliberately. Faced with an over-complicated situation, the old man failed miserably, a victim of numerous circumstances, amongst them the fact that he was out of touch with Venezuelan reality. His irascible and authoritarian personality also impaired his political effectiveness. Bolívar had met him in London and, judging him against that background, had urged him to return to Venezuela, not foreseeing the difficulties that would arise. Forty years is a long time and Miranda by then was out of place in his own country.

Miranda was unwilling at first to allow the young militia colonel Bolívar into the army, but he eventually gave way and had him by his side in the difficult capture of Valencia on 13 August 1811, in which Bolívar distinguished himself. He was sent to Caracas with the report of the victory, returning to active service in May of the following year. Shortly before, there had been an earthquake in Caracas, and his courage had averted panic in the Plaza de San Jacinto when the forces of obscurrantism preached that the earthquake was a sign of divine displeasure at the independence movement. On 4 May, he became political and military commander of Puerto Cabello. On 30 June the garrison of the castle of San Felipe mutinied, releasing Royalist prisoners and attacking the town with their artillery. After five days of fighting, under attack also by Monteverde's troops from Valencia, Puerto Cabello fell to the Spaniards. The failure of the Marquis del Toro in Oriente, the fear that Caracas would be captured by the slaves who this time had risen up at the instigation of their reactionary masters, the attitude of Guayana and Maracaibo, persistent sabotage and the wave of ill-feeling against Miranda, who instead of taking the offensive had settled into a defensive position: all this indicated that the end was near. There were desertions, rumours, insubordination, difficulties in obtaining military material. Miranda surrendered to Monteverde on 25 July. He did not betray his country or his companions; he was defeated by his mistaken appraisal of the effectiveness of the forces at his disposal and the calibre of the enemy, a mistake based on ignorance of local circumstances. His confidence in his enemies' observance of the conditions of surrender was another example of his remoteness from the crude and barbarous times in which he lived. He fell into the hands of the enemy and died after languishing for four years in Spain. One of the foremost authorities on his life has written: 'It was a great adventure, illuminated always by danger and tragedy. He should be understood and admired in a historical context and in the context of Latin America, for he is the supreme example of a figure whose importance went far beyond the boundaries of his own country. He was ... an 'adventurer', but one who ennobles the meaning of that word.'[10]

At this tense and difficult moment, the people gave no support whatsoever to the new order. The government had given no satisfaction to popular aspirations. They merely abolished the tribute levied on the Indians and announced on 4 August 1810, that is, four months after taking power, that 'it is forbidden to import negroes into this province'. Slavery was still functioning. From the political point of view, the Constitution promulgated in 1811 served the interests of the *criollo* nobility. It was a combination of the French and North American systems. There was a federal structure, as suited to the geographical and historic realities of the country. Political rights and civil liberties were instituted, such as equality before the law, the abolition of titles and privileges, an end to discrimination, freedom of thought. The State promised to safeguard property, thus fortifying a system clearly based on injustice since the Conquest and colonisation. In religious matters the régime was cautious and conservative. In other words, it was a foreign and rather abstract type of democracy, remote and incomprehensible to the masses, none of whose aspirations were answered. They had no reason to support the new order, and without their support it could not survive. The same mistake was repeated in the Second Republic and it suffered the same fate: collapse.

Thanks to the generous intervention of his Spanish friend Francisco Iturbe, Bolívar obtained a passport from Monteverde which enabled him to leave the country. He went first to Curaçao and then to Cartagena in New Granada, ruled at this time by an autonomous government. There he wrote his famous *Cartagena Manifesto*, addressed to 'the people of New Granada by a native of Caracas'. In this manifesto he revealed himself to be a profound political thinker, despite his youth. It is an important work for establishing his significance as a thinker and understanding the vision which guided him at the start of his career. His analysis of the causes of the recent collapse of the Republic is masterly.

In New Granada, Bolívar also took part in some military activity, not caring where he fought, so long as he was fighting for freedom. He obtained there the necessary support to organize another attempt to free Venezuela, the campaign later known as the *Campaña Admirable*. On March 1813, the government of New Granada, established in Tunja, conferred on Bolívar the rank of Brigadier-general and made him a citizen of New Granada. Two months later, he was on the Venezuelan border and on 14 May the campaign began. On the 15th he entered San Cristóbal and on the 23rd he was acclaimed as 'Liberator' in Mérida. On 15 June, in Trujillo, he issued a proclamation of war to the death, which brought some clarity to the situation, for it meant that the Republic was accepting war on the royalists' terms. Bolívar stated that the issues were clear: it was freedom against oppression, the people against the throne, independence against colonialism. He urged that there was only one possible choice for Venezuela, and pleaded for unity and an end to sterile and suicidal internal divisions. He even used the threat of revolutionary terror, but to no avail. His movement was unpopular, it seemed to lack any concrete aims, there was no mention of any improvement in the condition of the exploited classes; on the contrary, it seemed to promise simply a strengthening of *criollo* domination.

Nevertheless, the year 1813 brought victory. While Bolívar began his campaign in the west, a group of forty-five men, amongst them Piar, Bermúdez, Valdés and Bideau, led by Santiago Mariño, attempted to free Oriente with the Chacachacare Expedition, whose proclamation vindicated the noble name of Miranda. Mariño was in Cumaná when Bolívar entered Caracas on 6 August. The two commanders, each supreme in his own half of the country, met on 5 April 1814 in La Victoria. Not long afterwards, they were both forced into exile, with the collapse of the Second Republic.

Once again, the Caracas *cabildo* had taken upon itself the right to speak for the whole country. On 14 October 1813, it declared Bolívar Commander-in-Chief of the armies and confirmed the title of 'Liberator' already bestowed on him by Mérida. The government was reorganised; it had been a year of bloody fighting and even more sacrifices would be required in 1814, but in one of the rare intervals of calm in the city, on 2 January, Bolívar called a Popular Assembly, to which he rendered a detailed account of his actions and from which he emerged with unlimited powers.

Despite Bolívar's and Mariño's magnificent triumphs, royalist reaction had not died out. Maracaibo and Guayana kept it well supplied with men and material, and it was by this route that vital equipment reached the royalists from Cuba, Puerto Rico and some of the English West Indian islands. 1814 was a black year for the Republic. The masses had been won over to the monarchist cause, and were pressing the rebels, who could not obtain fresh supplies of arms. The U.S.A. were helping the Spaniards, as were the English, who were too afraid of Napoleon to quarrel with Spain, despite the tempting offers of substantial trading profits held out by the Latin Americans.

The Asturian José Tomás Boves became a leader of the royalist troops. As they were better armed and better fed than the patriots, they were generally successful in their attacks, which won Boves immense prestige among the poverty-stricken and illiterate *llaneros*, inhabitants of the *llanos* or grassy plains in the south of Venezuela. They were *mestizos*, having some Carib Indian blood, and being accustomed to the harsh life of cowhands, they were famous for their endurance and courage. Boves allowed his band of *llaneros* and *pardos* mainly from the lower classes to loot from the enemy and exact revenge for centuries of exploitation. Destruction and death were the order of the day amongst these people who had nothing to lose but their poverty and Venezuela was the scene of dreadful deeds. So Boves liquidated the short-lived Second Republic. His half-naked *llaneros*, riding without saddle or harness and with no weapon but their lances, made the cavalry the decisive force once the war was carried to the plains where animals were plentiful. In fact, the artillery was little used in the independence campaigns, due to the difficulty of obtaining guns, powder and shot.

Bolívar and his associates were once more forced into exile, though only temporarily. As the historian Augusto Mijares writes: 'The marvellous thing in Bolívar's life is to see him rise from the depths of misfortune to the heights of glory, carried upwards by his strength of character, which was reinforced by defeat.'[11] The situation seemed grim for the independence movements at this point. Ferdinand VII, re-established on the Spanish throne thanks to Napoleon's defeat, in February 1815 sent to America an expeditionary force of more than 10,000 well equipped veterans, commanded by Pablo Morillo. He was resolved to bring the continent back under Spanish domination, denying even the liberal principles and decrees set forth by the Spanish authorities during the recent crisis. Morillo occupied Margarita and temporarily subdued Venezuela and New Granada.

Bolívar had escaped in September 1814 via Carúpano to Cartagena. In Tunja he informed the Congress of his defeat. That body re-affirmed its confidence in him and confided certain military tasks to him, which he successfully carried out. Since it was impossible for the moment to go back to Venezuela, he went in search of support to the West Indies, remaining in Jamaica for seven months, during which time he read and meditated and wrote his famous Jamaica Letter. The historian Guerrero writes: 'In the Prophetic Letter, Bolívar becomes the historian of the future ... and he elaborates a philosophy of history ... He analyses economic, political, social and ideological factors before arriving at his conclusion: that America will eventually divide into fifteen or more independent Republics: that Mexico will be a representative Republic, with a President who will retain office for life providing he performs his functions adequately and justly, or a monarchy supported by military and aristocratic interests. Three attempts at Empire, with Iturbide, Maximilian and Porfirio Díaz, followed by the one-party rule since the Revolution, demonstrate the accuracy of these predictions. The Central-American Confederation: the Panamá Canal and the proposals for that of

Nicaragua: anarchy and *caudillismo* in the River Plate region, the Rosas dictatorship and the power of the land-owning élites: the political stability of Chile, thanks to the iron hand of Portales and the lessons of Bello: the soft, luxurious life of Lima, to which even Bolívar fell victim: the betrayals of Torre Tagle and Riva-Agüero: the development of Gran Colombia: the O.A.S. and Latin America's wariness towards her imperialist neighbour: all this was predicted in Bolívar's letter, which combined two apparent opposites, reason and intuition.'[12]

In December 1815, Bolívar arrived in Haiti. The decision to move to Port-au-Prince was a fortunate one, as it turned out. President Pétion, Luis Brión from Curaçao and Robert Sutherland generously helped him to prepare the Los Cayos expedition. There were a large number of Venezuelan exiles on the island, quarrelling bitterly amongst themselves over politics. Thanks to Brión's support, Bolívar assumed the leadership of this group, and a select group of officers set sail with him, amongst them Mariño as Chief of Staff and Brión as Admiral. Bolívar had spent the whole of 1815 gathering arms and munitions. In Venezuela, numerous guerrilla groups were harassing the royalists, but Bolívar was convinced that outside help was necessary. He reiterated his offers of commercial privileges to Great Britain, offering, for example, concessions in relation to the canal linking the oceans. He needed twenty or thirty thousand guns, £1 million sterling and fifteen or twenty ships. He even approached the North Americans in his attempts to gather these resources, without which there could be neither freedom nor independence, but did not obtain any help from them. Being more intent on preserving their neutrality and their friendship with Spain, they had shown the same indifference towards the Latin American independence movement as in the case of Palacio Fajardo to whom they addressed an 'icy reply which one day', according to the recipient, 'will set the tone for our replies to them'.[13]

The Third Republic was born with the arrival of the Los Cayos expedition in Margarita in May 1816, though it quickly suffered defeat at Ocumare and was forced to retreat again to Haiti. It was at this point that Pétion won his title of Benefactor of Venezuela, for he did not abandon his unfortunate friend, nor did he adopt the convenient expedient, suggested by Bolívar himself, of simply supplying him with the means to escape to North America, England, Mexico or Argentina. The Haitian historian, Paul Verna, in an excellent study, gives the text of Pétion's noble reply to the suggestion: 'If Fortune has betrayed you twice, perhaps she will smile on you the third time. That at least is my presentiment, and if I can do anything to lessen your sorrow and grief, count on me to the limit of my capabilities. Come quickly, then, to this city and we will discuss the matter.'[14] This was in September 1816 and there followed about three months of intense preparation. With the support of Pétion and Sutherland, Bolívar got ready his final attack, the expedition that was to culminate in the irreversible triumphs of Carabobo and El Callao.

There now began a series of successes for the independence fighters. The movement adopted a new language, more social than political. Bolívar had learned from his reverses, he had understood the reason for the royalist successes. In Jamaica he admitted: ' ... the Independence movement did not offer complete freedom, unlike the Spanish guerrillas.'[15] So, in a gesture that was in full accordance with his ideas, as well as those of Pétion, he freed all the slaves and, almost immediately afterwards, ordered a redistribution of land in favour of men who had fought in the independence campaigns. The themes of equality and social injustice became the centre of his declarations. Within the patriot armies, the possibilities of promotion for soldiers from 'the people' were enlarged. The guerrilla struggle over the years had already done the work of selecting the fittest, thus enabling men of humble origin to rise to positions of power. Morillo wrote that any of the independence *caudillos* 'who found himself in an area where there were no royalist troops immediately alerted all the citizens, freed slaves and within a few days had formed a new army.'[16] Ex-slaves became excellent officers and the independence movement found an inexhaustible source of men in the poverty-stricken rural masses. Boves had died in 1814 at the battle of Urica, and now another leader won the fervent adhesion of the warlike *llaneros*: José Antonio Páez, who brought them over to the Republican side by a promise of land-reform which Bolívar was quick to endorse. It was translated into the abolition of the *latifundios* or immense privately-owned estates in the *llanos*, the declaration of the right to graze anywhere and the distribution of land to soldiers.

The final defeat of Napoleon improved prospects for the Latin Americans, for once that danger was past, British manufacturers and merchants pressed for a change of policy in relation to Latin America. There was no need to nurture the friendship with Spain, and they were very interested in commercial possibilities. Moreover, England at this point was over-stocked with old war-material that could be sold at a profit to Latin America, while the latter's products, such as cocoa, coffee, fruit, leather and mules were much appreciated in England. The actual trading could easily be carried out in the West Indies, where the preparations for the independence campaigns were also in train. Thus the supply of arms grew steadily better, the independence armies were no longer dependent on whatever arms they could capture, nor were they forced to pay the exorbitant price previously demanded by unscrupulous traders taking advantage of the situation of shortage.

There was a significant difference between this campaign and previous ones, in that Caracas was not the principal target. When the expedition first arrived from Haiti, Piar was one of the first to realise the importance of capturing Guayana. Resources were concentrated on this aim, and he organised the Battle of San Félix which won this important province for them. Angostura became the geographical and political centre which had hitherto been lacking; its strategic location, the possibility of contact with the outside world via the Orinoco, its ease of defense and the abundance of resources made it a valuable capture. Thanks mainly to the efforts of the Franciscan Missions, Guayana was an extremely rich province; at a time when practically the whole country was devastated by the war, Guayana was unscathed, having been almost constantly in royalist hands. The Spanish General Morillo later confirmed Piar's intuition when he called Guayana 'an emporium where the enemy have a fortune stored'.[17] For him, the loss of this important region implied the eventual fall of Caracas and Bogotá, and it is true that once the independence armies had secured Guayana they did not suffer any significant defeats. The road forward to a Republic now seemed clear.

The struggle spreads

From Angostura, Bolívar set out to liberate the whole of South America. First, however, he reformed all the institutions of the Republic, creating a Council of State, a deliberative Congress, (which confirmed Bolívar as Supreme Commander of the independence forces) and an Executive Power, with its attendant Secretariats or Ministries. Another important step was the creation of a newspaper, the *Correo del Orinoco*, to spread the message. In the chancelleries of Europe it began to be understood that a serious, progressive, civilian and constitutional state was joining the club of free peoples.

At last, by the middle of 1818, the independence fighters had all the arms and material they needed. Moreover, they had installed arsenals in many towns. The admirable feat of crossing the Andes and the subsequent liberation of New Granada strengthened Venezuela. Crossing the highlands with *llanero* soldiers was another amazing feat, crowned by the victory at Boyacá on 7 August 1819, one of a series of triumphs that distinguished this period. Morillo, veteran of the Spanish struggle against Napoleon, did not conceal his admiration for the courage and endurance of Bolívar's troops, who overcame deficiencies in their arms and equipment through their indomitable will to fight for a more just, egalitarian and free society.

The year 1820 was crucial. The mutiny led by Riego y Quiroga in Spain, which forced Ferdinand to swear loyalty to the Constitution of 1812, prevented the dispatch of new troops to Latin America and even brought significant changes in Spanish policy. In Venezuela, in the meantime, the royalists had been losing the sympathy of the masses who had originally supported them. The large contingent of Spaniards under Morillo followed a suicidal policy of harassing the general population. The role of the *llaneros* in the independence armies, the superiority in numbers of the latter and the improvement in their equipment turned the tide of battle. Morillo was ordered to negotiate and at his instigation a six-month armistice was signed, during which a final peace-treaty would be negotiated. In the meeting which took place on 27 November and which would have seemed impossible a year before, Bolívar proposed that the treaty should contain references to the conventions of war, a proposal which showed that Gran Colombia considered herself a sovereign nation, equal to Spain.

From April 1821, after the breaking of the armistice, Spanish power grew weaker and weaker in Venezuela. The victory of Carabobo in June set the seal on independence, at the cost of more than two thousand dead. The independence forces consisted of Páez and his *llaneros*, the ex-dissident Mariño, Cedeño and Plaza, who died in battle, Briceño Méndez, Salom, British volunteer legionaries and officers and soldiers from all over Venezuela, 6,400 men in all. The Spanish forces consisted of 5,200 men, half of them Spaniards, half Venezuelans, commanded by Miguel de la Torre. They managed to retreat to Puerto Cabello with one batallion, emerging in December to occupy Coro, which was freed again, however, in May 1823. The last significant action by the Spanish forces was the naval battle of Maracaibo. The Spaniard Morales surrendered on 3 August, and Páez took Puerto Cabello on 10 November, allowing generous terms of surrender to the commanders, Calzada and Carrera. The remnants of the Spanish armies, 56 officers and 539 men, were permitted to leave the country with full military honours. The war was over in Venezuela.

The following nine years in Bolívar's career will be examined in detail in the main part of this study, for in that period his thought is of more significance than his actions. For the moment, a brief résumé of the years 1821–30 will suffice. After Carabobo, he returned to New Granada, finally liberated by the battle of Bombóna on 7 April 1822. He then initiated the Southern Campaign (1822–26), realising that Gran Colombia was not safe while its most vulnerable flank was exposed to attack from the Spaniards. It was a hard necessity that forced him to turn his attention to the south of the continent, for it brought the destruction of his work in the North. In the end it cost him his power, though he still retained it nominally, and it brought the Republic by 1826 to a state where it was 'a horrible labyrinth', and 'an edifice like the Devil's, on fire everywhere'.[18]

On this new crusade to the south, Bolívar was accompanied by officers and troops from Venezuela and New Granada, the most outstanding figure being Antonio José de Sucre. Ecuador and Peru were liberated by the battles of Pichincha on 24 May 1822, Junín on 6 August 1824 and Ayacucho on 9 December 1824. In Guayaquil, Bolívar had reached an agreement with José de San Martín: the Argentine leader had begun the fight in the south from his own country, Bolívar with his superior forces was to carry the fight to Peru. Sucre went ahead and ignoring the principle of *uti posseditis juris* he presided over the creation of a new republic: Bolivia. The Liberator disapproved at first of the initiative, but later agreed to accept the *fait accompli*, when he realised that Gran Colombia by this means would have an affiliated state in the south.

Bolívar carried out important constitutional and diplomatic tasks in this period. He personally directed the Mosquera and Santa María missions, he composed and presented proposals for a Bolivian Constitution, he convened the Congress of Panamá, he had an audience with envoys from the River Plate region, who invited him to become the protector of the whole of Latin America, he wrote about education and social justice.

This was Bolivar's and, through him, Gran Colombia's finest hour. Yet the seeds of decay were being sown in his absence, confusion was growing and finally anarchic *caudillismo* and the machinations of the oligarchy forced his return to Caracas. It was Bolívar's destiny to be constantly forced to begin again from the beginning. Stoically, he forced himself to depart from Lima. As one historian has written: 'The fact that he dragged himself away, by an effort of will, from a social milieu in which he had found honour, pleasure and delight, in response to the call of patriotic duty, when there was no longer the stimulus of victory nor the acclamation of the crowd, and when he could have rested on his laurels, is one of the best demonstrations of the fact that his life was ardently dedicated to ... his dominating passion.'[19]

The discord between Páez and Santander was a clear prefiguration of the conflict that would split Gran Colombia. Bolívar was unable to overcome the oligarchy, which grouped itself around Páez, while Santander also had powerful support for his plans to help the *caudillos* and *mantuanos*. Gran Colombia fell victim to politicians avid for riches and power. A loan negotiated with England gave rise to an immense scandal, which did not prevent the men who had negotiated it from waxing rich. For a time it seemed that Bolívar might have succeeded in calming Páez, but the malaise lay too deep. A special convention was called in Ocaña, which attempted to analyse the situation calmly, but with little success. Bolívar was forced to adopt dictatorial powers, in a last desperate throw of the dice. It was not a dictatorship of the type that later became so common in Latin America; rather, it was a dictatorship in the Roman sense, of a crisis government. Far from being a reversion to reactionary principles, it was a last attempt to make the revolution work, as Bolívar's actions at this time in favour of the slaves and the Indians, in economic policy and in relation to the Church, show. In fulfilment of his promise, he handed over power in 1830 and left Bogotá on his last exile, following Sucre on the bitter path of ingratitude, incomprehension and disillusionment. Yet he forgave his compatriots at the moment of his death. With their fanaticism and stupidity they had embittered his last months, execrating his name and exiling him from the country that he had set free: yet he wrote: 'After my death, I desire my remains to be desposited in Caracas, my native city.'[20] Ramón Díaz Sánchez has written of Bolívar's last days: 'Bolívar's life was exemplary ... Surrounded by material wealth from birth, he died poor. But those who survived to see him buried ... were they any happier? Dying, like living, is relative. A man lives or dies ... by his works, not by the wealth he has accumulated. Bolívar lived more intensely than the selfish people who persecuted him. The approach of death brought him a tremendous lucidity. Then he understood everthing more clearly. His heart was free of hatred and rancour because his spirit and his conscience were full of light.'[21] The distinguished dean of Venezuelan historians, Cristóbal L. Mendoza, to whom I owe the inspiration for this work, commented: 'Throughout Bolívar's life, one is aware that all his thoughts and actions were obsessively bent towards the task of emancipation ... More than anyone else, he recognised the profound nature of the transformation, knowing so well the country and its circumstances ... The triumphant dawn of hope sheds its light over the figure of Bolívar.'[22]

Chapter III References

(1) 'Transcripción del Expediente Original de la Real Audiencia de Caracas, sobre domicilio tutelar del menor Don Simón de Bolívar, originado por la fuga de éste de la casa de su tutor, Don Carlos Palacios y Sojo, en el mes de julio de 1795,' *Boletín de la Academia Nacional de la Historia*, Caracas, no. 149, enero–marzo 1955, p.22.

(2) A. Rumazo González, *Bolívar* (Caracas-Madrid, 1955), p.39.

(3) Perú de Lacroix, *Diario de Bucaramanga*, pp.226–230.

(4) V. Lecuna, *Catálogo de errores y calumnias en la historia de Bolívar* (2 vols. New York, 1956), I, 160.

(5) Perú de Lacroix, *Diario de Bucaramanga*, p.229.

(6) *Itinerario documental de Simón Bolívar* (Caracas, 1970), p.14.

(7) *Vida de Bolívar* (N.Y. 1883), I, 7.

(8) C. L. Mendoza, *Las primeras misiones diplomáticas de Venezuela* (2 vols. Caracas, 1962), II, 127.

(9) *Constitución Federal de Venezuela, 1811* (Reproducción facsimilar de la edi-

ción de 1812, Caracas, 1961), pp.18, 38.

(10) J. Nucete Sardi, *Aventura y tragedia de Don Francisco de Miranda* (Venezuela, 1964), pp.395, 406.

(11) *El Libertador* (Caracas, 1964), p. 108.

(12) L. B. Guerrero, 'Bolívar, historiador del futuro', *Candideces* (Caracas, 1967), pp.8, 10.

(13) C. Parra-Pérez, *Una misión diplomática venezolana ante Napoleón en 1813* (Caracas, 1953), p.20.

(14) *Pétion y Bolívar* (Caracas, 1969), p.256.

(15) *Obras completas*, I, 180.

(16) A. Rodríguez Villa, *El teniente general don Pablo Morillo* (2 vols. Madrid, 1920), II, 18.

(17) Rodríguez Villa, *El teniente general don Pablo Morillo* II, 80.

(18) Bolívar, *Obras completas*, I, 1432–44.

(19) R. Bernal Medina, *Ruta de Bolívar* (Cali, 1961), p.182.

(20) *Obras completas*, II, 988.

(21) *El caraqueño* (Caracas, 1967), p.138.

(22) 'Discurso en el sesquicentenario de la Batalla de Carabobo', *Boletín de la Academia Nacional de la Historia*, Caracas, no. 214, abril–junio, 1971, p.165.

IV Ideas

In twenty years of public life, in his writings and actions, Bolívar constructed a programme for the revolution that would create a new South America. He did not invent all the elements of that programme; he invented some, and the rest he inherited from a long and vigorous tradition that had developed during the years of frustrated effort. His contribution and his significance lay in his ability to synthesise all this into a unified and coherent whole. Simón Rodríguez summed up the case from the viewpoint of his seventy years: Bolívar gave America 'many of his own and other people's ideas, propagating those most likely to convert into free men those who were formerly slaves'.[1] Some very significant ideas came from classical culture, as the historian Julio Febres Cordero has shown.[2] He also took a considerable amount from contemporary thought, showing his familiarity with a wide range of writers. His real contribution, however, was in bringing all these influences together like the spokes of a single wheel, in struggling and working right to the time of his death on behalf of independence and in giving careful attention to every detail, without ever losing his sense of priorities. Moreover, he expressed other people's ideas in a fresh and precise language. Beginning with the ideas on autonomy of the *criollo* aristocrats, but going far beyond them to the radical ideas of his last fifteen years, he built up a complete programme for the new America. He was not, however, a mere populariser or propagandist, for of all the Latin American leaders he was the one who went furthest in carrying out the programme.

The political situation in Venezuela before 1800 was similar to that in the rest of Latin America, the characteristic feature being that political decisions relating to the colony were taken by the Spanish authorities. As late as 1809, Martín de Garay, in the name of Ferdinand VII, declared to his subordinates in America: 'At no time has unity between the metropolis and the colonies been more essential. Now is the time to rectify abuses, to remove obstacles to progress and encourage it by every means, to put the relationship between the colony and the metropolis on a proper basis of justice.'[3] This was on the eve of independence, with Spain facing a crisis as a result of the Napoleonic invasion. The Bayonne Congress, tacitly recognising the realities of three hundred years of colonial rule, promised that in future 'the Spanish provinces and kingdoms in

America will enjoy the same rights as the metropolis'.[4] Yet it was only at the end, under the precarious government of the Regency Council, that Spain consented to end the injustices of those three hundred years. In an act of repentance, the Regency Council repeated the convocation issued by the Central Junta of Seville of a meeting of the *Cortes* or Spanish parliament at which the American colonies would be represented, and recognised that Latin America's problems arose from the arbitrariness and incompetence of the officials of the old régime'. It went on to promise solemnly: 'From this moment, citizens of Spanish America, you are raised to the dignity of free men. You are no longer, as before, bent under the yoke which grew harder to bear, the further you were from the centre of power, ill-treated through greed or indifference, destroyed through ignorance. Remember that once you have spoken or written the name of the man who is to represent you in the national congress, your destiny will no longer be in the hands of ministers, viceroys or governors, but in your own hands.'[5] Note the vocabulary: 'bent under a yoke', 'greed or indifference', 'destroyed through ignorance'. The Spanish confession exempts us from seeking further proofs.

The independence movement was opposed to colonialism and absolutism, and in favour of democracy, self-government and freedom. Without the seizure of power, that is without possession of the means of governing and the levers of authority, nothing could be done, and this had led certain far-seeing spirits in various parts of South America to conceive of the idea of independence and even to sacrifice their lives to it. Miranda had thought of it ever since 1781, when he was fighting for the United States. *Tiradentes*, Espejo and Nariño had also imagined an autonomous order which would recognise the separate personality of the Latin American people and win them a place amongst the adult countries of the world.

We have already referred to a document from 1781–2, in which revolutionary principles can be glimpsed for the first time: the document in which Bolívar's father, together with the Marquis de Mijares and Martín de Tovar described the 'unbearable and infamous oppression' that they suffered from the 'tyrannical decisions' of the Intendant and begged Miranda 'with outstretched arms and on bended knee ... for the love of God' to be the '*caudillo* who would end this general state of desperation and rescue [us] ... from this accursed slavery'.[6] Chirinos' rebellion in Coro was motivated by French political ideas of Republicanism and freedom, learned from the Haitian Jacobins, but after Miranda it was Picornell, Gual and España who best understood the ideological, preparatory phase of the Revolution.

It could be said that Bolívar inherited the mantle of the men of 19 April and 5 July. He had a double objective: to destroy the old system and to build a new one, to liquidate the despotic and oppressive régime, break the chains that bound them in subjection to the Spanish Crown and win independence. Control over public affairs must be won for the Latin Americans, whose condition he described in the Jamaica Letter: 'serfs to do the work, pure consumers, though even this function is hedged about with unacceptable conditions.' 'In Europe,' he continued, 'we are not considered a nation: simply a country of producers and consumers.'[7]

Sovereignty of the people
The new order was to be based on the will of the people. In a letter to Pétion, Bolívar reaffirmed his belief in this principle, congratulating the Haitian leader for having been elected by 'the willing acclamation of your fellow-citizens, the only legitimate source of power'. Since 1812, he had been living in hope of a new order, and when he initiated the Magdalena campaign he sketched out the plans for this new order for the citizens, magistrates and clergy of Tenerife, in terms which recall the Regency Proclamation cited above: 'Now you are free men, independent of all authority other than that set up by your own votes, subject only to your own will; you will vote according to your conscience, in the legal manner prescribed by the constitution you are about to recognise and accept, a constitution which guarantees the property, life and honour of every citizen [and] ... gives [him] ... the opportunity to exercise his talents and industry, with all the advantages that can be obtained in a free society, the most perfect state to which Man can aspire on this earth.'[8]

Sovereignty, then, resided in 'the will of the citizens', meaning the mass of the people, and it was imprescriptible, that is, it could not be claimed that the king had the right to it through usage, even though the people had not hitherto exercised it. Bolívar said this quite clearly at Angostura, and he reiterated the principle when he left Lima on his way south in 1824, this time stressing the neutrality of the Executive in relation to the mass process. He ordered the Government Council to 'diligently ensure that the will of the people is carried out in relation to elections for the new Congress. I want the whole nation to be convinced that the government has no other role in the elections than that assigned to it by the constitution, of permitting the people to choose freely, according to their conscience. I urge this point simply in order to show my concern that the elections should be held in as free a manner as possible.'[9]

Bolívar frequently gave signs of this concern. There was his statement to his faithful confidant, Pedro Briceño Méndez, from whom he had no secrets: on 14 August, 1822, he wrote to him from Guayaquil: 'I will act in the elections in the south as I have always done everywhere. I mean that I shall not intervene in any way ... the people must decide for themselves and so must the electors. All that interests me is the freedom of my country and that enemies do not seize hold of her: to prevent that I am always ready.'[10] In 1826, in the face of difficulties with regional loyalties that seemed likely to destroy the nation, Bolívar's only proposal was 'the solution of the people: let them decide whether to act well or badly.' Even three months before his death, he replied energetically to those who suggested that he should return to power in defiance of the law: 'Tell your constituents that while the people have acclaimed me Head of State, they did not do so with the massive majority which alone could justify the step you mention ... Tell them that if that majority is attained, I will sacrifice without hesitation my peace of mind, my existence, my very life, for the sake of my country.'

He insisted on the need for regular consultation: 'Frequent elections are necessary in popular systems, for there is nothing so dangerous as leaving power in the hands of one individual. The people grow accustomed to obeying him, and he grows accustomed to giving orders: this leads to the usurpation of power and to tyranny.' When Bolívar proposed the creation of an Electoral Power to the Constituent Congress of Bolivia, this was because he was convinced that 'nothing is so important to the citizen as the election of his legislators, magistrates, judges and spiritual leaders'. By voting, each citizen contributed to the creation of the law, thus exercising his proper function as a member of the sovereign body. The act of voting annulled differences between individuals, making them equal. Nevertheless, in an attempt to compensate for low cultural standards inherited from the long years of colonial rule in these primitive communities, Bolívar proposed in Angostura the distinction between active and passive citizens, a distinction based, not on wealth, but on type of profession or work and educational level: 'Those people should be citizens who have the necessary qualities and abilities, even if they have no wealth. [However] the man who cannot write, who does not pay taxes, who has no known occupation, is not a citizen.' His formula did look forward to a time when all citizens would be active, and some years later, in Bolivia, he abolished the distinction, while reaffirming his opposition to other types of discrimination: 'Knowledge and honesty, not money, are what the exercise of public power requires.'

A phrase from Bolívar's last proclamation has often been misinterpreted, sometimes deliberately, since it seems to suggest that he was opposed to one of the bases of democracy. 'If my death contributes to the decay of parties and the strengthening of the Union,' he declared 'I will go to my grave happy.'[11] It is quite clear that Bolívar was not referring to political parties in the modern sense, since these were unknown at the time, only appearing towards 1850. He was referring to what elsewhere in the document he calls 'local antipathies', that is, manifestations of an unhealthy regionalism which, in accordance with a usage still current in the Andean region, he called 'parties'. Faithful to democracy, which is based on consent, participation and representation of the citizens, Bolívar aspired to overcome local rivalries and consolidate the Union of the three Republics so that Gran Colombia could surge ahead, respecting internal differences while hoping they would not rend it apart.

Bolívar did not fulfil his desire to see a democratic government established, even in the limited, pragmatic form he had envisaged, though his life was one long campaign in its favour. He was a genuine democrat, but not a naive one, like those of the dawn of independence, whom he vigorously denounced in the Cartagena Manifesto, claiming that their excessive idealism was the cause of the collapse of the First Republic. In determined efforts to bring some sense into politics, he tried to moderate absolute democracy, bringing it into line with the peculiarities of the Latin American situation. 'The government must, as it were, take its lead from the character of the circumstances and the men around it.' Experience taught him a number of lessons in this field, and in 1815 he enunciated his conclusion: 'Events on the mainland have shown us that perfectly representative institutions are not suitable for our character, customs and present level of understanding ... Until our compatriots acquire the talents and political virtues that distinguish our brothers in the north, entirely representative systems, far from being helpful, will, I fear, bring us to our ruin.' 'Is it feasible that a people recently freed from its chains should immediately fly into liberty without its wings, like those of Icarus, melting and plunging it into the abyss? Such a miracle cannot be imagined ... There is no reasonable basis for hope on this point.' He found abundant examples to support his judgement on the weakness and ineffectiveness of absolute democracy in the annals of Athens, Sparta, Rome, England and France and eventually concluded that neither the theoretical basis nor the practical mechanics of a government were really important: what mattered was that it should be suited to the nature and tendencies of the community for which it was established.

Bolívar thus believed that at that time and in that place, the right to vote should be curtailed. He also made it clear that some matters should not be exposed to the uncertainties of elections. Even in societies with a higher educational level and more political experience, mistakes could be made, for 'let us be clear on one thing: the majority of men do not know what is in their own best interest and they constantly go against it.' There were other problems with elections. 'Popular elections, with primitive country people and cynical town-dwellers, are yet another obstacle to unity amongst us, for the former are so ignorant that they vote mechanically, while the latter are so ambitious that they turn everything into a contest.' There was also the question of local autonomy, which tended to be divisive and in the end caused anarchy and chaos. This divisive spirit had been present ever since the first constitution and when he came to analyse the failure of 1812, Bolívar did hot hesitate: 'Internal factions were without a doubt the fatal poison that brought death to our Republic.' In 1828, the Ocaña Convention was split by the same desires for regional autonomy.

Despite his recognition of the limitations imposed by his circumstances, Bolívar's faith and enthusiasm for the struggle never waned. He was confident of the redemptive power of education, and anyway he recognised that tolerance of different points of view, attention to public criticism and respect for public opinion were essential in a democratic society, as he pointed out in a letter to Páez in 1820: 'He who rules over a large family has to put up with many things, not all of them pleasant. You should not be annoyed by others' opinions. I hear them every day and am not annoyed, for a leader must listen to the truth, even if it is hard, and after he has listened he must learn to correct the deficiencies that cause error. All moralists and philosophers advise princes to consult their wise vassals and follow their advice. How much more necessary this is in a democratic government where the leaders have been put there by the people to do as much good as possible and no harm.'[12] The long tradition of absolutism had produced arrogance and suspicion which lingered even under Republican governments: 'Men in public life are subject to censure by the citizens, especially under an elected government. If complaints by the people were a sufficient reason to abandon the task of government, I should have left it long ago, for not only have I been criticised, but anathemas were launched against me in Bogotá, I was banished from Cartagena, and in the province of Cumaná treated as an enemy.'

The concept of freedom

Bolívar defined freedom in the Angostura proposals as 'the right of every man to do anything not prohibited by law'. The most important aspect was freedom of thought and expression, 'the most precious gift of nature which the law itself cannot take away'.[13] The censorship to be exercised by the Moral Power over books, magazines and all printed matter, must be after publication, so that the Moral Power would serve as a guide, but would never suppress freedom of thought. There were, of course, sanctions against those who abused freedom of expression by disturbing public order or attacking the material and moral heritage of the nation. Bolívar insisted on the practical aspect of the question: 'In practice, freedom consists of the proper administration of justice and the rule of law, so that the just and the weak are free from fear, and merit and virtue are rewarded.'[14] The exercise of freedom demanded a tremendous effort of education, for as he said: 'Freedom is light, but it is also difficult to balance, even for the most cultivated and civilised nation.' He claimed the right to speak frankly about his own nation: 'Our peoples have many vices, many preoccupations and little love for real liberty, which is only attainable through the practice of virtue.'

Bolívar considered that the state should be neutral in religious matters, merely guaranteeing freedom of worship, without supporting any particular sect. 'Religion is a matter of conscience. In a political constitution there should be no prescribed religion ... Religion is for the individual in his own home ... within himself ... ' In this role as head of state and therefore inheritor of patronal rights over the Church exercised by the Spanish king, he decided in 1817 'as Supreme Head of the Republic, to invite with all cordiality, and if necessary with the force of my authority, all members of the distinguished clergy of this diocese, to appear within fifty days before their legitimate authorities in the capital, to discuss the needs of the Holy Church and in particular to nominate an eminent cleric to take charge of fulfilling them.'

He was well aware that with the revolution, political activities and discussion would come to the fore, and he was not afraid of this exercise. The use of freedom, he often said, was not easy, it required practice, which could never be acquired under an autocratic régime. Nothing was more opposed to freedom than the artificial calm and inertia that existed under tyrannous rule. He referred on one occasion to the 'sweet agitation of freedom', and he considered that the greatest satisfaction a people could obtain was 'the glory of living ... under laws dictated by their own will'. He was not afraid of chimera: 'The fire and agitation of freedom, seen from a distance, resemble civil disturbance or war.' Nevertheless, he realised that they were living on the edge of a crisis and that freedom and democracy could easily disappear. 'The diverse origins of our people', he said at Angostura, 'mean that the hand that guides them must be tactful but firm: otherwise, this heterogeneous society will fragment and divide at the slightest conflict.'

Another basic principle was that governments, as institutions emanating from the people, should be composed of capable men from normal civilian life. Bolívar insisted on the differentiation of functions within the state and his analysis of the role of the military is masterly. On the difficult questions of recruitment, conditions and tenure in government service, he announced: 'Fellow citizens, there is to be a long-needed reform in relation to the number of employees in the public service and their salaries. Our spending must be in relation to our earnings, if our country is to be saved. There will be no lack of virtuous men in every branch of service who will be content with sufficient money to live: these are the men on whom I rely to maintain an efficient public service.' He was severe, though just, in the punishment of offences committed by public servants. In 1824, he referred to the criteria for dismissal of Treasury personnel, insisting that there must be proof of misconduct, incompetence or neglect. On the other hand, he clearly stated: 'I do not think it just, if someone is doing his work properly and he has experience and intelligence, that the job should be taken from him and given to another, for that is contrary to the spirit of democracy.'

With his innate sense of justice, Bolívar did all he could to eliminate nepotism. No accusation has ever been made against him, for none of his close relatives ever occupied a high position in public life; in fact, in some cases, his scrupulousness almost became injustice. As he declared in Bucaramanga: 'No-one can ever accuse me of having raised up and placed in high positions members of my own family: on the contrary, I may be accused of having been unjust with some of them who were in the army. For example: my first aide-de-camp Diego Ibarra, who was by my side from 1813, nevertheless for many years remained a captain, then a lieutenant-colonel, then a colonel. If he had not been a relative of mine, he might now be a general, like others who have perhaps done less that he: I should have rewarded his courage, his firmness and loyalty, his patriotism and dedication to duty and even the friendship and warm admiration I have always felt towards him: but he was a relative and a friend of mine, he was by my side and these circumstances are the cause of his being overlooked for an important post in the army. My nephew Anacleto Clemente has never risen beyond the rank of lieutenant-colonel.'[15]

Centralism and federalism

Bolívar favoured centralism, in opposition to the federal system which had been set up in Venezuela in 1811, in response to the fragmentation inherited from colonialism. In the Cartagena Manifesto he declared: 'It is my opinion that if we do not adopt strong central government in Latin America, our enemies will reap the advantage ... The federal system, though it is the most perfect and the most able to procure human happiness in society, is nevertheless not in the interests of our newly-created states.'[16] In August 1813 he again insisted: 'The only powerful and respected nations are those that have a strong central government ... the division of power has never been the foundation of long-lasting régimes, only the concentration of power can win respect for a nation, and if I liberated Venezuela, it was to inaugurate this system.'[17] In meditations during his Jamaican exile, his thoughts on these matters became more precise and in his famous Jamaica Letter to Mr. Cullen he wrote: 'Out of all the democratic and representative systems I reject the federal one, because it is too perfect and demands political talents and virtues greatly superior to ours ... Since we cannot aspire to the most complete and perfect forms of Republic, let us at least avoid demagogic anarchy or dictorial tyranny. Let us seek a middle way between these two extremes, either of which would lead us to disaster ... and dishonour.'[18]

Over the course of his career and in the light of his experience of the geographical, historical and social realities of the country, this principle grew firmer, and he stated in 1829: 'There is no other course open to Colombia than to organise as well as can be done a centralised system properly adapted to the size of the territory and the character of the inhabitants ... Because of the difficult nature of the topography and the ignorance of the people, we shall be forced to strengthen our institutions more than is considered necessary in other countries. Imagine our problems, in trying to rule over a vast empire with a government that is scarcely able to govern a province ... '

In any case, Bolívar was more interested in results than in the outward forms of government. He stated in the Jamaica Letter: 'The most perfect form of government is the one that gives the greatest amount of happiness, security and political stability.' He also declared: ' ... the excellence of a government does not reside in its theoretical basis, nor in its form or mechanism, but in its being suited to the temperament and character of the nation for which it is established.' He would wish, quite simply, for 'a government under which the law would be obeyed, the magistrate respected and the people free: a government which would prevent the denial of the general will and desires of the people.'

The balance and coordination of the powers, rather than their separation, was another of Bolívar's basic principles. He had studied the question in Aristotle, Locke and Montesquieu, and believed that certain branches of the government should be assigned specific areas; however, he did not go so far as to say that they should be completely separate. He preferred to say that they should be united, and that mutual respect should exist and grow amongst the different organs of government. He felt that this organic type of government would be republican and democratic, yet simple, morally strong and effective, capable of defending and completing the process of revolution. He had described the proposed system early in his career: 'The Supreme Head of State ... is endowed with all the moral and intellectual qualities required of a leader ... The Senate, composed of wise and learned men, keeps constant watch over the conduct of magistrates and judges. The legislative body, which represents the sovereignty of the people, defends its rights with rectitude and justice ... The legislators are the fathers of the people ... There is a judiciary which deals out justice impartially, showing favour to neither the powerful nor the intriguer: ... no-one is deprived of his natural and legitimate rights through an arbitrary sentence or a malicious interpretation of the laws.'

The two constitutions proposed by Bolívar, one at Angostura, the other for Bolivia, were mainly based on Locke and Montesquieu, more the former than the latter. In Angostura, he proposed the usual bicameral legislature, but with a hereditary Senate. For the Executive he proposed a popularly-elected President, answerable to the electorate and obliged to submit to an election at the end of his term. It was in the proposals for Bolivia that the idea of a life-President appeared. Now, it must be emphasised that Bolívar was always opposed, in theory and in practice, to the concentration of power in the hands of one individual. Although experience had shown the weaknesses of collective governments, whether triumvirates or juntas, he did not recommend the creation of autocratic or dictatorial forms of government. He insisted on the creation of Government Councils and State Councils side by side with a single President: when *de facto* unlimited power was offered to him, his protests were sincere and effective. This became clear during his period as Dictator in 1828 and during his government of Peru: although he had been invested with complete powers, he was scrupulous about consulting the inhabitants of the country and leaving to them decisions about the most basic and serious questions, even if it meant — as in fact it finally did — the loss of his hopes for Panamerican union.

Both in Angostura and in Bolivia, he proposed an independent judiciary. In Angostura he declared that two conditions were essential for the success of this power: stability and independence. In the case of Bolivia he treated the matter at great length: 'The judicial power I propose enjoys complete independence, more here than elsewhere. The people puts forward candidates and the legislative body chooses which individuals are to serve. This is the only method which enables the judiciary to protect the rights of the individual, liberty, equality and security, the guarantees of social order. The real constitution is the civil and criminal codes: and the most terrible tyranny may be that exercised by the courts, in using the fearful instrument of the law. Normally, the Executive deals only with matters of state, whereas the courts are the arbiters in personal matters and individual cases. The judiciary can bring about the happiness or the misery of the inhabitants of the Republic and where there is liberty and justice they come from the judiciary. At times, the form of political organisation is unimportant if social institutions are perfect, if the laws are scrupulously obeyed and considered as ineluctable as fate.'

In the Angostura Address, without doubt the most brilliant and wide-ranging exposition of Bolívar's thoughts, his theory on the relationship between the powers is clearly stated: 'Nothing is so contrary to harmony amongst the powers as their mixture; nothing is so dangerous for the people as the weakness of the Executive and if it has been considered necessary to make it ... strong in a Monarchy, how much more necessary it is in a Republic.' Bolívar's aim was to achieve a strong democracy, with vigorous powers, competent in technical and political matters, patriotic and morally scrupulous, to carry out the revolution for which the people were waiting. His measures always showed an awareness of long-term as well as immediate issues. 'Let the whole system of government, then, be strengthened and the balance between the powers be such that it cannot be lost, without, however, being a source of weakness. For the very reason, that no form of government is so weak as a democracy, its structure must be as solid as possible, and its institutions designed for stability. Otherwise, we will find that we are experimenting, not setting up a permanent form of government: we will see our society grow restless, rebellious and anarchic, rather than happy, peaceful and just.' Bolívar was thus drawn to the difficult task of inventing institutions and drawing up legal formulae without being a specialist in law. In both his proposed constitutions, to the classic schema of the three powers, he added a fourth: in Angostura, the Moral Power, and in Bolivia, the Electoral Power. Moreover, in the Bolivian Constitution, he proposed that the legislative body should have a third chamber or house, that of the Censors, to which he would assign the functions of a Moral Power. Dr. Luis Prieto Figueroa recently published a study of this highly significant point in Bolívar's thought.[19] He interprets the Moral Power as a counterweight to the strong Executive which Bolívar considered necessary in the Latin American situation. In this interpretation, it serves as a check on the government and as a substitute for the right of the people to resist oppression, a right which, though figuring in the 1811 Constitution, was omitted by Bolívar from his two later proposed constitutions. Thus the Areopagus, as it was called in Angostura, or the Bolivian House of Censors, was designed to attenuate the power of the Executive.

The force of circumstance

Certain political acts of Bolívar's during the Dictatorship have given rise to a reputation as a 'reactionary'.[20] It is true that, faced with the urgent need to strengthen the régime, Bolívar took certain measures, but in the majority of cases, despite appearances, they can be shown not to have harmed the cause of democracy but to have advanced it. For example, a number of respected historians have criticised severely the suppression of the municipal governments, seeing it as a manifestation of autocratic centralism. The whole question was analysed by Bolívar after the failure of the Ocaña Convention, and it is worthwhile repeating his words, to show how unfounded is the prejudice against this measure: 'The municipal governments which could be useful as councils for provincial governors have scarcely ever performed their real function: some have dared attribute to themselves the sovereignty which properly belongs to the nation, others have engaged in sedition: and almost all the new ones have hindered rather than helped food supplies, public works and hygiene in their respective towns. Such corporations are not carrying out properly the tasks assigned to them: they are hated for the taxes they impose and for the burden placed on members elected to them, who in many cases can find no-one willing to replace them. This is the main objection, the harm done to citizens forced to become magistrates for a year, a task which costs them time and money and often compromises their peace of mind and even their reputation. It is not unusual to see people voluntarily leave their homes, to avoid being elected to one of these onerous offices. I only say what everyone thinks, when I state that no measure would be more popular than the abolition of the municipal governments.'[21]

It has also been said that Bolívar attacked freedom of speech, by insisting on the application of the law against the abuse of freedom of the Press. Historians have pointed to the rise in the study of Latin and Theology, the banning of secret societies on the grounds that they were a cover for conspiracy and the prohibition on teaching certain texts, such as Bentham's *Introduction to the Principles of Morals and Legislation*. Like other measures of the same period, these must be seen in the context of a revolutionary situation. Bentham's work, for example, was not only contrary to Catholic dogma: it was also prejudicial to the idealistic and generous spirit of the revolution. It tended to found culture on utility and profit, and the rich élite which was conspiring against Bolívar in Bogotá found inspiration in these ideas to defend the concepts of usury and imprisonment for debt, and to reject angrily any intervention in the economy by the state. There was a move towards the Church during the Dictatorship, but it was neither very profound nor very effective: the government promised to protect Catholicism 'as the religion of the inhabitants of Colombia', a far cry from the 'state religion' to which many commentators have referred. It is true that patronal rights over the Church were not revoked, and that the Archbishop was included in the Council of State, but one could argue that it made sense for Bolívar to win over the influential clergy to his side in this moment of crisis. He did not compromise his own independence, for he deliberately emphasised that the State was supreme in religious matters and in a decree of 24 November 1829 he reiterated that the Chancery of the Republic was the only proper medium of communication between Archbishops, Bishops, the secular and regular clergy, even private individuals and the Holy See.[22]

The main problem Bolívar faced was that of stability. He was living in an unstable, anarchic situation where the revolutionary process was impeded. His efforts to secure stability were unremitting. In 1829, when the situation could not have been gloomier, he said: 'If America does not retrace her steps, if she does not take account of her own insignificance and impotence, if she does not return to order and reason, there is very little hope for the continued existence of these governments: a new colonial servitude will be the inheritance we pass on to our descendants.' In Angostura he had already commented on the weaknesses of Latin American societies. It was in an attempt to counter-balance this political instability that he invented institutions like the hereditary Senate, and the life-Presidency, both intended as temporary expedients. In this sense, they are not part of the Bolivarian canon. They were created in response to a crisis, but do not form part of his theoretical system.

There can be no doubt that the hereditary Senate was the most aristocratic of all the institutions conceived by Bolívar. To some extent, the absence of able people justified its creation. He hoped that it would be 'a neutral body, which would always be on the side of the weak against the strong ... a counterweight to the government and the people, an intermediate power or buffer for the blows these two groups incessantly direct at each other. In any quarrel, a calm third party can bring about a reconciliation, and thus the Venezuelan Senate will be the main beam of our delicate edifice, so vulnerable to violent attack: it will be the Iris who calms the storm and maintains harmony between the limbs and the head of this body politic.'[23] It should be noted that a hereditary Senate was never mentioned in his later writings.

The life-Presidency, similarly, was a concept that was opposed to the general lines of Bolívar's thought, but was forced on him by necessity. In any case, one should not confuse his idea of life-President with the perpetual autocrats Latin America has known ever since. The Constitution expressly stated that 'the President may not deprive any Bolivian citizen of his liberty nor impose any sentence ... he cannot prevent the elections nor any other institution decreed by law.'[24] The Vicepresident of the Republic was the real head of government and the three Secretaries of State were under his orders. Bolívar hoped that the life-Presidency would 'preserve order and discipline amongst the citizens, with firmness and consistency'.[25]

In any case, his true preference was for republican institutions. He recommends vigilance as the only guarantor of civil liberties, and was fascinated by the example of Washington: 'The lesson taught us by this citizen and hero, the father of the great American Republic, should not be ignored. The people wished to re-elect him to the position of power, but he, virtuous general ... pointed out the dangers to the citizens of power remaining indefinitely in the same hands. He was heard, and the people obeyed: the American Republic is today an example of the glory, freedom and the happiness that comes from virtue.' Bolívar had enunciated this idea constantly throughout his career: 'What virtue is required to possess immense power without abusing it. Can any people wish to place itself under one man?' The temporary nature of the life-Presidency can be seen in the fact that it was conceived with a particular individual in mind. Bolívar suggested it, not as a general principle, but in relation to the particular qualities, above all the integrity, of Sucre. 'Unhappy Bolivia', he declared, 'with four different leaders in less than two weeks.' He felt that only Sucre could efficiently guide the first steps of the new Republic, without endangering democracy. As he wrote to Unanué from Chuquisaca: 'I am no longer needed here. I have promulgated a number of organic decrees, and framed a Constitution as the Assembly requested, and therefore I believe General Sucre will do the rest as well as or better than myself.' To Santander he declared: 'General Sucre is necessary for this Constitution, without him it is nothing: therefore, I ask you to urge that he be given the opportunity to accept the position for a number of years.' Notice the phrase 'a number of years': it is evident that Bolívar did not intend that Sucre should be President for life. It is more likely that he had in mind about a decade, the usual period envisaged before the revision of the constitution. For even constitutions were not seen by Bolívar as restricting garments that should curb the growth of the young Republics. Constitutions change, they are not drawn up to thwart the people's aspirations, but to take them along the path of national prosperity. Life-Presidency, like the rest of the Bolivian Constitution, was not meant to be eternal. In new societies, like those of Latin America, the laws and even the constitution must be subject to frequent revision, to allow them to adjust to the demands of the historical moment.

Bolívar drew a strict division between military and civilian affairs, right from the beginning of his career: 'I am a soldier, and my duty advises me blind obedience to the government, without questioning the wisdom of its actions.' In the midst of the grievous crisis of 1828, he explained the reasons for the military *pronunciamiento*, and made a solemn promise: 'The army's only desire is to safeguard the will and the rights of the people: in so doing, it merits the gratitude and esteem of the citizens ... The army has been our basic guarantee, and will be so in the future. That I promise, in the name of the army, of which I am the leading soldier, if I may be allowed that boast. I know the army will never go against the will of the people, because I know its feelings. From now on, it will simply be subject to the law and the will of the nation.'

These sentiments were perfectly in accord with his belief that sovereignty resided in the will of the people, and nothing was more repugnant to him than the application of the military spirit to civilian government: 'Force is not government.' In fact, he argued that military duty and the task of administration were incompatible: 'Although a soldier may save his country, he is rarely a good head of government.

Accustomed to the rigour and cruel passions of war, his administration is tinged with the harshness and violence of his profession of death.' When he spoke to the Constituent Congress of Bolivia, he was adamant: 'The army's task is to protect the frontier. God forbid that it should turn its arms on the population. Internal order is the task of the national militia.'

The problem facing Bolívar was to conciliate two forces, the general will and the authority of the government. The citizen must enjoy as much freedom as was compatible with respect for the government, if the latter was to have a basis of authority with which to carry out the general will. The aim of the revolution had been 'to reconcile the existence of the Republic, and the rights of the citizens, with the stability of institutions, to give the people maximum happiness and freedom and the government maximum energy and strength'.

Agrarian reform
In the colonial period, plantations and mines had been established through the use of slave-labour. Even Indian handicrafts were the object of unscrupulous speculation on the part of the Spaniards, so much so that attempts had to be made to put a stop to it by law, for example, in the regulations for *encomiendas* drawn up by Juan de Villegas in Venezuela in 1552. However, even the regulations of the *Leyes de Indias* were ineffective in relation to Indian labour, for the very authorities charged with administering the regulations were the ones most interested in the continued exploitation of the Indians. Throughout the colonial period, the poverty and humiliation of the Indian, the servitude of the negro and the unjust and depressing treatment given to the *pardos* meant that large sections of the population turned against a socio-economic system which constantly harmed them and denied them any possibility of improving their situation, and the majority of uprisings, rebellions and protests in Venezuela during the three hundred years of colonial rule were motivated by the injustices of this economic system.

In the initial phase of the revolution in Venezuela, the sectors that came to power were expert in the protection of their own interests and postponed indefinitely any consideration of the basic needs of those at the bottom of society. For example, no significant steps were taken to improve the lot of rural dwellers, though they formed the immense majority of the population. Men like Sanz had cried aloud for an agrarian reform that would serve the ends of justice and at the same time stimulate development, but the Caracas aristocrats were not interested in a serious reform of property: so one looks in vain amongst the acts of the Supreme Junta, or of the first constitutional government, or even of the brief and agitated administration that grew out of the *Campaña Admirable* for any ruling on this question. Instead, one finds a discreet and cautious favouring of the inherited interests of the wealthy 'revolutionaries'. One of the first measures was to reduce taxation, a measure which mainly benefited the rich. In fact, the abolition of the heaviest taxes had already taken place, when the fiscal machinery of the Spanish administration was dismantled: this led to a breakdown in order, and soon no-one would pay any taxes. The same situation arose during the prolonged hostilities of 1810–30. Naturally, this sudden drop in public revenue had serious consequences for the republican administration. After 19 April, the existing funds were soon exhausted. Bolívar described this critical phase in the Cartagena Manifesto, showing that the issue of paper money caused serious damage to the new régime they were trying to build.

With the collapse of the colonial system, the natural reaction of all sectors of society was to take advantage of the circumstances to try to improve their own situation, and so the people themselves began to attempt an economic revolution. The *llaneros*, who were at this time the poorest section of Venezuelan society, and the *pardos* from the city rallied to Boves, an astute analyst of rural poverty, who permitted and even encouraged looting. Boves promised land to his followers, and this, on top of the years of humiliation, was a powerful incentive to join the royalist forces. Many joined in the hope of redeeming themselves from poverty and hunger by expropriating the wealth of the *criollos*. José Antonio Páez, who shared the background and the mental outlook of Boves and his followers, learned his lesson, as Briceño Méndez explained very well in July 1821: 'When General Páez occupied Apure in 1816, finding himself isolated in the midst of enemy country, without support nor any hope of obtaining it, and without even being able to count on the good will of the people of the area, he had to promise his troops that all the land belonging to the government in Apure would be generously distributed amongst them. By this and other means he won over his soldiers and increased their numbers, for all came running to participate in these advantages. General Páez was so convinced of the importance of this step, and of the worthwhile effects it had had, that when the time came to acknowledge the authority of H.E. the President, who was then Supreme Commander, he made no other demands than the ratification of this promise. His Excellency could not deny it to him, and believing it to be just in principle, though too extensive and unlimited, he decided it should be modified, but at the same time extended to the whole Army.'[26] It should be noticed how easily the two leaders accepted land reform, as though they recognised in it the culmination of the work of the revolution. Bolívar, moreover, lent it the full weight of the law and tried to implement it in such a way that it would really work.

The decree dictated in Guayana on 3 September 1817 was the first of many revolutionary decrees on this subject and it is clear and explicit.

'All wealth and property of any kind, moveable and immoveable as well as credits, shares and titles belonging to any person of either sex who has joined the enemy by leaving the country, or actively serving in the enemy troops, are ... confiscated and become the property of the state ... All lands and properties belonging to the Capuchin friars and other missionaries who have made a vow of poverty, are confiscated and become the property of the state ... Equally, all the properties of the Spanish government and its servants are confiscated, whatever their country of residence.'[27] Another decree, twenty days later, set up the Expropriations Tribunal, and named the officials who were to compose it. On 10 October, a law was finally passed on the distribution of national lands amongst the soldiers of every rank who had fought in the independence armies of Venezuela.

Some historians have declared that Bolívar's aim was simply to buy the loyalty of the soldiers. Yet it cannot be denied that the masses benefited by the measure. As Bolívar said: 'In Colombia the army is the people.'[28] The question was an important one, as he recognised: 'For a long time, we cannot be anything other than an agricultural people.' He explained his point of view in his message to the Council of State on 1 November 1817: 'Men who have faced every danger, who have abandoned all they possessed, and suffered every privation, should not be denied the reward due to their unselfishness, their courage and their virtue. Therefore, in the name of the Republic, I have ordered the distribution of lands belonging to the nation amongst the defenders of the nation. The law determining the limits and conditions of this land bonus is the document I have most satisfaction in offering to the Council. To reward merit is the noblest act within human power.' Fifteen months later, the same ideas were given a more literary elaboration in the Angostura Address, where he rounded them off with a dramatic appeal: 'If I have earned any debt of gratitude from the people, I beg their representatives to listen to my request, as the reward for my feeble services. The Congress should order the distribution of the national lands in accordance with the law which I, in the name of the Republic, have decreed in favour of the Venezuelan soldiers.' This military land bonus and the abolition of slavery were two of the most essential and concrete revolutionary measures, and the main ones Bolívar felt obliged to present to the Congress. They were, he said, 'the most important in my period of government ... the most important resolutions of recent times'.

It is clear that a large number of Bolívar's soldiers were peasants, for on 5 September 1817 he wrote to José Félix Blanco: 'I am informed that your squadron is quartered at San Antonio and that the soldiers are complaining because they are being kept from their farms and work for no good reason. The complaint does not seem unreasonable, for it is true that they have nothing to do for the moment and could usefully be employed in the cultivation of their fields until the time comes to move.' According to the new law, land was to be distributed in accordance with military rank, as it was felt that the rank achieved in battle was an undeniable demonstration of the different services performed by each individual in the army. There was a twelve-point scale which went from general, with the right to land worth 25,000 *pesos*, to private, with the right to 500 *pesos*' worth. In cases of exceptional merit, larger amounts could be assigned.[29]

The well-known North American specialist in the economic and social history of Latin America, Charles G. Griffin, considers it perhaps 'somewhat exaggerated to call a system of bonuses for soldiers an "agrarian reform"'.[30] In his estimate, the number of people who could have benefited from Bolívar's decree was extremely low, between 15,000 and 20,000 people out of a rural population of at least ten times that figure. One could still argue, however, that the measures were the basis of a radical transformation, and that if they had been carried out as planned, the history of Venezuela might have been very different. The immediate success of the measures would seem to indicate that Bolívar's instincts were right. If Páez's offer had been effective in winning over the *llaneros*, who merely wanted free use of the *llanos* for pasture and the departure of the big landowners, then similar measures must have been even more effective in other parts of the country, where actual ownership of the land was more important. Bolívar did not approve of the distribution of small pieces of land, as this would have been harmful to the increased production for which he hoped, to cover both internal consumption and export. He encouraged beneficiaries of the scheme to band together and take on common ownership of a large property, which thus became a kind of collective farm. This tacit opposition to the *conuco*, a form of minifundio or small land-holding derived from the Indian system, shows his revolutionary tendencies. He was attempting to open the way to a type of large-scale capitalist production, with the peasant as paid labour, which would mean the destruction of feudal institutions such as the *encomienda*.

Property had been defined in the proposal for a constitution at Angostura as 'the right of the individual to enjoy and freely dispose of his possessions and the fruits of his talents, skill or labour'. Bolívar accepted that the state should protect and guarantee property and indeed he placed it beside equality, freedom and security as the fourth great human right that must be defended, influenced in this by Locke and Hume, who had inspired the French Encyclopaedists and the Declaration of the Rights of Man. Due, however, to certain imperatives of the particular historical moment, Bolívar made some changes in the concept of property. He pointed out that there were questions of equity and justice involved, and that a revolutionary state should only protect property considered legitimate in the light of revolutionary justice. It would be absurd and contradictory for the new democratic régime to protect property which was the result of usurpation and violence, and which prolonged a situation of injustice by preventing an improvement in the condition of the masses who had fought to install the régime. He therefore recognised the legitimacy of expropriation when required by 'public necessity or general utility, duly proven' and noted that 'compensation should be paid, where circumstances allow it'.[31] The full extent of these changes can be appreciated if we compare his wording with that of the Abbé Sieyès, reproduced in the Declaration of the Rights of Man: 'The right to property being an inviolable and sacred one, no-one may be deprived of it except when public need, duly proven, clearly requires it, and compensation should always be paid in advance.' Bolívar omitted the words 'sacred' and 'inviolable', he extended the conditions in which expropriation was justified by including the concept of 'general utility', less imperative then 'public necessity', and he released the State from the need to pay compensation with the phrase 'where circumstances allow it', and the abolition of advance payment.

The redistribution of land was the most tangible and immediate of Bolívar's measures, but he did introduce others aimed at a revolutionary advance in economic and social matters. For example, he abolished internal levies on the transportation and sale of fruit, arranged credit to encourage agriculture, forbade the export of cattle and horses, established a commercial bank, restored the *consulado* on a new basis and arranged for gifts of land to immigrants, 1,000,000 *fanegadas* of uncultivated land being destined by law for this purpose. Nor were these measures confined to Venezuela. Considering it a matter of urgency to correct abuses committed in Cundinamarca in relation to the Indians' lands, he dictated a decree on 20 May, 1820, which read: 'All reserved land belonging to the Indians must be handed back to them as legitimate owners ... without regard for any deeds held by the present owners ... Any liens on the said lands are abolished, even though they may have existed since time immemorial ... The *jueces políticos* will distribute to each family as much land as each can comfortably cultivate, having regard to the number of persons in each family and the total area of the reserved lands.' An unusual point, and one that serves to demonstrate Bolívar's sincerity, was that he added: 'The present decree will not only be published in the normal way, but the *jueces políticos* will [also] instruct the Indians about its content, urging them to claim their rights, even against the *jueces* themselves, and to complain about any infractions of the law.' Any remaining land was to be rented out and the money used to set up an educational programme for the Indians.

After his insistence before the Council of State and the Angostura Congress, Bolívar followed with interest the fortunes of his measures on the distribution of land to the soldiers, for he wished to ensure that it was really effective. While he was in El Rosario, he heard that the Congress had approved his decree, but with some alterations. As he wrote to Santander: 'They have made certain changes in the decree, so I understand, though I have not seen it. They have ordered the soldiers to be given national bonds, to be sold in auction to the highest bidder.'[33] Needless to say, Bolívar understood the dangers of this move and quickly had the law restored to the form he wished.

In January 1821, he gave Páez carte blanche to carry out the agrarian reform in Venezuela, conferring on him 'all the authority which by the Law of the General Congress on the Distribution of Government Land is invested in the President', and giving him simple instructions: 'The legal forms should be kept as short and simple as possible, avoiding the danger of bonds being distributed instead of land.' Once the distribution had begun, he was to 'ensure that the recipients do not dissipate it, to their loss and that of their families, and contrary to the intention of the law.' On 12 February 1821, Bolívar found himself obliged to reiterate his decree of the previous year concerning the Indian lands in Cundinamarca. This time, he asked the Governor and General Commander of Tunja to oversee the distribution and ensure that the other regulations were respected. He was determined on 'restoring the Indians to the enjoyment of all the reserved land to which they are entitled, no matter who the present owner may be. Distribute all the reserved land to the Indians, so that they have as much land as they can cultivate and can thus escape from the miserable condition to which they have been reduced ... Make a point of including in the land to be distributed, that which is richest, most fertile and easy to cultivate, so that it is the Indians who enjoy these advantages of their land and not others.'[34]

On 13 January 1823, in Pasto, he decreed that government lands should be distributed to the soldiers who had liberated that part of the south. One decree confiscated certain lands, and another of the same date created a commission to carry out the distribution.[35] When he arrived in Peru, where the situation was fundamentally similar, he naturally adopted the same measures. On 8 April 1824, he decreed in Trujillo: 'The lands known as 'communal lands' will be divided, according to the regulations, amongst all the Indians who do not possess any other land, and they will become the owners ... The share will be according to the situation of each individual, the married men receiving more that the single.'[36] On 4 July of the following year, he announced in Cuzco that 'despite the provisions of the ... laws, the distribution of land has not been carried out properly: the majority of the Indian population has never enjoyed possession of the land: a great part of the land ... intended for the Indians has been usurped on one pretext or another by the *caciques* and tax-collectors.' He reminded the Peruvians of the decree published in Trujillo and insisted that it must be observed. This Cuzco decree contains a number of provisions aimed at preventing the usual evasions. 'Every Indian, of either sex and of any age will receive one and a half leagues of the good, irrigated land and three leagues of the dryer, less fertile land.' A system of compensation was established for those who had lost their lands at the time of the colonisation. In order to prevent the transfer of lands to religious or semi-religious bodies, who exerted psychological and spiritual pressure to obtain them, it was laid down that the Indian's absolute right to the land was granted 'on the understanding that he is not free to dispose of it until 1850, and never into mortmain, under pain of confiscation'.[37] Similarly, in Bolivia, on 14 December 1825, he ordered land to be given to 'the Indians and those who have done most to serve the cause of independence, or have suffered damage because of it'.[38] A period of one year was granted, after the donation of the land, for the new owner to cultivate it. If he did not do so, 'he will be deprived of the deeds of ownership of the land, which will be assigned to others, who will cultivate it properly.' In the search for equity, impartiality and efficiency in the process of distribution, it was laid down that it should be carried out by 'honest and intelligent persons'.[39]

When Bolívar visited his native country for the last time, he was greatly disillusioned to find that his long absence had caused the almost total frustration of his ideals. At each step, he found that he had indeed 'ploughed the sea' and he concluded that it was impossible for 'one man alone', as he put it, to transform the older order, when the very inhabitants were their own worst enemies. He complained to Brión that his work 'was destroyed by the very people for whom it was intended'. He saw himself as Sysiphus, condemned constantly to renew a useless and sterile labour. In Caracas, he was forced to press for confiscations which had been ordered ten years previously. The instructions sent on 19 February to the Intendant of the Department of Venezuela are sad, showing the waste of a decade. 'The Liberator desires that everything should be done to effect ... very quickly the confiscation of the lands indicated. Since your Excellency informed me that the delay is due in great part to a lack of diligence on the part of the notaries, who are officially carrying out the confiscations, the Liberator has resolved that they are to keep a record of the amount due to them according to the agreed scales and that the cost will be met by the person who finally receives the house, farm or land.'[40]

Bolívar's insistence on the points mentioned above shows his determination to effect a real change in the economic structure of the countries under his control, and the same could be said of his policy in relation to the mines. In a continent like South America, which was almost exclusively a provider of raw materials, these were of fundamental importance. In Pucará and La Paz, in August and September of 1825, it was decreed that 'all neglected or abandoned mines belong effectively to the State, [and will be] used to pay the national debt'.[41] These were antecedents to the decree issued on 24 October 1829, in Quito, which nationalised the whole mining industry. Incidentally, if the Quito decree was significant at the time, it was more so in the future, for it renewed certain provisions of the Regulations for the Mines in New Spain, introduced in Colombia in 1703 and valid for Venezuela from 1784. Under the *Leyes de Indias*, non-metal mines had belonged to the owner of the ground. The Spanish Crown changed this, and Bolívar followed that lead. He did so because he recognised the unique importance of the mines: nationalising the mines meant not only that the state was the owner, but that the state actively intervened in the organization of their activity. It is almost as though his genius had foreseen the immense wealth that lay under the soil of Venezuela in the form of petroleum and other combustible materials. Certainly he solved for the future inhabitants of Venezuela the problem of the ownership of these riches.

Bolívar brought about a change in social attitudes, by exalting labour as essential for the revolutionary task of national reconstruction, sweeping away centuries of contempt for manual work. There is an interesting demonstration of this in his thoughts on the future of his nephew Fernando, who was like the son he never had. If the young man decided to learn a skilled trade, Bolívar said, 'I should be very happy, for we have an abundance of doctors and lawyers, but we lack good tradesmen and farmworkers, which is what the country needs to advance to prosperity and well-being.'[42] He constantly encouraged and rewarded the industrious and energetic and criticised the lazy, always stressing the idea of usefulness to society. 'We must work hard to regenerate the country and establish it on a firm basis: what is needed is patience and more patience, determination and more determination, work and more work, to build our country.'

Bolívar referred on a number of occasions to the difficulty of finding qualified people to run the Treasury. In general, he followed the principle of giving the job, not necessarily to the person who wanted it, but to the one he judged most able to carry it out. 'The way to be popular and to govern properly is to employ honest men even if they are enemies [of the régime].' It must be remembered that this kind of work had not enjoyed prestige or esteem amongst the Spaniards. Bolívar pointed out the difficulty of finding a Minister of Finance despite the fact that this was a post 'upon which the life of the country depends'. When he asked Revenga to take on this responsibility, he stressed the importance of the task: it would be 'the principal base on which all State reforms would turn'. He expressed the vital importance of economic health in a series of organic metaphors which recall mercantilist and physiocratic formulae, some old-fashioned even in his time, some still contemporary: 'Taxes are the nerves of the Republic'; the life of the state 'cannot be nourished except by the gold running through its veins'. He told Santander: 'Remember that one of the principal causes of the French Revolution was the poor state of public finance.' Finally, he considered that the economic argument was the best justification for the independence of Latin America, as he explained in the Jamaica Letter: '16,000,000 Latin Americans are defending their rights: they are oppressed by the Spanish nation, which though it had once the largest empire in the world, is now impotent to dominate the New World, or even maintain its position in the Old. And is civilised Europe, the lover of liberty, to permit an old serpent to devour the fairest part of the earth, simply to satisfy its own poisonous malice? ... Is Europe deaf to the clamour of its own interest? What madness is this in our enemy, to attempt to reconquer America, without a navy, without resources and almost without soldiers ... Can such a nation preserve a commercial monopoly over half the world, when she has no manufacturing industry, no agriculture, no science, no arts ... ?'

Latin American unity

So long as Latin America formed part of the Spanish Empire, it was as though she did not exist on the international plane. Until the beginning of the nineteenth century, the great powers, or occasional combinations of powers such as the Holy Alliance, disposed of the world at will. Spain had a double image of Latin America, and for that reason its treatment of the colonies was highly contradictory. Latin America was one unit, when it was convenient to see it that way, that is, for purposes of domination, monopolistic exploitation or mercantilist interventionism. There was one unquestioned centre of government and the economies of the various countries were complementary, so that they formed one unit from the Spanish point of view. But in the Latin Americans themselves, the idea that the Spaniards tried to inculcate was that of an archipelago, a labyrinth of jurisdictions. With a care that would not have disgraced a worthier cause, Spain set out to construct a series of legal and cultural barriers to disguise and even destroy the unity they did not want their subjects to perceive. For example, they tried to impose a strict quarantine on the whole of the New World, by making access difficult for foreigners. Even the inhabitants were forbidden to move from one province to another without royal permission. The *Leyes de Indias* forbade trade with foreigners, under any pretext. In part, this was an inheritance from the peninsular mentality, for Spanish 'unity' was itself imposed on a mosaic of conflicting sensibilities and prejudices. The process was aided by geographical factors, such as the immensity of the continent, the presence of high mountains and impenetrable forests and the difficulty of communications, factors which isolated the Latin American countries and kept them apart. If there was one salient characteristic of the colonial period, it was distrust and suspicion between peoples, frequently giving rise to aggression. Common dangers, such as attack by pirates or natural disasters, often acted as a cohesive agent, but as soon as the emergency was past recalcitrant individualism grew up once more. In the majority of Latin American countries, and in the case of Venezuela in each province, there grew up a federalist or isolationist mentality which precluded all hope of unity. One cannot ignore the problem of the immense distances separating one community from another, a factor which militated against union. Andrés Bello illustrated this point in 1811, though he managed to draw an edifying moral from the circumstances: 'Caracas receives news of Buenos Aires almost always via the United States, and Buenos Aires gets its news of Caracas from the English newspapers. However, for those who have experienced the natural and political obstacles to communication, it will always be a subject for astonishment that the sense of Latin American unity should still have arisen at both ends of this huge continent, with a uniformity not always found even amongst peoples who have had the time and the opportunity to concert their efforts.'[43] Bolívar corroborated this from Peru in 1825: 'We know the news from Russia before the news from Caracas: reports from Junín reached us from England before they reached us from Caracas: and sometimes we receive papers dated the same day from London and Bogotá.'[44]

Different witnesses testify to the fact that one characteristic of the Venezuelan people, from the beginning of its history, has been its tolerance and receptivity to ideas, an open and liberal mentality which contrasts forcefully with the narrow views of other communities in Latin America. There may be factors in Venezuelan history which would explain this tendency. The high degree of *mestizaje* in Venezuela, for example, may have been a factor: another could be the favourable geographical situation of the area, on the Caribbean and close to the Dutch, English and French possessions. Smuggling was a regular activity and the Venezuelans had frequent contact with progressive Protestant ideas and with representatives of the nations considered most tolerant and liberal at the time. The relative lack of metals meant that Venezuela aroused little interest in Spain, avid for gold and silver, so that Iberian fanaticism lay rather lightly on Venezuelan society and the Inquisition was a source of anecdotes rather than a real object of terror. The

Venezuelan territories were the only area of the Latin American continent ever rented to anyone other than a Spaniard, in this case the 'Welsers'. José de Oviedo y Baños, in the first history of Venezuela, published in Madrid in 1723, said of the people of Caracas: 'They are of a lively and quick intelligence, courteous, amiable and diplomatic: they speak the Castilian language perfectly, without the strange sounds which ruin it in other American ports ... in general, they are lively in spirit and of stout heart, and so inclined towards anything political that even the negroes (if born in America) are despised if they do not know how to read and write.'[45] In 1800, having travelled extensively in Venezuela and observed the inhabitants, Humboldt was struck by having found in Caracas 'more knowledge about political relations between peoples, and wider views on the state of the metropolis and the colonies' than in any of the many Latin American towns he had visited, with the exception of Havana.[46]

Francisco de Miranda was the first Venezuelan to express his sense of Latin American unity, in 1781, while he was helping to free the North American colonies. He had already established pre-revolutionary links with groups of people in his native province who were dissatisfied, but it was in the United States, as he himself admits, that he first had the idea of redeeming the whole of Latin America. Two years later, back in the United States again, he contacted all the most prestigious and influential figures in the new democracy and spoke to them with enthusiasm of 'the future destiny of Spanish America'. He told the French diplomatic representative in Philadelphia: 'Our kingdoms of Spanish America will soon experience a revolution similar to the one you are witnessing.' In New York he drew up for Alexander Hamilton his plan 'for the independence and freedom of the whole Spanish American continent'. The basic idea behind the Picornell, Gual and España plot in 1797–8 was also the unity of the continent, and the phrase most often repeated in the insurgent texts was 'the people of America'. During Picornell's lectures on the subject in the La Guaira prison, his fascinated listeners were told again and again in each session that Latin America must be for the Latin Americans, and in his *Ordenanzas* there were detailed instructions for the conduct of the initial phase of the Revolution: 'The inhabitants are to be as well armed as possible and divided into various squadrons, each led by a corporal whom they will elect; they are to raise in every street and square the cry: Long live the American people.' In one of his proclamations we read: 'The day has come, Fathers of my country, when the freedom of the American people can be announced'. The *American Sonnet* composed by Manuel Cortés de Campomanes reads: 'People of America/The day has come/When the party of tyranny/Dies forever'. Another propaganda poem, this time with the title *Song of America*, reads: 'Tremble, infamous King/Tremble, perfidious Carlos/All of your crimes/Will now be punished./The terrible sword/Of the American people/Will destroy your pride/Bloody despot.'[47]

The idea of Latin American unity was expressed in Venezuela only one week after the coup of 19 April, when the Supreme Junta of Caracas invited all the *cabildos* of all the capital cities of Latin America to collaborate in 'the task of [creating] the Spanish American Confederation'. 'The task is one', the invitation read, 'our slogan must be one: Loyalty to our unhappy monarch; war on his tyrannous oppressor; fraternity and determination.'[48] (We have noted that 'Loyalty to the unhappy monarch' was merely a temporary expedient.) Bolívar first put forward on paper his ideas on continental unity during his visit to England as head of the first diplomatic mission. He wrote in the *Morning Chronicle* of 5 September 1810: 'On the day, which is not far off, when the Venezuelans become convinced that their moderation, their evident desire to maintain friendly relations with Spain, even their financial sacrifices, have not won them the respect or the gratitude to which they feel entitled, they will raise the flag of independence and declare war on Spain. They will not neglect to invite all the peoples of Latin America to join together in a confederation. Those peoples, already prepared for this plan, will quickly follow the example of Caracas.'[49]

Venezuela persisted in this effort and achieved a brilliant success. Through her initiative, the first treaty in the annals of the two nations was signed between Venezuela and her neighbour, Cundinamarca, on 28 May 1811. The Caracas representative, José Cortés de Madariaga, thus laid the foundation for Gran Colombia, the nation so dear to the hearts of Miranda and Bolívar. In the same year, in the first Venezuelan Constitution, there was a fervent call for understanding amongst all the Latin American nations. Bolívar's voice also rang out in the hall of the Patriotic Society, inviting them to fearlessly 'lay the foundation-stone of American liberty'.[50]

Bolívar was a convinced and efficient agent of Spanish American nationalism, a stance perfectly compatible with his universalist vision, in which peace and understanding between all men was the supreme goal. The conversion of *de facto* unity into a legally-established working reality would benefit not only the Latin Americans, but all of mankind. We must remember that Latin America was formed from the presence of several races, and the independence movement freed everyone, regardless of race, creed or colour. In the difficult but creative conditions of his Jamaican exile, Bolívar calmly analysed the reality of the continent, weighing the pro's and con's of union: 'It is a magnificent concept, to wish to form a single nation out of the whole New World, with a single centre linking all the parts to each other and to the whole. Since it already shares one origin, one language, one religion and one set of social customs, it should have one government, to confederate the different states that are about to form, but this is not possible, because differences in climate and situation, conflicting interests and the clash of characters all divide America.'

Bolívar mentioned common origins. It is true that at the time of the Conquest, there were many different types of society in America, but it could be argued that Columbus brought them all on to the world stage at the same moment. Certainly, the processes of conquest and colonisation were experienced more or less contemporaneously all over the continent. It is significant that the first notions of independence emerged at the same time in different places, and even after independence the same anarchy gripped the whole continent. These are indications that the same situation prevailed everywhere, so that similar causes brought similar consequences. The principal unifying factor was the language, which had been used by the Spaniards as an instrument of domination. Through language, a culture and even a style of thought are implanted. Of course, when Bolívar referred to the linguistic unity of Latin America, he was excluding Brazil and the areas occupied by France, England and Holland. In the convocation to the Panamá Congress, he indicated that he was addressing 'what was formerly Spanish America'. This does not mean that he was devoid of affection for other parts of America: 'Let us see to it', he said, 'that chains of love link all the sons of Columbus's hemisphere and that hatred, vengeance and war are driven from our breast and carried to our frontiers, to be turned against the only true enemy, tyranny.'

Religion, another unifying element, had also been imposed by the conqueror. At the time of the Emancipation, Catholicism was the dominant religion all over the Iberoamerican sphere. Naturally, religion had also a unifying effect on morality and social traditions and customs, and even on the law and the economy. Contrary to Spanish intentions, the continent was also unified by its political aspirations: to be free of Spain and to unite in the quest for peace and progress. There were also solid political reasons for union. The league prescribed by Bolívar, amongst other advantages, had that of being a stabilising element. Inspired by Rousseau, Bolívar intuited a law of what we have elsewhere called 'political physics', whereby the weight of the whole was felt to counteract tendencies towards disorder in the parts. Once Spanish America had been established as one unit and socio-economic problems solved, the chaos in each part would disappear, authority would be strengthened and the *caudillos* would learn that the exercise of power involved more than local skirmishes and parish intrigues. Petty quarrels and rivalries would lose any sense they might once have had, for the state would have at its disposal sufficient force to guarantee stability and prevent anarchy: it would be a step towards peace and dignity in public affairs.

Another argument in favour of unity was the need for outside recognition. During the independence wars, Bolívar noted, almost with desperation, the indifference of Europe and North America, explicable to some extent by the multitude of governments involved. In the eyes of the great powers, Latin America was a constellation of disorder, a shapeless bunch of conflicts. They did not understand that it was in fact one nation, struggling for emancipation: they saw a number of small nations, engaged on an unequal struggle with a great imperial power. Apart from what this represented for the Latin American countries in terms of wasted energy, the continent was not winning the respect or even the attention it deserved for its proposals for political and economic interchange. If unity had been effective from the beginning, the Emancipation would have cost less in lives, time and resources, including social and cultural resources, for it would have been easier to arrange outside help. Bolívar said in 1819: 'The lack of unity and cohesion and above all the lack of resources that followed from the separation of the republics is, I repeat, the real cause of the lack of interest shown until now by Europe and our neighbours in our destiny. Sections, fragments which, though vast, have neither population nor resources, could arouse neither interest nor confidence in those who might wish to establish relations with them.'

In a document from 1813 which clarifies the creation of Gran Colombia, Bolívar explained to Mariño, not only the dangers of fragmenting Venezuela, but also the advantages of a union between that country and New Granada, to be the foundation stone for the eventual unification of the whole of South America: 'If we set up two independent powers, one in the east, the other in the west, we create two distinct nations which by their insistence on appearing as such ... will look ridiculous. Venezuela joined to New Granada is only just able to form a nation capable of inspiring in others the courteous respect she deserves. Why should anyone wish to divide them? Our security and our reputation as an independent government impose upon us the duty of becoming one nation with New Granada. This is the wish now of the people of Venezuela and New Granada and in search of this union, so useful to both, the brave sons of New Granada have come to set Venezuela free. If we unify everyone in one nation at the same time as we extinguish the flames of agitation, we will be consolidating our forces and encouraging mutual cooperation in the achievement of our aims. Divided we shall be weak and less respected by our enemies and by neutral powers. Unity beneath one government will make us strong ... in the eyes of all.'

The most decisive argument in favour of unity was genuine community of interests. The alliances proposed by Bolívar rested on solid advantages to all members. He foresaw that the demographic development of the Latin American countries would mean that they would one day have the largest number of inhabitants in the whole American continent, and he felt this would bring them into the vanguard position. He was opposed to the idea of a foreign power, big or small, signing a bi-literal agreement with any of the Latin America states. Instead, he felt they should negotiate with the whole bloc. He had also learned the lesson of Washington's testament to the United States, in which he advised them to reject even favourable treaties with the powerful nations who could dispense wealth and prestige. The Latin American nations must keep in mind at all times that it is madness for one nation to expect disinterested favours from another, and that everything received as a favour will be paid for sooner or later with a part of one's independence. It was clear, therefore, that Latin American unity must be achieved, if equitable and just treaties were to be signed with the great powers, for 'once a pact has been signed with the strong power, the weaker power is eternally under an obligation'. Bolívar drafted a comment on an initiative of Santander's regarding an alliance between England and the future Hispano-American federation: 'At the moment, I believe that the alliance with Great Britain would bring us respectability and prestige and that in her shadow we could grow to manhood and wisdom, strengthening ourselves to appear amidst other nations with a degree of civilisation and power necessary for a great people. But these advantages do not dissipate my fears that this powerful nation might in the future take over consultation and decision in the assembly: her voice might be the most persuasive, and her will and interests might become the main focus in the confederation, which would hesitate to oppose her, in the fear of creating an irresistible enemy. This, in my opinion, is the greatest danger in involving a strong nation with others that are weak.' We should note that Bolívar made these remarks in relation to Great Britain, a country with which he always had the greatest sympathy. Another important point with respect to the solidarity of the union was that an offence against any one of the members would be answered by the ensemble, which should cause outside powers to hesitate before attacking any of the republics.

The story of Bolívar's efforts on behalf of Latin American unity began in March 1813 with his attempts to integrate Venezuela with neighbouring Cundinamarca. On 2 November 1812 he first used the term *Colombia* to refer to this alliance and later, in January 1814, through Muñoz Tébar, he expounded brilliantly on the factors favouring such an association: 'During three centuries of ignominy, a continent richer and more densely inhabited than Spain was the victim of the perfidious plans of the Madrid Cabinet: if the latter, from a distance of 2,000 leagues, and without any great effort, could keep the whole of America, from New Mexico to the Magellan Straits, under its domination, why should a solid alliance between Venezuela and New Granada not be possible? And in fact, why should not the whole of South America come together under one central government? ... We require our nation to have the strength to resist successfully any aggression prompted by European ambition: and the giant we must become, in order to face up to a giant, can only come from the union of the whole of America in one nation, so that one central government can apply the whole of its resources to one single end, resisting outside attacks, at the same time increasing mutual cooperation internally, so that we reach the highest levels of power and prosperity.'[51]

As Bolívar told San Martín: 'My first thought, on the field of Carabobo, when I saw my country free, was for Your Excellency, and the liberation army in Peru ... Your Excellency must believe me: next to the well-being of Colombia, nothing preoccupies me so much as the success of your forces, entirely worthy to carry their glorious banner to wherever men are slaves, that they may shelter in its shade.'[52] He sent the flower of Venezuelan manhood to New Granada and to the West Indies, to help set those areas free. The unity of the continent became his obsession, an obsession that was shared by Manuel Palacio Fajardo and Pedro Gual, the outstanding diplomats of the period, as can be seen from Palacio Fajardo's *Bosquejo de la revolución en la América española*, a defense of the movement published anonymously in English, French and German between 1817 and 1818.

During this period of romantic deeds, a number of idealistic Venezuelans took part with other Latin Americans in the adventure of the 'Florida Republic', which reinforced Venezuelan tendencies towards integration. At the end of June 1817, they seized the port of Fernandina, on the island of Amelia, just off the North American peninsula. There they proclaimed the Republic of Florida, which lasted seven months and whose flag, like that of Venezuela and later that of Colombia, was inspired in the ensign raised by Miranda at Jacmel on 12 March 1806. Soldiers like MacGregor, Aury and Codazzi and civilians like Roscio and Gual came together in this venture. The last-named wrote: 'Here, we are doing something that will benefit the whole of South America. This is the one aim that binds us closely together ... The establishment of a Republic in Florida commands the attention and the support of all true friends of South America.'[53] Their intention was to establish a bridge-head in the north to help the revolution, especially their colleagues in Mexico and Central America.

Bolívar concentrated all his energy and prestige on making Colombia a reality. When circumstances grew less difficult, he summoned the Angostura Congress to create the constitution of the new Republic. For Bolívar, the existence of Colombia was a guarantee of liberty for the whole of South America. He was anxious that the Republic should be worthy of this responsibility and planned the most advanced state, morally and politically, of the time. Issues of democracy, justice and liberty were argued and fought for, being translated into the distribution of land, the abolition of slavery, the defense of absolute equality and the establishment of a progressive, representative and legal régime. Morality and culture were given pride of place, so that one could say Bolívar built up the first nation in Latin America, first, not in the chronological sense, for many had emerged earlier, nor in the material sense, for Peru was richer and Brazil larger. Venezuela was the first country to experiment in union with another, not with any ambition to gain territory or hegemony over other states, but simply in pursuit of the policy of unification.

Bolívar was a believer in the law, and so he felt the need of a legal doctrine and institutions to accompany the unification. These he set about establishing himself, and the legal principles he evolved are a precious part of the inheritance passed down to the present day. His system bore no resemblance to the famous European alliance, for what was being attempted was not a close union of states brought together by violence under the leadership of great power for purposes of aggression: instead, it was an instrument of defense, and a means of unifying political advance. The 'balance of power' in Europe was a balance of appetites, set up to neutralise rival ambitions. Bolívar developed the notion of a 'world-balance', rather more positive in its aims, as he explained: 'The lessons of experience must not be disregarded: the spectacle offered by Europe, running with blood from defending a balance that is constantly at risk, should [lead us to] correct our policy, in order to avoid these blood-stained reefs. Beyond this continental balance, which Europe seeks where one would least expect to find it, in the midst of war and disturbance, there is another balance: this is the one which interests us: the world-balance. The ambition of the European nations carried the yoke of slavery to the rest of the world: all those other parts should try to establish a balance between themselves and Europe, to destroy the latter's domination. This is what I call world-balance, and it should be a factor in Latin American policy.'[54] Bolívar's originality here is striking. In proclaiming the unity of Latin America, he anticipated the principle of nationalities developed somewhat later by Mazzini, which proclaimed that there were natural frontiers, easily defined. For Bolívar, the logic was unquestionable. The independence wars had shown, despite occasional friction between *caudillos*, that the peoples of Latin America had a sense of solidarity and recognised an implicit pact in the identity of cause and interests.

The territorial principle to be followed under the new order was: 'The republican governments are based on the frontiers of the former viceroyalties, captaincies-general or presidencies.'[55] On the same principle, it was felt that the former Spanish American Empire also formed a natural unit. The frequent repetition of this principle shows the importance attributed to it by Bolívar. The term *uti posseditis juris* was first used by Pedro Gual in 1823, and achieved the joint aim of marking clearly the limits of each state, thus avoiding conflict over frontiers, and guaranteeing mutual defense, destroying forever the possibility of another colonisation of Latin America. Unity negated dependency.

The prestige attached to Bolívar's name brought the adhesion of many areas to the ideals for which he struggled. The Panamanians declared their independence on 28 November 1821. Realising the dangers that threatened their small nation, they adopted Bolívar's solution, confident in the strength of his reputation. They established qualified popular representation, centred on the Panamá *cabildo*, promoter of the Junta. Interpreting and executing the general will, it decreed that 'the territory of the provinces of the Isthmus belongs to the Republican State of Colombia, to whose Congress their deputy will go to represent them at the appropriate time'.[56] Bolívar did not conceal his delight at this move, and even before he was officially notified, he hastened to say, with his usual sincerity: 'I cannot express the feelings of joy and satisfaction I felt on hearing that Panamá, the centre of the earth, has been redeemed by its own efforts and freed through its own merits. Panamá's Declaration of Independence is the most glorious monument in the history of any American province.'[57] In the West Indies also, where Bolívar suffered the grief of exile, though without ever losing his determination and hope, his epic achievement in destroying the old order and building the new found an echo. José Núñez de Cáceres declared himself President of the Independent State of Spanish Haiti on 1 December 1821. The Constituent Act of Government prescribed alliance and federation with Colombia, that part of the island becoming one of the states in the Colombian Union. Although Boyer immediately dealt a severe blow to these hopes by fusing the two halves of the island, nevertheless in 1824, while he was President, he attempted a diplomatic *rapprochement* with Colombia.

Bolívar was forced to dedicate the last quarter of his public life to the countries in the south. This was a great sacrifice, but there was no way out of the dilemma: if he remained in the south, his work in the north would be lost, but if he went north, the south would fall into royalist hands. His absence cost him the loss of perhaps the best part of his work: Colombia collapsed, power escaped from his hands, the oligarchy and *caudillismo*, in collusion, were enthroned, and the revolutionary tendency was swamped by reaction. Bolívar thought that the greatest danger to the revolution lay in the Spanish resistance in Peru, which must be crushed, if independence in the north were to be secured. He set out on the Southern Campaign, accompanied by his best officers and by troops from

Venezuela and New Granada. It was an arduous task: the very peaks of the Andes seemed to be conspiring against the revolution. Yet patriotic tenacity overcame all the obstacles and victory crowned their efforts. In May 1822, the triumph of Pichincha brought the people of Quito into Colombia. On confiding the delicate diplomatic negotiations to Sucre, Bolívar emphasised that he should reassure the Ecuadorians 'that we are not attempting to dominate them, but to form one great unit, composed of completely equal parts'. The negotiator should try 'to convince them of the general advantages to the Republic of their adhesion and of the particular advantages to themselves of belonging to a great Republic which will secure, protect and defend their existence, without harm to their rights or political representation'.[58]

The case of Guayaquil was different. An independent province since 1820, although included within the Presidency of Quito since 120 years earlier, Guayaquil was courted by both Peru and Colombia. She decided in favour of the latter, and Bolívar, who arrived in the city on 13 July 1822, placed it under his protection. The interview between the two great leaders, Bolívar and San Martín, took place there on the 26th. The most bizarre interpretations have been offered of that meeting. Legends have grown up attacking one side or the other, legends which cannot be sustained in the light of present-day historical knowledge. An eminent Argentinian historian has given a definitive account of this important meeting between the two great figures of Latin America: 'San Martín did not go to the beautiful Pacific city in order to incorporate it into Peru. Extensive documentary sources show that he always maintained Guayaquil must decide its own destiny. Therefore, when he learned that Bolívar had annexed it to Colombia and he lost hope of its being annexed to Peru, he was sorry, to some extent; but he did not make a major issue of this point, considering it a secondary one to the main motive which took him to Guayaquil. San Martín went to Guayaquil to discuss with Bolívar the union of the Peruvian and Colombian armies, with the aim of ending the war as quickly as possible ... San Martín's renunciation was not a renunciation, nor was it due to his defeat over Guayaquil, nor even less to any ambition on Bolívar's part. San Martín had decided, when he assumed command in Lima, not to govern for more than a year, and four months before he left for Guayaquil he agreed on the details of his renunciation or retirement ... with his Minister of State and Foreign Affairs, García del Río.'[59] There could be no petty rivalries between these two great men, comrades whom destiny had entrusted with the task of liberating an entire continent. 'I call you friend', Bolívar said to San Martín, 'and this is the title we should continue to use all our lives, for we are brothers in the struggle, in thought and in the task we face, and should be joined by bonds of friendship.'[60] The latter replied: 'Dear friend: may success and happiness never leave your side: these are the wishes of your constant friend, J. de San Martín.'[61] A portrait of Bolívar painted by San Martín's daughter was with him at the moment of his death on French soil in 1850. As another great Argentinian leader wrote: 'Even before Pichincha, Bolívar, triumphant in the north, was stronger: after Pichincha, he was the decisive voice, and he could dictate the conditions of his aid to the south.'[62] San Martín retired as he had arranged. Guayaquil solemnly declared its incorporation into Colombia, which now encompassed Venezuela, New Granada, Panamá, Quito and Guayaquil. Bolívar continued along his chosen path, one that led him to pain and grief as well as satisfaction. Of the two leaders, it was he who shouldered the greater burden.

At this point, Colombia undertook four diplomatic missions, all under instructions from Bolívar and followed very closely by him. Three of these missions achieved relative success, the only failure, and that not complete, being the mission to Buenos Aires. Mosquera and Santa María, the Colombian plenipotentiaries, signed treaties with Peru, Chile and Mexico. The first two were signed in 1822 and the third, due to the fluctuations in Mexican affairs, in the following year. Bolívar's diplomatic policy aimed to achieve something more than simply bilateral agreements between Colombia and her sister nations. He had already decided upon his plan of continental integration and these missions were a first step, and a very important one, towards that greater goal. The central idea in each of the agreements was the promise made by each country to 'interpose its good offices' with the other countries of Latin America to persuade them to accept the union of all in a permanent confederation. Peru gave Bolívar a special welcome, showering him with honours as well as offering him unlimited powers. The Peruvian Constituent Congress, in a law of 12 February 1825, recognised him as Liberator.

It should be emphasied that Bolívar's diplomatic initiatives signified the creation of a new legal framework. In this sense, he left a very positive inheritance to Latin America and to the whole of humanity, in that he showed how a peaceful and just settlement could come about, both at a regional and at a continental level. He believed firmly that international relations must be founded on dignity, respect and peace, and that agreements must be honoured. This explains his attitude to the national debt and his solemn recommendation to the legislators: 'The national debt is the repository of the faithfulness, honour and gratitude of Venezuela. Respect it as you would the Ark of the Covenant, for it contains, not so much the rights of our benefactors, as our own reputation. Let us perish rather than break a promise which has been the salvation of our country and her sons.'[63] He insisted that a good reputation and international credit were the greatest asset of any country, and suggested an enforced isolation of countries which failed to honour their promises. He felt that relations between states could be built on no stronger foundation than voluntary submission to the collective will and self-imposed restraint in certain areas covered by an agreement. If the basis of trust was missing, the association would collapse, so that it could be considered a crime to defy treaties: 'The nation that infringes a solemn agreement incurs general proscription. All communication, all relations with her must cease: she has attempted to break the political links of the group, and the group is entitled to break her.'

Reciprocal recognition of national autonomy was another important point discussed by Bolívar. He was convinced that the correct way to achieve unification was through mutual interest rather than force. Miranda gave little importance in his plans to the consent of the various countries, assuming that their decision would be favourable to unification, since the advantages were so obvious. Bolívar, having triumphed militarily, and with the prestige he enjoyed all over Latin America, could easily have imposed the kind of union he desired on a large part of the continent, but his devotion to democracy and to the principle of national autonomy, as well as the dynamic of the revolution, made him choose a different path: that of seeking consent. He awaited the constitution of the various states, so that they could send representatives to a free assembly where these matters could be discussed frankly and without undue haste. This intense respect for individual nations did not exclude the possibility of intervention in extreme cases where the defence of continental unity was involved. Bolívar had a scale of priorities on which survival held the top place. The aims of justice, freedom and democracy came close behind, and in the interests of achieving these aims, other principles might be temporarily compromised: 'I believe', Bolívar stated to Santander, 'that we should imitate the Holy Alliance in everything relating to political security. The difference should reside in our adhesion to the principle of justice. In Europe, everything is obtained by force, here by free will ... To bring ourselves up to the level where we can sustain the struggle, we have no choice but to adopt the same measures.'

The repudiation of war as a means of resolving disputes was yet another of Bolívar's tenets. His ideology was sincerely pacifist, in line with the needs of his continent, whose greatest tasks were internal ones: the conquest of nature, economic development, social, moral and intellectual progress. Bolívar stressed repeatedly his abhorrence of war for war's sake. He accepted it, and waged it, but only as a means to an end. Paradoxical as it may seem, he reached the stage of conceiving of the army as the principal guarantor of peace. To his military companions he said in 1823: 'All the armies in the history of the world have been set up to defend kings and the powerful: you are set up to defend the weak and the just ... In your rifles, together with the bayonet, carry the laws and liberty and you will be invincible.'

The integration Bolívar was seeking would have given rise to a common Latin American citizenship, a natural development for this group of politically and socially homogeneous republics. The response of the different countries to Bolívar's suggestions is well-documented. In Costa Rica, for example, the birth of Colombia evoked sympathy and admiration. In February 1823, don Rafael Osejo, a Nicaraguan intellectual and teacher resident in Cartago, suggested the union of Costa Rica and Colombia, as a means of avoiding incorporation into the new Mexican Empire. Osejo wrote to Bolívar while the latter was travelling through Ecuador to the south. Enthusiastic demonstrations in San José, Aserrí, Tres Ríos, Ujarrás, Cartago, Curridabat, Escazú, Pacaca and Alajuela, practically all the towns of the Costa Rican central valley, except Heredia, acclaimed the idea of federation with Colombia. Problems of communication and above all the enormous unresolved problem of the south, Colombia's vulnerable heel, prevented Bolívar giving this important matter the attention it merited. Nevertheless, Colombia was the ideal which mobilised the population of Costa Rica, guided by Osejo, in favour of emancipation. The First Costa Rican Constituent Congress, of which Osejo was the secretary, in the end established a separate government from Mexico, Guatemala and León.

In Cuba, Bolívar's epic struggle inspired a conspiratorial movement with the title *Suns and Rays of Bolívar*. The lack of immediate, practical possibilities and also, to a large extent, the implications of European and North American policy in the Caribbean, again obliged Bolívar to postpone measures he had planned for the liberation of the larger Spanish islands, whose inhabitants wished to follow the example of the mainland. He referred to the people of Cuba and Puerto Rico in the Jamaica Letter: 'Are the inhabitants of these islands not Americans? Are they not badly treated? Do they not aspire to well-being?' Then while he was in Lima he received the visit of a Cuban, José Antonio Aranjo and a Puerto Rican, Antonio Valera, both refugees belonging to the *Suns and Rays*. Bolívar wrote to his agents in Panamá, Gual, and Briceño Médez, reminding them of a plan that was to be executed jointly with Guatemala and Mexico: 'This plan envisages: i) defending any part of our coasts attacked by the Spaniards or other enemies ii) sending an expeditionary force to Havana and Puerto Rico iii) marching on Spain with greater forces, after taking Puerto Rico and Cuba, if the Spaniards still refuse peace even then.[63a]

The people of the southern part of the continent were liberated by Bolívar's forces, under the expert command of Sucre. After the battle of Ayacucho, Peru took its place amongst the independent nations of the world. Bolívar's influence on the social and economic structures of the country was soon felt (it is visible even today). Sucre, on his own initiative, and in an act of penetrating political lucidity, achieved the creation of Bolivia. There, too, as we have seen, steps were taken to re-distribute the land, abolish slavery and servitude, reform the educational system and initiate a rule of law and virtue.

At this, Bolívar's finest hour, plenipotentiaries from the River Plate came up to the Bolivian plateau to invite him to Argentina to join their struggle against the Brazilian Empire.[63b] The Argentinian emissaries, General Carlos de Alvear and Dr. Miguel Díaz Vélez, offered Bolívar the protectorate of America, that is, the supreme glory of winning freedom for the whole continent. He had never received such a signal honour. Bolívar's prestige was immense, and he had the support of some of the most influential leaders in the River Plate, amongst them Pueyrredón, Necochea, Monteagudo, Alvear, Guido, Alvarado and above all Manuel Dorrego and Gregorio Funes. Rivadavia, however, had reservations about the plans for federation, and for this reason frustrated to some extent the aims of the Colombian diplomatic mission, by signing, not the treaty proposed by Colombia, similar to those already signed with Peru and Chile, but a treaty of 'Friendship and Alliance' drawn up by himself.

Bolívar also dreamed of redeeming Paraguay, where Rodríguez Francia had installed an abominable dictatorship which closed off the country (and, it must be recognised, saved it from the rapacity of its powerful neighbours). At this point, there was not a single country unaware of Bolívar's reputation, of what he had accomplished and of his plans for the future. He addressed words of praise and encouragement to Central America, which he hoped to see form a solid association: 'This area, magnificently positioned, between the two great oceans, could in time become the warehouse of the world: its canals will cut distances, strengthen commercial links between Europe, America and Asia, and bring to this fortunate area tributes from every part of the globe. It is perhaps the only place where one could establish the capital of the world ...'[63c] Guatamala drew from him in 1824 expressions of strong affection: 'I hope that time will concede me an ample period to extend my activities to Guatamala, as is my earnest wish.' ('Guatamala' at that time meant the present-day country, plus Costa Rica, El Salvador, Honduras and Nicaragua.) Bolívar was also approached by Brazilian exiles, the defeated remnants of the popular revolution of 1817 in Recife. (Abreu y Lima, the son of one of the martyrs of this movement, fought bravely for the freedom of Colombia.) The monarchical régime was successful in Brazil and the civilized and moderate José Bonifacio de Andrade e Silva initiated a process of evolution after 1822. Nevertheless, there was still discontent and the aspiration towards a Republic on the model of Colombia.

The culmination of Bolívar's efforts on behalf of Latin American unity was the Panamá Congress. Incidentally, Bolívar was quite clear about the territorial limits of the type of union he desired, though his views have sometimes been distorted by historians. In the convocation issued in Lima in 1824 and addressed to the governments of the Republics of Colombia, Mexico, the River Plate, Chile and Guatemala, he affirmed the principle twice: 'It is now time that the interests and relations which unite the American Republics, *previously Spanish colonies*, should be put on a solid basis which will assure the continued existence of these governments ... Such an ... authority can only consist of an assembly of plenipotentiaries, named by each of our Republics and brought together under the auspices of the victory obtained by our arms against the Spanish power ... The government of Peru (and that of Colombia) have promised to interpose their good offices with the governments of *what was formerly Spanish America* to persuade them to enter into a pact and attend an assembly of the whole confederation.' He chose Panamá for geographical reasons, referring to it as the centre of the Earth, almost equidistant from Asia, Africa and Europe and the two poles, and comparing it to Corinth in Greek times.

The Congress was to be the central institution of the union envisaged by Bolívar. Amongst the functions attributed to it, two are particularly important: i) the Congress would unify foreign policy and coordinate defense; ii) it would be an organ of conciliation and understanding between the various nations of America, an example to the world of pacific regulations. It was hoped that large issues affecting the whole of the New World would be debated at Panamá, that supra-national laws would be drawn up and that the efforts of all would be concentrated on the achievement of the ideal expressed in 1822: 'The great day has not yet come for America. We have driven out our oppressors, broken the tablets of their tyrannical laws and founded legitimate institutions. But we still need to lay the basis of the social pact which will make of this continent one single nation, formed of many Republics.' Bolívar's imagination leaped over the centuries, inspired by hope: 'When, one hundred centuries from now, posterity seeks the origin of our public law and recalls the treaties that sealed its destiny, the Isthmus protocols will be remembered with respect. In them, will be found the plans for the first alliance ... our first steps in relations with the rest of the world. What, then, will be the isthmus of Corinth, in comparison with that of Panamá?'. He wanted the Congress to be permanent, with regular meetings and its own federal army and navy. All the complementary institutional organs were likewise to be permanent and supra-national in character and to have permanent headquarters.

This Hispanoamerican League envisaged by Bolívar would have been an excellent basis for economic development. It was foreseen in the agreements that countries within the union would accord preferential commercial treatment to other members. Andrés Bello had propounded a similar notion as early as 1810, when he declared to the Supreme Junta of Caracas: 'In my opinion, it is most important that the peoples who have already thrown off the old yoke should join common cause, form a close federation and meet together often to reach an understanding: they should not sign separate agreements.' In 1811, he insisted yet again on the need to deepen the relationship between the various peoples: 'The promise not to enter into any separate agreements and the elaboration of a clear, uniform policy should in my opinion be the first aims of the association ... It is always desirable, where rights and interests are the same that public declarations and action should be the same also.'[64] It was thus that the 'favoured nation' clause in Chile came to be called the 'Bello clause'. His idea coincided with Bolívar's, that union should be close and total and that no member should be able to contract alliances with countries outside the union without the consent of the others. The Panamá Congress was the first and, until now, alas, the only example in the history of the world, of a number of autonomous democratic nations coming together without pressure or haste, seeking only mutual understanding. Colombia, the promoter of the Congress, had no desire to dominate the other members.

Simón Bolívar was thus Head of State of one of the most respected Latin American republics and famous as the leader of the war of continental liberation. A romantic idealist, he employed terms rather foreign to the orthodox language of politics, such as the Christian and humanistic use of 'brothers' and 'brotherhood'. The chronology of this usage is revealing in that it became more frequent as the idea it enshrined grew more important to him. At the end of 1812, a critical year for Venezuelan independence, the idea appeared for the first time in an explanation given to the Congress of New Granada: 'Caracas, the cradle of Colombian Independence, can only be redeemed, like a new Jerusalem, by new crusaders who are faithful republicans: these can be none other than men who, seeing close at hand the torments suffered by Venezuelan victims, would be filled with the sublime determination to become the liberators of their captive brothers.'[65] Around the same time, he had used the term 'Colombia' for the first time in writing: he used it again in the Cartagena Manifesto, where he spoke of 'the tree of liberty of Colombia' and also begged the people of New Granada not to be 'insensible to the lamentations of your brothers'. A couple of years later, when adversity brought him back to Cundinamarca, he stated in the famous Pamplona proclamation: 'I am merely a soldier who has come to offer his services to this fraternal nation.' In 1818, from Angostura, he called with enthusiasm and gratitude to the people of New Granada: 'Join your efforts to those of your brothers: Venezuela is marching with me to liberate you, as you in years past joined with me to liberate Venezuela.' After serious quarrels, in 1826, he sent a message of reconciliation and harmony to all the peoples of Colombia: 'Once again I offer you my services, the services of a brother. I have not tried to find out who did not play his part. I have never forgotten that you are my blood-brothers and my companions at arms. I embrace you all ... my arms encircle ... the people of New Granada and of Venezuela, the just and the unjust alike, all of the liberating armies, all citizens of the great Republic.' On 2 May 1820, he sent the government of Chile a copy of the Constitution then operative in Colombia, so that the Chilean people might see the system by which their brothers in Colombia were ruled. He always held O'Higgins in high esteem and in August 1821 he wrote to the Chilean leader to propose the unification of the Colombian armies with that of Chile, adding that 'wherever these brothers in arms [meet up for the first time] there will arise a spring of liberty that will flow to all the corners of America'.

A similar spirit is evident in an eloquent note to the Supreme Director of the United Provinces of the River Plate signed by Bolívar in Tunja on 4 February 1821: 'My sole object is to give a guarantee of loyalty from Colombia to Your Excellency, bringing it to the attention of Your Excellency and of the heroic people you rule, in testimony of the sentiments of union and friendship I wish to see grow in our relationship, not as between two different nations, but as between two brothers who support, protect and defend each other.' He told the plenipotentiaries Alvear and Díaz Vélez: 'The Argentine people can rest assured that our hearts will never be indifferent to their fate in the future: that our liveliest interest and our sincerest affection will always go out to the nation that set out on the noble path of liberty at the same time as ourselves.' He demonstrated a similar attitude to the people of Ecuador. When he was about to march south on the crusade that was to carry him to Potosí, he explained his intentions to the Congress: to march without delay 'to the ends of Colombia, to break the chains that bind the sons of Ecuador and to invite them to become part of Colombia, after they are free. I hope you will authorise me to unite with us through bonds of benevolence, peoples whom nature and destiny have given us as brothers.' This was on 3 October 1821, and a week later he expressed similar sentiments in relation to Mexico: 'Let Colombia and Mexico appear before the world with joined hands and, even more, with joined hearts. Destiny united us in misfortune, our courage unites us in our plans for the future, nature gave us but one being so that we might be brothers.' A similar tone is evident in the instruction given at the end of 1821 by Chancellor Gual to the Colombian diplomats Santa María and Mosquera: the confederation they were trying to achieve 'should not be formed as an ordinary alliance for defense and attack: it should be a closer alliance than the one recently formed in Europe to oppose the freedom of the people. Ours should be a society of brothers ... temporarily separated ... by the course of human history, but united, strong and powerful to resist the attacks of foreign powers.'[66] When Bolívar addressed the Peruvian President Unanué, he echoed the message sent to Argentina in 1821: 'Our republics will be joined in such a way that they will not seem two distinct nations, but instead two brothers, joined by all the links that bound us in the past, but with this difference, that then we obeyed one tyrant, whereas now we shall be united in embracing freedom, though we may have different laws and even different governments.'[67]

Bolívar's concept of fraternity also extended to the citizens of the United States, whom he called in the Jamaica Letter 'our brothers in the north'. A similar formulation appeared in an official note of 1819. Finally, on 30 March 1830 when he received the Brazilian diplomatic representatives in Bogotá, Bolívar took advantage of the opportunity to state that the arrival of an emissary from the court at Rio de Janeiro 'will ensure forever the most perfect friendship between our neighbouring and fraternal countries'.

It should be pointed out that unity amongst the countries of Latin America is not incompatible with the idea of universal solidarity, nor is it contrary to such noble aims as world peace and cooperation between nations. The formation of smaller groupings is an important initial step towards these ends. On this point, it is instructive to look at Bolívar's immigration policy. His first public act in Venezuela was to extend an open invitation to foreigners without discrimination of any kind. 'Firstly: we must again invite foreigners, of any nationality or profession, to come and settle in these provinces, under the direct protection of the government. We offer this protection, secure in the knowledge that the fertility of our soil, its varied and useful produce, the pleasantness of our climate and a régime which guarantees individual security and property must give settlers all the advantages or facilities they could ever hope for in their own country.' Years later, in Peru, he granted trading facilities to foreigners, stating that they should enjoy the protection of the law just as much as Peruvians and pay the same taxes, for obstacles put in their way would be in contradiction to the liberal principles that presided over the formation of the Republic and the practice of the most progressive nations. Bolívar desired immigration as a means of populating the empty zones and also of hastening development through the example of more advanced nations. 'Venezuela', he said, 'has ... invited ... all men fit to work who wish to seek shelter amongst us and help us by their industry and knowledge, without enquiring into which part of the globe gave them birth.' The

Angostura Congress consecrated the almost total equality between foreigners and nationals: the criteria for obtaining citizenship were probably the widest and most liberal in the entire constitutional history of America. In 1813, Bolívar declared that any foreigner who had fought in the ranks of the liberation army was automatically a citizen and in 1815 he spoke to Hyslop about regions of America which 'await only their freedom, to welcome into their midst people from the continent of Europe, to form in America, in the space of a few years, another Europe'.

In 1818, he reminded General John D'Evereux of the sympathy with which America regarded those 'virtuous and magnanimous foreigners who preferred freedom to slavery and who, abandoning their own country, came to our continent, bringing science, the arts, industry, talents and virtue'. In 1824 he spoke at length about the relationship between immigration and progress: 'We must foment', he said, 'immigration from Europe and North America, so that these people will settle here, bringing their arts and sciences with them. These advantages, plus an independent government, free schools and intermarriage of our people with Europeans and North Americans will change its entire character, making it learned and prosperous.'[68] He wanted foreigners who would be the authors of material advance and was confident that in the future 'order will be established and the government strengthened by ... European and Asian immigration, which must necessarily increase the population'.[69] He explained this point of view to Pedro Gual, urging him to carry out the necessary work of propaganda. 'The protection afforded by the Government to honest foreigners who wish to settle amongst us will compensate for our lack of population and give us virtuous citizens. Please spread these ideas amongst respectable foreigners, pointing out the advantages that await them.' Even to Spaniards, he extended a welcome: 'If you wish to be Colombians, you shall be Colombians, for we need brothers to swell our family.' It goes without saying that Bolívar harboured no racial prejudice. O'Leary's impression of Bolívar's stay in Haiti and his relations with Pétion was mistaken, as recently discovered documents show. There exists, for example, a letter from Bolívar to the Haitian leader: 'I hope, Mr. President, that the similarity of our sentiments regarding the defense of our common native country will earn me the benefits of Your Excellency's inexhaustible benevolence.' A historian of the period remarks: 'In respect of the Liberator's supposed hesitations over the embarrassing consequences that could derive from his association with the Haitian leaders, the letter reveals that not only did he not fear, he positively welcomed the association as an aid to the achievement of his aims in the emancipation movement. His declaration about the similarity of his and Pétion's sentiments concerning the defense of the rights of their common native country is a clear indication of his attitude to the racial question.'[70] In general, Bolívar considered physical racial characteristics unimportant, referring to the colour of the skin as an 'accident'. His immigration policy was not concerned about pigmentation or cranial measurements, but about moral qualities. He was well aware of the complex racial composition of the Latin American people, which he considered an advantage.[71] 'I look upon America as a chrysalis,' he said in 1822. 'There will be a transformation in the physical life of her inhabitants: finally, there will arise a new race out of all the old races, which will produce a homogeneous people.'[72] In Angostura, he urged: 'The blood of our citizens is different, let us mix it together to make it one.'[73]

Bolívar thus sought the unity of Latin America through racial integration, but he went even further: he believed that America could communicate its revolutionary fervour to Africa and Asia, and destroy the yoke of servitude that Europe at this period had hung upon the rest of the world. He aimed at a kind of link which would be closer than the ephemeral alliances hitherto known, even looking forward to a united world, where the principles that had given birth to America would reign: 'With the advance of time, there could exist, perhaps, one single nation, embracing the whole world — a federation.' It is worth noting that although Bolívar was a confirmed centralist so far as the internal politics of each state was concerned, in inter-American affairs he was a federalist. He considered these two separate problems and proposed two different solutions, realising that continental federation was a very different matter from federation at a national level: 'The former means the union of large forces, the latter the fragmentation of each of these forces into tiny parts.'

The American Federation advocated by Bolívar was unique. It was hoped that it would have a unified foreign policy and mutual cooperation in internal defense: 'The New World will divide into independent nations, joined together by an agreement which will unify their foreign policy and provide a stabilising agent in the form of a permanent general congress ... The forces of all would go to the aid of any member under attack from an external enemy or from anarchic factions.' It was not a federation, however, in the sense of having a common Executive. It was closer, in fact, to a confederation, in that 'internal order will be preserved, amongst the different states, and within each one. None will be weak in relation to another, none strong.' Realising that the old labels were inadequate to describe this new reality, but feeling this was a minor issue, Bolívar used both terms, 'federation' and 'confederation', without distinction, and on one occasion stated that he preferred the term 'union', for its moral and social, rather than strictly political or legal connotations. In August 1826, disillusioned by the failure of the Panamá Congress, he turned to the more feasible aim of integrating Colombia,

Peru and Bolivia. The fusion of these countries, to which he had given freedom, represented a respectable area, some 5,000,000 square kilometres, equal to half the area of Europe, and in terms of population a sizeable part of Latin America.

This did not mean that he abandoned hope of unifying the whole country. Even when the meagre gains of Panamá were threatened by the refusal of all the countries except Colombia to ratify the agreements already signed, he continued to affirm his faith in the principle he had always followed. His communication of August 1828 to the Mexican President shows this quite clearly: 'Colombia will never abandon the American Confederation, which must be of such benefit to all the nations of this continent, in assuring their independence and unifying their policies, bringing them closer together: confident of the support of our brothers and allies in the Republic of the United States of Mexico, Colombia will not fail to promote, in better days and in happier circumstances, the meeting of plenipotentiaries to discuss our common interests.'[74] In a last attempt at unification, during the Dictatorship, he sent Pedro Gual and Miguel Santa María as Colombian plenipotentiaries to the second American Assembly. This vain attempt to save the Republic closed the chapter on his attempts to give a concrete reality to the idea of unity, for by then Bolívar was close to death.

The idea of unity had preoccupied him throughout his public life. It appeared in his article in a London newspaper, to which we have already referred. The people of Venezuela 'will invite all the peoples of America to join them in a confederation. These nations are already prepared for such a plan and will hasten to follow the example of Caracas.' His earliest surviving speech, to the Patriotic Society, contained a similar argument: 'How could those who are most aware of the need for unity promote division? What we wish is that this union should be effective and that it should encourage us in the glorious enterprise of winning our freedom: to unite only in order to rest, to sleep in the arms of apathy, was a fault yesterday: today it is crime.'[75] In the Cartagena Manifesto he warned: 'Our internal divisions, not Spanish arms, will restore us to slavery.' In the Carúpano Manifesto, the theme is also present in the main idea of the text, that divisions had also led to the failure of the second great attempt to establish a democratic system. 'Thus it would seem that heaven has decreed, to our shame and our glory, that our victors are our brothers, and that our brothers can triumph only over us.' In the Jamaica Letter he wrote: 'I will tell you what can put us in a position to drive out the Spaniards and found a free government: unity.' To the Angostura Congress he urged: 'Unity, unity must be our watchword', and he reminded the Ocaña Convention that 'no nation won respect without the unity that fortifies'. The farewell with which he ended his public life could not be more moving: 'Fellow countrymen: Hear my voice for the last time, at the close of my political career: in the name of Colombia, I ask you, I beg you, to remain united, not to be the assassins of your country and your own executioners.' From one extreme to the other of the continent, Bolívar came to represent unity. José Gervasio Artigas, for example, said: 'Intimately linked by bonds of nature and mutual interest, we struggle against tyrants who try to trample on our most sacred rights.' José Cecilio del Valle concurred with this view and stretched out his hand to 'place our destiny, and that of our descendants, under the protection of a solemn union, and at the same time serve our mutual interest, establishing bases as solid as our sincere wishes'.[76]

Anti-slavery legislation

We have seen that colonial society in Latin America was characterised by inequality and we have examined the struggle against inequality that took place from the sixteenth century onwards. Picornell, Gual and España proposed not only the equality before the law prescribed and divulged by the French Revolution, but also equality of what they called 'caste', that is racial equality. In Picornell's text he declared: 'Slavery, of course, is abolished, as contrary to humanity.' So also was the payment of tribute by the Indians, to whom land would be given and 'means of existence, so that they may live as happily as other citizens'.[77] The first revolutionary government of Caracas took only very timid steps towards equality, by abolishing the privileges and exemptions that distinguished certain social groups, such as having special laws and even special judges. Hereditary titles and distinctions were also abolished, as was the use of the particle 'de' in surnames. The terms 'Excellency', 'Your Grace', 'Sir', and so on were replaced by a uniform 'Citizen' and the normal Spanish form of address, 'Usted'.

The condition of the *pardos* improved slightly under the First Republic, but, although they represented the vast majority of the nation, they were still excluded from public affairs and there was no clear commitment to the long awaited decrees that would abolish such iniquities. The Supreme Junta did the absolute minumum: it abolished the Indian tribute, but it did not abolish slavery or the slave trade, though it did consent, after much vacillation, to 'prohibit the importation of negroes into these Provinces, it being clearly understood that this prohibition does not apply to those expeditions which have already been authorised: these orders will enter into effect once those expeditions have returned.'[78] Miranda had invited *pardos*, negroes and even slaves to join the Patriotic Society, wishing to establish a platform of popular support in his country, where he was really a stranger. But although he proposed the abolition of the tribute and forbade racial discrimination, he did not make any decisive statement on the question of the abolition of slavery. At the time of the *Campaña Admirable*, Bolívar still believed that military success was the vital factor. Moreover, his Republican principles were abstract and remote from the material aspirations of his people. His Republic fell because the people did not defend it, but they had no reason to do so, for until then it had been nothing but words, with no practical content and no concrete results. His West Indian exile, though hard and painful, was fertile in showing Bolívar the reasons for his earlier failure. Pétion gave him vital assistance, on the understanding that the black slaves on the mainland would be freed. This encounter in Port-au-Prince had a profound influence on the direction taken by the Venezuelan revolution after the Los Cayos and Jacmel expeditions, in that the revolutionary process thereafter was more conscious. The success of Monteverde and Boves, with all the ill consequences for the patriotic movement, had been a powerful lesson. As soon as Bolívar arrived in Margarita, on 23 May 1816, from Villa del Norte, he announced the good news of the end of slavery: 'There will be no more slaves in Venezuela, except those who wish to be slaves. All those who prefer liberty to repose will take up arms to defend their sacred rights and will be citizens.'[79]

Ten days later, in Carúpano, he made a more formal declaration: 'Considering that justice, political coherence and our country cry out for [the recognition of] this inalienable natural right, I have come to decree, and do hereby decree, absolute freedom for slaves who for three hundred years groaned under the Spanish yoke.' A month afterwards, he reiterated to the inhabitants of Caracas, which was the province with the largest slave population: 'That unhappy portion of your brothers which groaned under the miseries of slavery is free. Natural justice and political coherence demand the emancipation of the slaves. From now on, there will be only one class of men in Venezuela: citizens.' The revolution set only one condition for the emancipation of the slaves, a condition justified by the political situation: that they fight to defend their rights. 'Is it just that only free men should die to free the slaves?' Otherwise, Bolívar showed himself in favour of unconditional emancipation. The style of his speeches to the Angostura Congress demonstrates how profound this conviction was. 'I implored the protection of the God of humanity and then the Redemption dissipated the darkness, slavery broke its chains and Venezuela found herself surrounded by new sons, grateful sons, who transformed the instruments of their slavery into instruments of freedom. Yes, those who were formerly slaves are now free men: those who were formerly enemies of a cruel step-mother are now the defenders of their country. It is useless to insist upon the justice, the necessity, the benefits of this measure ... you know that no man can be both a slave and free, without violating all natural, political and civil laws.' The fate of his other measures was a matter of indifference to Bolívar, compared with this one which, as it were, contained all the others. 'I leave to your sovereign decision the reform or revocation of all my statutes and decrees: but I beg you to confirm the total emancipation of the slaves, as I would beg for my life, or that of the Republic.'

In his proposal for a constitution, Bolívar defined freedom as 'the right of every citizen to participate in the making of the laws, as a member of the sovereign body', and proposed that the constitution should contain the words: 'true equality can only exist in the making of the law and before the law, that is the law should apply equally to all, without exception, both in rewards and in punishment.'[80] The principles of popular sovereignty and equality before the law are not, of course, a denial of the real inequalities which exist between individuals: the purpose of the law is to correct this inequality and push it in the desired direction towards equality. As Bolívar states: 'Legal equality is highly necessary where there is physical inequality.'[81] In other words, for Bolívar, equality is something produced by the law, not something which previously exists and is merely recognised by the law. He was in advance of his time in his adherence to this principle, that the law was an instrument which should be used to compensate for inequality, though this subsequently became a generally accepted principle.

In some ways, it represented a return to distributive justice, which advocated, not similar treatment for all, but unequal treatment to compensate for disadvantage. Such a notion fitted very well with the rest of Bolívar's ideology and accorded with his preference for concrete realities rather than abstract theorising, however admirable. In the Angostura Address, he dwelt with pleasure on the fact that Venezuela had decreed equality and explained the reasons for the inclusion of the words quoted in the constitution: 'The citizens of Venezuela enjoy under the Constitution, the interpreter of nature, perfect political equality. Even if such equality had not been an item of dogma in Athens, France and America, we should still be bound to bring it into operation, to correct the obvious differences which do exist. It is my opinion, Legislators, that the fundamental principle of our system depends directly and exclusively on equality as established and practised in Venezuela.' He had come to realise that the abolition of slavery was necessary, impelled by the logic of his revolutionary beliefs. 'I think it madness', he said, 'that in a revolution for freedom there are people who wish to maintain slavery.' Páez echoed this thought in his autobiography of 1867: 'To think we believed it feasible, or even possible, within the logic of events, to liberate a country while leaving a part of the inhabitants in servitude, is an absurdity into which the Liberator of Colombia would not have fallen.'[82] Bolívar did show that he had learned his political lesson: 'It is shown, therefore, in the political maxims drawn from examples in history, that any free government which commits the absurdity of maintaining slavery is punished by rebellion and sometimes extinction.'[83]

Bolívar considered the Indians an oppressed and degraded section of the population, whom he wished to see obtain concrete benefits from the revolutionary measures. The first of his decrees favouring the Indians appeared in 1818: 'I draw your attention to the ruling that [the Indians] should be allowed three days per week for their own work and should realise that they are now free men, not slaves as they were in the time of the Capuchins.'[84] On 20 May 1820, in El Rosario, he promulgated certain advanced laws: 'Neither the priests not the *jueces políticos* nor any other person ... will be able to use the Indians' labour in any way or under any circumstances, without first paying them a salary previously stipulated in a formal contract drawn up in the presence and with the approval of the *juez político*. Anyone who infringes this law will pay double the amount of the salary for the work done: the *jueces políticos* will demand payment of this fine, in favour of the injured party, whenever a complaint is made: where the *jueces* themselves are the guilty party, the *gobernadores políticos* will exact the fine.' Knowing how unworthy priests, speculators in faith, used religion as a means of exploiting the Indians, he laid down other severe and radical measures: 'From this moment, the practices of not administering the sacraments to Indian parishioners until they have paid their confraternity and stipendiary dues, or demanding from them parochial dues from which they are exempted by virtue of the state stipend paid to the priest, or obliging them to pay for feasts for the saints, all these practices must cease: they are contrary to the spirit of religion, to Church discipline and to the laws. Priests who contravene this law and continue these abuses ... will be dealt with very severely. The *jueces políticos* are to keep a careful watch over the conduct of the priests and give an account to the government of any misdemeanours in this area, so that the proper steps may be taken.' This amounted to a freedom charter for the Indians: Article 15 was a declaration of rights which would be enough in itself to prove Bolívar's revolutionary credentials: 'The Indians, like all other free men in the Republic, can come and go with their passports, trade their fruits and other produce, taking them to any market or fair they wish, and may exercise their industry and talents freely, in any way they choose, without hindrance.'[85]

The next step in the series of measures aimed at achieving social equality was Bolívar's appearance before the Cúcuta Congress, to which he spoke as follows: 'The children born to slaves in Colombia from this day on are free, for they belong only to God and their parents, and neither God nor their parents wishes them to be unhappy. The General Congress, authorised by its own laws, and even more by those of Nature, can decree the absolute freedom of all Colombians, through the fact of being born within the Republic. In this way, property rights, political rights and natural rights are reconciled.' Bolívar was taking advantage of a period of euphoria in the Colombian Congress to ask for a commitment to the abolition of slavery: it was all he asked, in this moment of victory, 'as a reward for the battle of Carabobo, won by the liberating army, whose blood was spilled in the cause of freedom'.[86] In general, one can say he never let slip an opportunity of presenting the abolitionist case. It was through his influence that in the instructions to the Colombian plenipotentiaries to the Panamá Congress there was a recommendation that the abolition of slavery should be included as one of the lofty aims of that body: 'The interest shown by the civilised world in the abolition of slavery and the slave trade with Africa demands that this Assembly should also deliberate the issue. The question presents our republics with a magnificent opportunity to give an example of the liberality and philanthropy of her principles.' The mission to Panamá was thus charged with 'achieving the abolition of the slave trade with Africa and declaring those engaged in this dreadful traffic guilty of the crime of ordinary piracy'.[87]

Bolívar's efforts were particularly useful in Peru, for in that country there existed the fateful combination, inimical to any just and liberal régime: gold and slaves. On 24 March 1824, in the city of Trujillo, Bolívar took a curious but significant decision. He decreed that slaves should be protected whenever they wished to change masters, 'whether they have cause or not, even if it is a mere whim'. His secretary communicated this decision to the Prefect of the Department: 'His Excellency commands you to afford the poor slaves all possible governmental protection, for it is the height of tyranny to deprive these unhappy people of the sad consolation of changing masters. By this order, His Excellency cancels all laws prejudicial to the slaves' right to choose a master as they wish.'[88] It is curious that Bolívar, having already made up his mind to end slavery, did not mention abolition on that occasion, but instead referred to a trivial right, that of changing masters. He had mentioned this right as a child and his guardian, Carlos Palacios, had described the notion as: 'improper for his age and, what is worse, and more dangerous, most impolitic and erroneous ... because no-one but an ignorant demagogue could teach that slaves are free to change masters and choose one to suit their fancy, an idea which, if it were to become established and widely held, would completely upset our republic and cause tragic damage, for which reason I consider it an idea opposed to good government and to our system of legislation.'[89]

Again in the city of Trujillo, on 8 April 1824, Bolívar arranged for the re-distribution of what were called common lands amongst the Indians who did not hold any other property. His aim was the foundation of new towns, and besides this public goal, he sought justice, that no Indian should be without his piece of land. On 4 July, he advanced even further in this task of restoring their rights to the descendants of the Incas. He had been in the city of Cuzco for nine days, and it had impressed him profoundly: 'Everything turns my mind towards high ideals and profound thoughts: my soul is charmed by the presence of primitive nature, giving forth its creations, inspired by its own internal rhythms, without interference from outside factors or advice, the caprices of the human spirit, or the contagion of the history of the crimes and stupidity of our human species. Here everything is pure and original, like inspiration from on high.'[90] Possibly it was this inspiration which led him to decree: 'No employee of the State is to demand, directly or indirectly, labour from the Peruvian Indians, without previously drawing up a free contract, specifying the payment for the work. Prefects of Departments, Intendants, Governors, Judges, bishops, curates and their assistants, landowners, mineowners and owners of textile workshops are forbidden to use Indians against their will in forced labour, or any type of domestic or other service ... The daily wage of labourers in mines, textile workshops and farms must be paid at the agreed rate and in cash, so that they are not obliged to accept goods in lieu, nor accept a lower than normal rate.'[91] These laws were surrounded by the usual safeguards to ensure that they were obeyed: violation would attract official attention and would be one of the specific points to be investigated in a *residencia* or enquiry into the period of jurisdiction of government officials.

Bolívar also laid down that the distribution of land arranged in Trujillo should be carried out. At the same time, he abolished the title and authority of the *caciques* or Indian leaders used by the Spaniards as instruments of domination against their own people: many of these unhappy creatures had grown thoroughly adapted to the corrupt system which degraded them into agents of a foreign power. Bolívar understood these complex relations very well, so that his decree stated that the former *caciques* should be treated by the Republican authorities as citizens worthy of respect, so long as this did not prejudice the rights or interests of the other citizens. From Cuzco and Urubamba, helped by the stimulating presence of Simón Rodríguez, Bolívar took other important social measures. Provisions were made with respect to education: some new teaching institutions were founded and others reformed. The distinction between the priests of Spanish congregations and those of the Indians was abolished. He founded two asylums, one for invalids and the other for beggars, and ordered the Casa de San Buenaventura in Urubamba to be used as a home for orphans and illegitimate children. He also took an interest in roads to facilitate social and commercial interchange. Measures similar to this were taken in Bolivia, in Chuquisaca. Bolívar announced there that 'the privileged classes have ceased to exist' and that 'any tax degrading to the citizen's dignity' must be eliminated. For this reason he abolished 'the duty levied only on the Indians and known as tribute, which ... falls on the poorest section of society' and proposed the inclusion in the Bolivian Constitution of the words: 'All those who until now were slaves are Bolivian citizens: as such, they are set free by the publication of this Constitution: a special law will determine the amount of compensation to be paid to their former owners.'[92]

It is difficult to find another subject on which Bolívar expressed himself with more passionate and emphatic sincerity than on slavery. In Angostura he declared: 'Slavery is a child of darkness: and an ignorant people is the blind instrument of its own destruction.'[93] At the Bolivian Congress he said: 'Slavery is contrary to all laws. A law to preserve it would be sacrilegous. What justification could anyone allege for its retention? From whatever angle one considers this criminal activity, one cannot imagine there is a single Bolivian, however depraved, who would attempt to justify this striking violation of human dignity ... To found rights of possession on ferocious assault is only conceivable if one abandons all normal legal principles and the most elementary notions of duty.' He wrote to Bentham in 1827: 'Unfortunately, the weight of slavery deadens the spirit and renders it unfit for freedom. It is for this reason that the study of the subjects you mention (the sciences) is so important, so that even in the midst of his chains, Man can at least discover that he has rights he can claim.'

A number of other measures demonstrate Bolívar's determination to eliminate distinctions and promote equality. In the reform of the rules of the University of Caracas, in 1824, for example, the doors were opened to all Venezuelans, without distinction, and he advised that this course should be adopted elsewhere. The *pardos* thus received from Bolívar proper recognition and the treatment to which they were entitled under a new and revolutionary order. He did not try to hide his satisfaction at the changed times he had helped to bring about: 'Before the revolution, the whites had access to all positions under the monarchy, they could attain the position of minister to the king or even of Spanish grandees. Through talent, merit or fortune, they could achieve anything. The *pardos*, reduced to the most humiliating condition, were deprived of everything. The holy priesthood was closed to them: one could say the Spaniards had managed to close to them even the gates of Heaven. The revolution has won them every privilege, every right, every advantage ... Everything wicked, everything barbarous, everything odious has been abolished and in its place we have absolute equality, even in domestic customs.' With complete moral authority Bolívar addressed his soldiers on the case of

Piar who he felt was promoting anarchy through racial struggle: 'As you know, equality, liberty and independence are our watchwords. Has not humanity recovered its rights thanks to our laws? Have not our weapons broken the chains of slavery? Have not hateful differences of colour and class been abolished for ever? Have not the national lands been distributed amongst you? Are not fortune, knowledge and glory awaiting you? Are your merits not rewarded abundantly, or at least adequately? What, then, did General Piar wish for you? Are you not equal, free, independent, happy and respectable? Could Piar obtain anything greater for you? No, no, no.' There was no discrimination within the army: this was a freedom that had been won by the people's insistence and Bolívar said of it at Bucaramanga in 1828: 'In the first years of Independence, we needed men who were above all brave, who could kill Spaniards and make themselves feared; negroes, *zambos*, mulattoes and whites, all were welcome so long as they fought bravely; no-one could be rewarded with money, for there was none; the only way of maintaining ardour, rewarding exceptional actions and stimulating valour was by promotion, so that today men of every caste and colour are amongst the generals, leaders and officers in our forces, though the majority of them have no other merit than brute strength, which was so useful to the Republic but which now, in peacetime, is an obstacle to peace and tranquility. But it was a necessary evil.'[94]

Nowhere in Bolívar's writings does one find a prejudice in favour of his native town or region, nor even of his family. He did not elevate any of his relatives to high office, and when justice demanded it, he ensured that strict penalties were levied against them. In April 1827 he wrote to Páez: 'In the last week, Caracas has witnessed a legal action which has contributed greatly to public morality, proving that the law is the same for all, since its force fell on an individual to whose defence even my relatives sprang: but I ... was inflexible.'[95] He reproved his nephew, Anacleto Clemente with special rigour: 'Are you not ashamed of yourself to see that some poor *llaneros*, with no education and no means of obtaining it, who have had no other school that the guerrilla war, have become gentlemen; they have been transformed into respectable citizens; they have learned to respect themselves simply through respecting me. Are you not ashamed, I repeat, that being my nephew and the son of a lady of impeccable virtue, you should be the inferior of some poor soldier who has no family other than his native country?' In relation to certain financial questions he wrote to his sister María Antonia: 'I do not wish to exceed my rights, for the higher my position, the more those rights should be reduced. Fate has placed me at the apex of power: but I wish to have no other rights than those of an ordinary citizen. Let justice be done, and if justice is on my side, then let me have my part. If it is not, I am content to accept the decision of the courts.' In Peru, on the occasion of choosing ten youths to be sent to Europe to study, he insisted that equity should dictate the decision: four students should be chosen from the Department of Lima, two from Trujillo, two from Cuzco and two from Arequipa. A similar line of thought led him to envisage abolishing the old frontiers. On one occasion he told Páez: 'I forgot to mention that we are thinking of joining two or three parts of the Departments of Boyacá, Zulia and Barinas, so that there would no longer be any frontier between Venezuela and New Granada: for it is this very division which is killing us and must therefore be destroyed.'

Bolívar's significance in his time has never been properly analysed. His revolutionary vision was bold and modern, in that he was seeking to put America on the footing that Europe would attain a few years later. While the Old World was still trying to implant liberal individualism, Bolívar was trying to implant real justice and equity and the proper revindication of the rights of the oppressed. Where England applied 'freedom of contract', thus failing to protect the economically weak, Bolívar struggled to give the South American revolution a truly collective dimension, using such terms as 'social guarantees' and 'social rights'. The suppression of the corporations in Europe after 1791 and punishment of any attempt to revive them meant that at the beginning of the 19th century there was no regulation of working conditions. There the situation of the nascent proletariat was, it seems, worse than that of the Roman slaves or the medieval serfs, becoming unbearable in the years 1825–35. At that precise moment, Bolívar was drawing up legislation in America, with regard to Indian labour, which was clearly interventionist and protective in its aims. This was not an isolated example of humanitarianism, but part of a coherent plan for political and cultural progress. In Europe, the avowed aim was the phantom of individual liberty, and it was felt that society, or any form of association, limited free will and denied the rights of man and the citizen. The state should be allowed to wither away, as an obsolete despotic authority. (Such a withering would, of course, have led to a return to a pre-social stage and the domination of the weak by the strong.) Bolívar asserted the contrary principle, that 'nothing is so dangerous for the people as the weakness of the Executive', and he worked towards a vigorous system that could communicate its strength to the whole of society. Both the positions outlined, the individualist one supported by traditionalists, and Bolívar's opposite one, had supporters within Colombia. Those who supported the individualist position in fact wished to make of the state an instrument of the privileged classes, whilst the others strived to make it a sovereign organism, active on the side of justice and of a profound socio-economic transformation in favour of the exploited masses. Bolívar remained obstinately true to the policies he had chosen, right to the end. When he went to Caracas for the last time, he ordered an official enquiry into the application of the Law of Manumission which had freed the slaves in 1821. He found that out of tens of thousands of slaves, less than three hundred had been freed in the whole Republic between 1821 and 1826. His energetic response can be found in a decree published in Caracas on 28 June 1827: any monies owed to the emancipation fund 'must be paid within a year'. For greater rapidity and efficiency, taxes intended to feed his fund were henceforth to be collected by the government tax inspectors. The liquid assets of people who died intestate were to go into the fund. Where a man died owing money to the fund, the debt must be paid out of his estate within one year of his death. There were severe penalties for officials who did not observe these rules. The rights of the slaves to food, medicine, clothing and shelter were explicitly confirmed, as were the rights of aged freed men. If further proof of his intentions were needed, three days after the Dictatorship brought him unlimited powers, he promulgated a decree with precise and urgent instructions for the Juntas in charge of freeing the slaves: they were to reorganise themselves 'within one week of the publication of this decree' and hold 'in every canton at least one session per week'. The *jefe político* of the canton or, failing him, the first municipal *alcalde*, would be responsible for seeing this was carried out.

If we look specifically at the Indian question during the Dictatorship, we see that Bolívar published an important decree on 15 October 1828, a decree which, incidentally, has been misinterpreted by historians. It has been said that Bolívar reinstated the personal tribute payable by the Indians: in fact what he did was to equate the Indians with all other citizens on whom the burden of maintaining the state fell. He did recognise in the text of the decree that the condition of the Indians, far from having improved, 'has grown worse, and their needs greater'. The decree contained a number of measures to improve the treatment of these marginal Colombian citizens. An attempt was made to relieve their poverty, they were exempted from military service unless they volunteered, and they were declared 'exempt from having to pay any parish dues or any national tax of any kind'. The courts of justice were to be 'general protectors of the Indians' and amongst other functions it would be their job to assure 'by whatever means are at their disposal, the establishment of schools for the education of the Indians' children and to urge parents to send their children to these schools as regularly as possible ... The priests and protectors must tactfully urge the Indians to work in common a sufficient area of land left over from the reserved land to invest the profits in projects which will benefit themselves.'[96]

Cultural measures

In the main part of this work so far, we have examined what we might call the achievement of Bolívar's ideals: independence for his people, democracy, justice, equality and unity; on the last point, it should be noted that any measure taken in one country was intended for the whole ensemble of countries, Venezuela, Colombia, Ecuador, Panamá, Peru and Bolivia, from the great cities to the tiniest villages scattered over this vast region. Bolívar was convinced that progress could only arise from 'creative construction', which was the term then used for what we would call 'development'. He hoped to replace the slave system in agriculture with salaried labour, as appropriate in a monetarist economy, but he also saw the distribution of the land to those who worked it as a measure which would improve agricultural efficiency. He was not afraid of state intervention and took the initiative in nationalising the mines. Bolívar was also an advocate of popular education, feeling that it strengthened the moral basis of society, contributing to the birth of a new man who would embody the great moral values of our civilisation. The importance of this attitude will best be understood by examining the situation in Latin America at the time of his arrival on the scene.

Inevitably, backwardness was the norm in the Spanish colonies. Spain herself, through her intransigence and theocratic fanaticism, did not benefit from the technical advances of the industrial revolution fostered in the atmosphere of free enquiry favoured by the Reformation. Spain's response had been the Counter-Reformation and the Inquisition. Her culture was especially backward in relation to science, but even in the artistic sphere, a particularly closed type of Catholicism held sway, affecting education, philosophy, architecture, the theatre, literature and even music and painting (the norms of the Council of Trent explain the absence of nudes). The situation was further complicated by Spain's uneven distribution of cultural institutions in the colonies. The richer colonies received preferential treatment, so Venezuela came near the botton of the list. Caracas was only granted a University in 1725, and a printing press in 1808, that is, more than two hundred years after the first arrival of these in America.

A general characteristic of Spanish cultural policy was rigid censorship. The Holy Office was in charge of the entry, distribution and use of all books. Any works containing propositions hostile to Catholic dogma, or offensive to decency or public morality, or with a tendency to undermine the respect due to the monarchy or the law, were prohibited. In the index of forbidden books in use at the end of the eighteenth century, the Inquisition had noted some 5,420 authors, besides an infinite number of anonymous works. Rigour in the application of this control increased as the absolutist régime perfected its repressive bureaucratic machinery. The Crown was particularly zealous in relation to books dealing with

America. The approval of the Council of the Indies was necessary before these books could come into America and no-one could publish, own or sell them without its permission. Despite these restrictions, some important libraries were built up; Bolívar's father owned a quite considerable collection.

Knowing the situation of general cultural backwardness, Bolívar insisted from the beginning on the importance of education. Joseph Lancaster, the English educationalist, recalled: 'I remember you, on the occasion when I had the pleasure of giving a lecture, with illustrations, to the Deputies from Caracas (of whom you were one) in General Miranda's house in Grafton Street, Piccadilly, London, around 26 or 27 September 1810. My system greatly aroused your interest.'[97] Then towards the middle of his career, in the midst of fighting, he stopped to underline the value of ethics and knowledge by creating the highly original institution of the Moral Power. In 1828, he promised the rector of Bogotá University that 'no object will be so dear to me from now on as training these young shoots, these citizens who are to inherit our rights, our liberty, our independence, to preserve these precious gifts by the exercise of virtues, talents, science and knowledge. From now on, I shall direct my steps towards the education of the people and the sons of the people.'[98] One week before his death, in making his will, he remembered affectionately the University of Caracas. He was aware that the life of the community depended on education, that without it there could be no sense of history or national identity to survive the ravages of time. The school, in his opinion, was both a touch-stone by which a society could be judged and a melting-pot in which the future was formed. In his proposals for constitutions, support and encouragement to education figured prominently. He declared to the Angostura Congress: 'Popular education should be the first care of the Congress in its paternal love.' Joseph Lancaster's method of mutual instruction was adopted by Bolívar for primary education. This system enabled the master, with the collaboration of the more advanced pupils, to take charge of up to 1,000 pupils and was, therefore, highly suitable for the Latin American situation, where there was a shortage of trained staff and scarce financial resources. Bolívar emphasised his adherence to this method, which he described as 'marvellous'. He reminded the Caracas Council in a reproachful letter that he had put 20,000 *pesos* at the disposal of Joseph Lancaster, and made him certain promises, to persuade him to stay in Venezuela and found institutes of mutual instruction 'but much to my surprise, I learned from the gentleman in question, that the honourable town council of last year, instead of encouraging the spread of this system, so useful to the young, had opposed it from the beginning'. Bolívar was writing 'with the aim of combatting an abuse I can still scarcely credit' and urging the council, instead of opposing the Lancastrian schools, 'to afford them the protection owed to any establishment whose end is to dispense knowledge, since they are of such immediate service to the people'. On 31 January 1825, he decreed in Peru the establishment of a Normal School for the training of teachers, based on Lancastrian methods, in every Departmental capital. He also accepted with pleasure an invitation to select certain students to be sent to Hazelwood School in England, where the method of 'practical education' had been recommended to him by Jeremy Bentham as being the most suitable for developing the spirit. He considered it important for the future independence and cultural development of the country that certain gifted students should be educated in foreign universities, as can be seen in his detailed advice to the Government Council in Lima regarding sending students to London to be trained in law, diplomacy and public administration. In the proposals at Angostura, he paid great attention to the arrangements for the education of future members of the hereditary Senate, describing a 'college specially created to instruct these pupils, the future legislators of the nation. They would learn the arts, sciences, and literature necessary for a holder of public office: from infancy, they would know the career for which Providence had destined them and from an early age would elevate their souls towards the dignity that awaited them.' On another occasion, he insisted: 'Education forms the moral man, and to form a legislator, one must educate him in a school of morality, justice and the law.'

Over a period of ten years, in many different places, Bolívar dictated more than forty decrees and resolutions on every aspect of education. On 17 September 1819, he arranged for the establishment in Bogotá of a school for orphans, fatherless children, or children of the poor, who were maintained by the state, and on 5 December 1829 he published a new national syllabus in Popayán. His first decree on the subject had summed up the basis of his educational philosophy: 'Public education and instruction are the surest guarantee of general happiness and the most solid basis of freedom for a people.'[99] In his last decree, he made a complete analysis of the question as it related to Colombia. He continued to rely on the Catholic Church for primary education, but made changes in other areas, particularly the universities. He legislated on school premises and teachers for the Indians, insisting that the Indians should be taught, amongst other things, the rights and duties of man and the citizen in Colombia, according to the laws. In Peru, education was made obligatory. On a number of occasions, he turned his attention to female education: in 1825 in Cuzco, considering that 'the education of young girls is the basis of family morality', he decreed the creation of a school where 'girls of every social origin, whether from the capital or the provinces, who have the necessary ability' would be educated.[100] In Caracas in 1827, recognising that 'the important aim of public education would be imperfect if that of girls were neglected', he gave definite encouragement to the education of these future mothers.[101] In Bolivia he arranged that 'the episcopal share of the revenue from the parishes of this Department, which has hitherto gone to the bishopric of La Paz, will be devoted to the colleges of science and the arts'. In Urubamba, he ordered that 'the convent of Recoletos and its income be used ... for a public educational establishment, where the youth of this province can receive the first stages of education'.[102] On several occasions, he changed private colleges and convents into public institutions: similarly, he arranged for state property to be rented out to finance education. Lancastrian schools were established in Colombia, Peru and Bolivia, and a naval college at Guayaquil. When he travelled through Peru with Simón Rodríguez, in 1825, the year of maximum activity on the cultural front, he spoke on various educational questions. Important decrees were dictated in Chuquisaca: all religious institutions must devote themselves to the task of education; in every departmental capital a primary school for both boys and girls was to be established; in the Andean capital there would be an academy of the arts and sciences, a military college and a seminary which would serve the whole Republic.

Bolívar had as much interest in educational methods as any practising teacher. Some recent original research has been done on the sources of his ideas, which contradicts traditional wisdom on the question. Beginning with José Gil Fortoul at the beginning of the nineteenth century and continuing with Mancini, a fervent admirer of Rousseau, the majority of writers have held that the latter was the principal influence on Bolívar's thought on education. However, in 1968, Luis B. Prieto Figueroa, a distinguished educationalist, published his *Magisterio americano de Bolívar* which shows that nothing could be further from the truth. The evidence consists, not of vague generalisations or superficial judgements, but properly documented demonstrations that Bolívar's true mentors were Diderot, Condorcet, Helvétius, Vives, La Chalotais and others. He was also influenced by some of his contemporaries and friends, especially Simón Rodríguez, José Rafael Revenga and Dr. José María Vargas. Rodríguez was with Bolívar in Peru when the latter wrote the first draft of a newspaper article on 'Public Education' which is published amongst his papers. In the same year, he sketched out a plan of education for Fernando Bolívar, at that time a student in the United States. He had a very humane concept of the school and the master. The latter need not be a scholar, but he did have to be a cultivated man. The school should be a place of stimulus, satisfaction and recreation for the child: it was time to leave behind the days when 'to say to a child "we are going to school or going to see the master" was like saying: "we are going to jail, or to meet an enemy"'. Concerning rewards for school work he declared: 'Moral incentives and punishments should be ... used with rational children: rigour and the cane with animals. This system produces spiritual elevation, nobility and dignity of sentiment and decent behaviour. It contributes in great part to the formation of human morality, creating within [the child] the inestimable faculty which renders him just, generous, humane, obedient, moderate, in a word, a good citizen.'

He did not lose sight of other social functions of the school, recognising that it must respond to the needs of the community and could not be the same for all children: 'It should always be adapted to their age, inclinations, character and temperament.' Besides the cultural, ethical, religious and civic role of the school, it had other lessons to impart, no less important for being modest: good manners, cleanliness, proper speech, the exercise of democracy from an early age. For example, children were encouraged to choose monitors from amongst their own ranks. In his thought on teaching methods, Bolívar was ahead of his day. In reading, he considered that the separate pronunciation of each letter was difficult and impractical and that children should be encouraged right from the beginning to read and pronounce whole words. He also gave great importance to play: 'Games and recreation are as important to children as food: their moral and physical health requires both.' Other views he expressed were: that the study of the dead languages should come only after knowledge of the living ones; that in history one should begin with contemporary events and gradually work backwards; that there must be a harmonious development of all the intellectual faculties, the child with a good memory having his faculty for understanding strengthened, and the child who easily grasped concepts being given tasks to exercise his memory. He believed that both memory and arithmetical ability were strengthened by exercise, and considered Mathematics an excellent subject for 'learning to think and reason logically'. In his desire to form rigorous yet elegant spirits, he did not neglect the complementary virtue of social ease. Contrary to those who believed that to be a revolutionary meant to be churlish and rude, Bolívar defended the principles and manners of a gentleman: 'The teaching of good manners or social customs is as necessary as any other.' Students should be fired with 'a love of cultivated society, where the fair sex exercises its beneficial influence: and that respect for older men of experience and social position which makes youth charming and associates it with hope for the future'.[103]

The Moral Power proposed at Angostura consisted of two Houses or Chambers, one of Morality and one of Education. Their work was to consist of: keeping a watch on public behaviour; rewarding virtue and castigating vice; propagating simple rules 'adapted to the intelligence of mothers of families' for the bringing-up of young children; encouraging the publication of works on education 'adapted to our habits, customs and system of government'; commissioning 'zealous, educated and leisured citizens to travel, research and gather information on the subject all over the world'. He showed even greater vision when, realising that 'our present schools are inadequate to carry out a large plan of education', he proposed that 'the Chamber should pay special attention to the task of deciding how many schools are required in the Republic and having them built'. A large number of factors were to be considered: type of construction, situation, elegance, hygiene, comfort, facilities in the area for the care of children, suitability of the terrain and so on.[104]

He made some brief remarks concerning the teacher, the key to the whole process: 'A man of genius who knows the human spirit and knows how to direct it, and a simple system, a clear and natural method, are effective means by which society can make extraordinary and brilliant progress in a few short days. Precepts and labour are useless without these prerequisites: all will be disaster and confusion.' Bolívar declared that the man who 'generously and patriotically sacrifices his leisure and freedom to devote himself to the laborious task of creating citizens for the state, to defend and enlighten it ... deserves the gratitude of his country: he has earned the respect of the people and the approbation of the government, which should encourage him and reward him with distinctions.'[105] For similar reasons, he respected intellectuals, feeling that scientists, artists and teachers form the moral character of a nation. Somewhat in advance of the appearance and triumph of Positivism, Bolívar expressed an enthusiasm for science, believing it an ally of freedom, since it enabled man to know, and claim, his rights. He considered scientific knowledge one of the major forces in dominating the material world, together with courage, wealth and virtue; he thus saw it above all as a source of power. He believed that scientists should be maintained by the state. As head of government he welcomed scholars and researchers, and there are letters of gratitude to him in the French Museum of Natural History, from renowned figures such as the German scientist, Eric Bollman, who was searching for platinum in Colombia, and the Irish explorer and geographer J. Barclay Pentland, who travelled to Peru and Bolivia with the support of the governments. Requests came to Bolívar for specimens of fossils, minerals and flora and fauna, Indian relics and information of every kind. Scientific writers and authorities in various fields and in many countries sent him copies of their works and corresponded with him, communicating the progress of their research. On one occasion, some teachers from the Lycée Louis le Grand in Paris proposed the foundation of an Academy of Mathematics and Physics in Colombia. In general, painters, publishers, journalists and politicians all took a lively interest in the new Republic that was being born in America.

In educational matters, we see a new demonstration of the distance separating Bolívar's conception of the role of the state from a simplistic liberal doctrine of non-intervention in anything other than defence and the administration of the law. In a *laissez-faire* system, education is left in private hands, but Bolívar rejected this solution. In June 1820, in El Rosario, he made an emphatic declaration to that effect: 'The supremacy of the state in education and the corresponding uniformity in syllabus and style, that is, the maintenance, direction and government of the colleges and schools in the Republic, belongs to the state, no matter what the original foundation may have been.' In this article, he specifically included 'seminaries anywhere in the Republic, whose heads, rectors, lecturers and other employees will depend on the government and be nominated by it'.[106] A year before, in Angostura, in his plan for a Moral Power, he gave exclusive permission to the Chamber of Education to 'establish, organise and direct primary schools for both boys and girls'. He could not accept that the state should hand over to any other body the responsibility for the education of future citizens.

Bolívar repeatedly stressed, that when an educational system is adapted to the society inside which it functions, it is successful. When, on the contrary, it is in conflict with the society, the results are unpredictable. 'A nation will be wise, virtuous and manly if these principles lie behind education: it will be ignorant, superstitious, effeminate and fanatical if these errors are cultivated in the schools. This is why progressive societies always consider education a vital institution.'[107] He advanced along the road to free education, now, of course, an accepted principle in democratic societies. It is the state's duty to meet the cost of education, giving an equal opportunity to all its members, thus placing culture within the reach of all. In Cuzco, however, faced with national bankruptcy, Bolívar was forced to decree that the daughters of wealthy citizens in public institutions should contribute to their upkeep. Another method of increasing the meagre revenues available for education was to accept donations from the Church and convert some convent buildings for use as schools. Bolívar travelled with this intention to the interior of Peru, where he saw to it that public finances were put on a sound footing, and state properties efficiently administered, in order to finance education. In Bolivia, thanks to his efforts, the government promised to assign to education any savings that might be made in the future in other branches of the administration.

Without ever having attended a University himself, Bolívar was solicitous with regard to these seats of higher learning. Not long before his death, he declared in his will: 'I wish the two volumes given to me by my friend General Wilson, and which once belonged to Napoleon,

Rousseau's *Contrato social* and Montecuccoli's *Arte militar*, to be presented to the University of Caracas.'[108] During his last stay in Caracas, he was occupied not only in overcoming the Cosiata conspiracy, but also in drawing up, with the assistance of Revenga and Vargas, a new Constitution for the University. Certain archaic rulings were rescinded, the institution was modernised, and the basis of a new system was set up, advanced for its time and based on principles, some of which remain valid to the present day. Under the new regulations, the University consolidated its autonomy, being given its own property and revenues and, therefore, independence in running its own affairs.

The new University Constitution established an 'open door' policy, in that no-one would be prevented from hearing a lecture by any professor. Students were given a share in running the institution and also a certain amount of responsibility for assessing members of the teaching staff, as well as being assessed themselves: thus it was laid down that besides the Rector's visits to lectures, which he arranged as he considered necessary, he must choose two students per term from each class to inform him about the work of the professor. Students were exempted from military service or any other duties which might distract them from their proper studies. They were held responsible just as much as the teaching staff for the prestige of their establishment: in the literary competitions, two students must participate each year with every teacher, in order to demonstrate to the nation 'the progress made by youth and the condition of studies in the University'. The reforms also opened the way for a system of recognition of credits and examinations, to equalise education throughout the country. The equivalence of the degrees of all the Universities of Colombia was recognised. For the recruitment of lecturers, the system of open competitive exams was used, and juries were recommended to 'act in accordance with justice, without fear or favour'. Bolívar wanted university lecturers to be teachers in the fullest sense, not simple transmitters of knowledge, but also 'a model for the young people entrusted to their charge: good behaviour, manners, etiquette, cultivated speech, all these must be seen in the teacher, so that this becomes a practical lesson and helps in the formation of good students.'[109] He felt it was important for members of the teaching body to be seen at official functions of the institution, and arranged for severe sanctions against habitual absentees. A system of full pensions for those with twenty years' service was established. As a stimulus to the production of textbooks, anyone who wrote or translated a useful work was rewarded with a type of credit which could count as years of service towards a pension. Bolívar laid great stress on this question of text books, for he was aware of the problem of staff shortages and felt they could be overcome, at least partially, with good texts and educational material. His interest is shown by the fact that in a decree to forbid the teaching of Bentham's *Introduction to the Principles of Morals and Legislation* he included the following: 'As it is very important to produce more basic texts, especially in subjects where there are none suitable for Colombian students, the Department of Education urges sub-departments and Universities to see that the most able lecturers produce courses, to be printed at the expense of the University, [the cost] to be recovered from the proceeds of the sale of texts.'[110] So far as the Rectorship of the University was concerned, he felt sure that it should be for a fixed term. He felt that the greater number of people who participated in the administration, the better for the institution, and so it was established that the Rector of the University should be appointed for three years only. He pointed to the humanist ideal of education, proposing, for example, that medical students should have obligatory classes in French, English, Fine Arts and Science. At the same time, he made provision for medical studies to be practical rather than theoretical.

Bolívar conceived of the University as the central force in the cultural life of the nation. In his last decree relating to education, signed in Popayán on 5 December 1829, he assigned to the Universities the leading role in organising and administering educational matters. 'The sub-departments of education are abolished in those places where there is a University, and their functions taken over by the Universities, either individually, or as a body, depending on the nature of the decision to be taken.' Moreover, 'the Universities are authorised to legislate on the physical, moral, religious and social education to be imparted to students in Universities and colleges'.[111] As we have said, Bolívar's reform of Caracas University consecrated its autonomy, for he assigned to it the income of the magnificent *haciendas* of Chuao, Cata and La Concepción, the latter with its sugar-presses; the property of the expelled Jesuits; revenues from pious foundations; and certain revenues left over from Indian reserved lands, from the defunct College of Advocates and some other sources. The nine statutes or constitutions relating to entry to the University abolished, of course, social, religious and racial discrimination by abandoning the 'pure blood' criterion. The increase in the number of teachers, especially in Medicine, signified a real reform. The old Medical Board was abolished and Medicine became a complete Faculty, with its own buildings, as did Mathematics. In 1827, similar reforms reached the University of Quito. Here, Bolívar's decree laid down that alongside the study of the main European languages, the Indian language Quechua should be studied. Three years earlier, he had ordered the construction of the University of Trujillo and in August 1825 had laid the basis for what would later be the University of San Agustín in Arequipa. In December 1827, he established in Antioquia College a university syllabus for law students, thus laying the basis for the University of Medellín. Since Bolívar's interest in educational matters was well known in scientific circles in Europe, a number of French professors, amongst them Brunner, the mathematician, Pelegrin, the grammarian and linguist and Avon, the chemist and pharmacist, offered their services to found what would later be the University of Colombia proper.

Bolívar considered newspapers a magnificent medium of mass education, a portable forum for the propagation of new ideas. One of his fiercest opponents, José Domingo Díaz, said that the printing press was Bolívar's 'major weapon'. He considered it as important as equipment for his troops. Pétion gave him a printing press, which was lost, however, at Ocumare. Nevertheless, the revolution was successful in its determination to have its own newspaper, the *Correo del Orinoco* (1818–21). A Haitian, Juan Baillío, was the printer to the 1811 Congress, to the first and second Republican governments and also to the expedition of 1816. Bolívar wrote pieces for the Press on a number of occasions and had many shrewd remarks to make on how newspapers could best fulfil their role by attention to style, as we see from his advice to General Santander: '*The Correo de Bogotá* has many admirable things, it amuses me greatly, the only defect is the monotony of its letters; it reads like a censored correspondence. Tell the editor to announce to the public that he will no longer publish articles submitted in the form of letters, but will place a headline at the top with a summary of the contents. There is not another newspaper in the world with the form of the *Correo de Bogotá*. Everything should have the form that corresponds to its nature, and those forms should be as pleasant as possible, to arouse admiration and delight. It is very important that this newspaper, having such good writers, should treat subjects regularly and professionally.'[112]

Bolívar's educational and cultural achievements were not the work of chance, they were the practical outcome of a genuine revolutionary ideology. Joseph Lancaster, a witness to Bolívar's interest in education from 1810 onwards, perceived this quite clearly: in one letter, Bolívar echoed a statement of Lancaster's that 'the emancipation of the mind is apparently the only measure lacking to crown liberty with the fullness of glory and honour'. In another letter, Lancaster joins with Bolívar in hoping that 'the people of Colombia will combine knowledge with liberty and will build their glorious liberty on a foundation of enlightened ideas'.[113] The concept of culture as a united and coherent whole, rather than an arbitrary and chaotic collection of unrelated phenomena, is evident in many of Bolívar's writings and actions. He stated quite clearly that if his nephew Fernando were inclined towards practical studies, he would be delighted, for 'we are abundantly supplied with doctors and lawyers, but skilled artisans and farm labourers are in short supply'. Here, he was undoubtedly exaggerating the abundance of members of the liberal professions in order to underline the lack of farm labourers and artisans, though it is true that even up to the present day the Latin American universities have concentrated on intellectual training to the exclusion of vital training in such important matters as the rational exploitation of the land and other natural resources, the scientific conservation of resources, the planning of cities and public works and services, and problems of man and society. Even today, and more so in Bolívar's time, there is a shortage of the type of doctor who believes that all human beings have the right to reach their full potential, or the type of lawyer who is willing to rescue justice from corrupt hands. It is clear that Bolívar's cultural preoccupations were not limited to educational institutions. A culture is the coherent ensemble of practices adopted by a community in its work and daily life. A culture both produces and is produced by a people. Thus the culture of Latin America is both a cause and a result of the continent's weaknesses. It is also something which is in the process of being formed constantly. Bolívar realised, from his travels in Europe and in the New World, that America had special characteristics, and the aim of his cultural programme was to sharpen and define these special characteristics. It was commonplace at the time to deny South America's separate identity, but Bolívar, on the contrary, emphasised it. He felt that he owed it to the Afro-Indian-American heritage to dedicate himself to the task of defining and strengthening the nascent personality of the country. Intellectuals had a vital role to play in this task of forging a nation's identity, creating a sense of history and culture, making sense of the past, the present and hopes for the future. In this, too, Bolívar was a liberator. South America was a young country, but it would have been wrong to consider this a virtue in itself. Youth does signify hope for the future, but it also signifies an uncertain grasp on reality. Bolívar appeared to foresee the avalanche of cultural influences which would arrive as a cover for economic interests, for voracious and oppressive imperialist aims which would threaten the Latin American sense of identity. He saw the Press, the educational system, intellectuals and artists as the best defences against these attacks. Education was perhaps the most vital arm in this cultural struggle: 'Nations advance towards greatness at the rate of their educational advance; if the latter is rapid, so is the march towards progress; if education slips back and if it becomes corrupted or neglected completely, the nation is plunged into darkness and disaster. These principles, [which are] the fruit of experience and have been formulated by ancient and modern philosophers and political thinkers, are now so widely accepted that there can scarcely exist an individual who is not convinced they are correct.'[114] Simón Rodríguez, Bolívar's mentor, addressed similar advice to the Latin American people, warning them of the dangers and showing the way forward: 'The leaders must realise that they will accomplish nothing unless they educate the people. Through considering Republican education a secondary question, the leaders have lost a lot of time, and they risk losing what little time is left. The basis of the Republican system is public opinion, which can only be properly formed through education. If a man is capable of being educated — if he needs to be educated — if it is easy to educate him — and yet he is not educated, the fault lies with those who should be arranging for his education. No-one can do a thing well until he has learned, therefore one cannot build a Republic with ignorant people, whatever system one adopts. And it is quite useless to half-educate — nothing should be left half-done, the intention should always be to finish the job. Republicans! Take heed. Educate the children if you want to build a Republic.'[115]

This chapter has studied the broad lines of Bolívar's ideas and proposals, while the earlier chapters described the background against which these came into being. The situation of Latin America was such that he had to effect a radical change in the whole structure of the continent, making it truly a New World. His ideal of independence did not refer only to politics, it went beyond that to a vision which embraced the whole society in all its aspects. Besides political independence, democracy and republican constitutionalism, Bolívar fought for complete equality for the negro, the Indian and the despised *pardos*. He also aimed for economic justice, in the restoration of wealth to those who produced it and the reform of property laws. He dedicated himself completely to the unification of Latin America, not for aggressive ends, but as a means to development and progress. The whole edifice of his thought was crowned by his vision of education and culture. His revolutionary programme should be seen, not as a jumble of disparate ideas, but as a coherent whole. The best key to its interpretation was given by Bolívar himself, when he wrote to White, concerning the Angostura Address: 'Be good enough to read my speech attentively, looking not to the parts but to the whole.'[116] In Bolívar's writings, America was given a programme which corresponded to the reality of the continent, offering an alternative in every sphere to the structures of the old order, and forming a unified plan for a new society. Much of what Bolívar proposed had already been formulated by other thinkers, either American or European. His merit lay in bringing all these ideas together and expressing them in appealing and convincing fashion, so that they constituted an invitation to action for his contemporaries, and a lesson still valid for ourselves, for whom action can no longer be delayed.

Chapter IV References

(1) *El libertador del mediodía de América y sus compañeros de armas defendidos por un amigo de la causa social* (Caracas, 1971), p.5.

(2) 'Arcaísmos institucionales e influencias románticas en el Libertador,' *Boletín Histórico de la Fundación John Boulton*, Caracas, no. 26, Mayo 1971, p.153.

(3) J. F. Blanco & R. Azpurúa, *Documentos para la historia de la vida pública del Libertador* (14 vols. Caracas, 1875–78), II, 232.

(4) C. Parra Pérez, *Bayona y la política de Napoleón en América* (Caracas, 1939), p.6.

(5) Parra Pérez, *Historia de la Primera República de Venezuela*, I, 379.

(6) Miranda, *Archivo*, XV, 68.

(7) *Cartas del Libertador*, XII, 377.

(8) *Obras completas*, I, 214: II, 1007.

(9) O'Leary, *Narración*, II, 340.

(10) This quotation and those following occur in *Obras completas* in the following order: I, 671, 1477; II, 1281, 1134, 1221; I, 1254; II, 1221.

(11) This quotation and those following occur in *Obras completas* in the following order: II, 1282, 774, 1002; I, 168, 169; II, 1144, 1002, 1003.

(12) *Cartas del Libertador*, XII, 183, 185.

(13) O'Leary, *Memorias*, XVI, 138.

(14) This quotation and those following occur in *Obras completas* in the following order: II, 1262; I, 176; II, 1258, 1227, 1116; I, 1153; II, 1137; I, 532; II, 1141, 1026; I, 439.

(15) Perú de Lacroix, p.157.

(16) *Obras completas*, I, 44.

(17) *Escritos del Libertador*, (Caracas, Series began to be published in 1967), V, 24.

(18) This quotation and those following occur in *Obras completas* in the following order: I, 170; II, 774, 1141, 1143, 1253, 1008, 1225, 1146, 1147.

(19) *El magisterio americano de Bolívar* (Caracas, 1968). Trans. *Simón Bolívar: Educator* (N.Y. 1970).

(20) See especially: J. Gil Fortoul, *Historia constitucional de Venezuela* (3 vols. Caracas, 1942), I, Ch. 4.

(21) *Obras completas*, II, 1251.

(22) *Decretos del Libertador*, III, 366.

(23) *Obras completas*, II, 733, 1144–45.

(24) *Documentos referentes a la creación de Bolivia* (2 vols. Caracas, 1924), II, 338.

(25) This quotation and those following occur in *Obras completas* in the following order: II, 1255; I, 1361, 25; II, 1302; I, 1254, 53; II, 1264; I, 222, 1364; II, 1226, 1404.

(26) O'Leary, *Memorias*, XVIII, 400.

(27) *Decretos del Libertador*, I, 76.

(28) This quotation and those following occur in *Obras completas* in the following order: I, 565; II, 1290, 1114, 1153, 1152; I, 262.

(29) See the complete scale in Blanco and Azpurúa, VI, 80.

(30) *Los temas sociales y económicos en la época de la Independencia* (Caracas, 1962), p.49.

(31) O'Leary, *Memorias*, XVI, 139, 140.

(32) Decretos del Libertador, I, 194, 197.

(33) *Obras completas*, I, 444.

(34) *Materiales para el estudio de la cuestión agraria en Venezuela* (Caracas, 1964), pp.283–284.

(35) *Decretos del Libertador*, I, 275.

(36) *Materiales para el estudio de la cuestión agraria*, p.379.

(37) Blanco and Azpurúa, X, 32.

(38) *Documentos referentes a la creación de Bolivia*, I, 422.

(39) *Documentos referentes a la creación de Bolivia*, I, 423.

(40) *Materiales para el estudio de la cuestión agraria*, p.489.

(41) *Obras completas*, I, 1176.

(42) This quotation and those following occur in *Obras completas* in the following order: II, 1296, 64, 293; I, 1207, 1395; II, 273, 1203; I, 1334, 162.

(43) 'Derecho Internacional, II', *Obras completas* (Caracas, 1959), XI, 91.

(44) *Obras completas*, I, 1070.

(45) *Historia de la conquista y población de la provincia de Venezuela* (New York, 1940), p.422.

(46) A. von Humboldt, *Viaje a las regiones equinocciales del Nuevo Continente* (5 vols. Caracas, 1941–42), II, 330.

(47) López, *Juan Bautista Picornell y la conspiración de Gual y España*, pp.348–385.

(48) *Textos oficiales de la Primera República de Venezuela* (2 vols. Caracas, 1959), I, 119.

(49) *América y el Libertador* (Caracas, 1953), p.7. See also *Escritos del Libertador*, IV, 63.

(50) This quotation and those following occur in *Obras completas* in the following order: II, 993; I, 172, 1012; II, 1080; I, 407, 81, 792, 1267.

(51) *Gazeta de Caracas*, no. XXX, 6 de enero de 1814.

(52) *Obras completas*, I, 582.

(53) H. A. Bierck, Jr., *Vida pública de don Pedro Gual* (Caracas, 1948), p.143.

(54) *Gazeta de Caracas*, no. XXX, 6 de enero de 1814.

(55) *Obras completas*, I, 1045.

(56) Blanco and Azpurúa, VIII, 221.

(57) *Obras completas*, I, 626.

(58) A. Silva Otero, *La diplomacia hispanoamericanista de la Gran Colombia* (Caracas, 1967), p.30.

(59) E. de Gandía, *Bolívar y la libertad* (Buenos Aires, 1957), pp.90, 91.

(60) *Obras completas*, I, 654.

(61) *Bolívar y su época*, (Caracas, 1953), I, 115.

(62) B. Mitre, *Historia de San Martín y de la emancipación sudamericana* (4 vols. Buenos Aires, 1889-90), III, 75.

(63) This quotation and those following occur in *Obras completas* in the following order: II, 1154, 1021; I, 1408; II, 1193; I, 162.

(63a) *Obras completas*, I, 1421. In Caracas, a year later, the fate of the two islands was still occupying Bolívar's attention. On 27 February 1827, his Secretary of State, General José Rafael Revenga stated to the Secretary of War: 'The Liberator believes that we should take advantage of the moment to liberate Cuba and Puerto Rico. Not only would we thus drive out of the hemisphere the last vestiges of Spanish power, we would be putting our troops into action, which would preserve discipline, and give a certain solidity to our existence as a nation and our reputation.' This time there was a concrete plan, and it was only frustrated, it would appear, by British opposition. Revenga gave details of the strategy which was once more to involve several countries of South America: 'The attempt requires: i) that all help in the form of troops, ships, arms and money requested by Your Excellency, through me, or during the march, be sent to La Guaira; ii) that 1,000 men be added, as well as any other ships there may be in Cartagena suitable for the attempt; iii) that the Mexican government be persuaded to threaten and harass immediately the island of Cuba. The resulting weakness of the Department of Magdalena may be remedied with troops not required in the Isthmus, or with whatever troops can be brought from Peru; if the Mexican Government effectively harasses the island of Cuba, while Your Excellency goes to work on Puerto Rico with the forces you receive from outside and those you can gather in this Department and in that of Maturín, this will prevent one island being helped from the other, so that they can be emancipated at a lesser cost, for once Puerto Rico is free, the great expedition required for Cuba can be equipped there.' (O'Leary, *Memorias*, XXV, 50, 51).

(63b) Uruguay was to be the beneficiary of this agreement. Bolívar's idea, in April 1828 was not to intervene 'between the Argentinians and the Emperor, except in the case of our being able to induce the latter to adopt the just policy of leaving the *Banda Oriental* free to form its own government'. (*Obras completas*, II, 301).

(63c) This quotation and those following occur in *Obras completas* in the following order: I, 171, 984, 1013, 619, 1014.

(64) 'Derecho Internacional II,' *Obras completas*, pp.75, 91.

(65) This quotation and those following occur in *Obras completas* in the following order: II, 998, 995, 1005, 1006, 1072, 1124, 1232; I, 584, 533; II, 1213, 1178; I, 598.

(66) I. Liévano Aguirre, *Bolivarismo y Monroísmo* (Bogotá, 1969), p.18.

(67) This quotation and those following occur in *Obras completas* in the following order: I, 1239, 168; II, 1278, 1027, 1038; I, 134, 340.

(68) Blanco and Azpurúa, IX, 324.

(69) This quotation and those following occur in the following order: *Obras completas*, I, 181, 219; II, 1181: *Escritos del Libertador*, VIII, 290.

(70) C. L. Mendoza, Preface to *Escritos del Libertador*, VII, xxxvii.

(71) J. L. Salcedo-Bastardo, *Visión y revisión de Bolívar* (Buenos Aires, 1966), pp.269ff.

(72) Gil Fortoul, *Historia constitucional de Venezuela*, I, 674.

(73) This quotation and those following occur in *Obras completas* in the following order: II, 1149, 1215, 19, 1214, 1215; I, 1423–24.

(74) *Cartas del Libertador*, XII, 354.

(75) This quotation and those following occur in *Obras completas* in the following order: II, 993, 1002, 1068; I, 174; II, 1149, 1253, 1276.

(76) *Bolívar y su época*, I, 59, 130.

(77) López, *Juan Bautista Picornell y la conspiración de Gual y España*, p.354.

(78) *Textos oficiales de la Primera República de Venezuela*, I, 214.

(79) This quotation and those following occur in *Obras completas* in the following order: II, 1092, 1094; I, 425; II, 1152.

(80) O'Leary, *Memorias*, XVI, 140.

(81) This quotation and those following occur in *Obras completas* in the following order: II, 773, 1140; I, 435.

(82) J. A. Páez, *Autobiografía* (2 vols. Caracas, 1946), I, 380.

(83) *Obras completas*, I, 425.

(84) *Materiales para el estudio de la cuestión agraria*, p.214.

(85) *Decretos del Libertador*, I, 196, 197.

(86) *Obras completas*, I, 576.

(87) O'Leary, *Memorias*, XXIV, 273–75.

(88) *Decretos del Libertador*, I, 290.

(89) 'Transcripción del expediente original ... ,' *Boletín de la Academia Nacional de Historia*, no. 149, p.22.

(90) *Obras completas*, I, 1116–19.

(91) Blanco and Azpurúa, X, 31.

(92) *Documentos referentes a la creación de Bolivia*, I, 456, 324.

(93) This quotation and those following occur in *Obras completas* in the following order: II, 1135, 1227, 16, 1106, 1110.

(94) Perú de Lacroix, p.216.

(95) This quotation and those following occur in *Obras completas* in the following order: II, 89; I, 1342, 1073; II, 455, 1146.

(96) *Decretos del Libertador*, II, 345; III, 86, 171ff.

(97) *Bolívar y su época*, I, 146.

(98) This quotation and those following occur in *Obras completas* in the following order: II, 1264, 1150; I, 1067, 1282; II, 1144; I, 442.

(99) O'Leary, *Memorias*, XVI, 464.

(100) Blanco and Azpurúa, X, 41.

(101) *Decretos del Libertador*, II, 343.

(102) O'Leary, *Memorias*, XXIII, 293, 294.

(103) *Obras completas*, II, 1292–97.

(104) *El Libertador y la Constitución de Angostura de 1819* (Caracas, 1970), pp.197ff.

(105) *Obras completas*, II, 1292–95.

(106) *Decretos del Libertador*, I, 205.

(107) *Obras completas*, II, 1290.

(108) *Obras completas*, II, 988. When Bolívar heard in 1824 of the gift offered to him by Sir Robert Wilson, he wrote to him from Chancay: 'The Vicepresident of Colombia has written to inform me of your kindness in honouring me with the magnificent gift of two volumes relating to the law and warfare: the *Contrato social* and Montecocculi, both having been the property of the great Napoleon. These books will be precious to me on numerous counts. Their

authors are famous for both the good and the ill they have done. The first owner of the books represents the heights and the depths of the human spirit. The second owner, who now presents them to me, I esteem above all men, for he has followed the precepts of Montecocculi with his sword and on his heart is engraved the Social Contract, not in words and in theory, but in deeds both philanthropic and heroic.' *Obras completas*, I, 1006.

(109) O'Leary, *Memorias*, XXV, 411–438.

(110) *Decretos del Libertador*, III, 54.

(111) *Registro Oficial*, no. 54, (Bogotá, 1829), p.428.

(112) *Obras completas*, I, 714.

(113) *Bolívar y su época*, I, 146; II, 30.

(114) *Obras completas*, II, 1291.

(115) *El libertador del mediodía de América*, pp.129–148.

(116) *Obras completas*, I, 442.

V The Betrayal

Chaos

The revolutionary programme had not taken into account one phenomenon that was to prove its undoing: the *caudillo*, or military leader who after the triumph of the independence movement became political boss. When revolutionary change was first mooted, the *criollo* leaders imagined that it could be restricted to the taking of political power. They were the main supporters of the movement, the only sector with coherent political ideas, and they acted in accordance with their own interests, paying no attention to the social, economic and cultural issues which in fact brought the mass of the people into the struggle on the side of the patriots. When the struggle began, no-one foresaw the sweeping changes it would bring.

The *criollos* already had all the social power and influence they required, what they lacked was political power. This was how Bolívar himself saw the question, initially. It is true that in 1813 he spoke of 'war to the death' and threatened even the 'neutral' with extermination, but on the other hand, he had nothing material to offer the *pardos*, nor the Indians, nor even less the negroes. The masses perceived this quite clearly in the early stages of the war and naturally lent their adhesion to the people who held out most hope, in this case Monteverde and Boves, representatives of a monarchy that was closer to the people's aspirations than the puffed-up *criollos*, whose main thought was to emphasize their own superiority. The failures of the First and Second Republics demonstrated the leanings of the population towards royalism, and showed Bolívar that the road he had followed up to 1815 was not the correct one. His exile in Haiti and Jamaica and the help he received from Pétion suggested other ideas, so that from the Los Cayos and Jacmel Expeditions onwards it became clear that the revolution had found its true path. The advice of Simón Rodríguez, as well as his own experience of the world, and his ability to modify his ideas in response to reasonable argument, made Bolívar a convinced adherent and the major leader of this new phase of the revolution. The people had shown the type of change that was wanted: social equality, economic justice and improved educational and cultural facilities. Bolívar adopted these ideals and added to them emancipation from Spain, the institution of a democratic Republic and the union of South America.

It should be noted that not all Venezuelans accepted the cause of independence. The Spaniards had sturdy defenders in Venezuela, and the independence war was also a civil war. Moreover it was a type of war which created its own scale of values, a scale on which ferocity and aggression rated very high. Tough, courageous and violent men were needed, and the toughest naturally became the leaders. After the success of the independence movement, there was a power vacuum, into which these *caudillos* stepped. They were, however, basically unprepared for this transition, and were easily manipulated by other groups, to whom they sold themselves in exchange for the trappings of power and material wealth. The end of the independence struggle heralded the beginning of a new reign of exploitation, of which the *caudillo* was the willing instrument.

It was Bolívar's tragedy that few of the revolutionary leaders understood, far less shared, his altruism and idealism. The majority kept up a rhetorical front of adhesion to revolutionary ideals, while they in fact pursued personal gain. That is why Bolívar died convinced of the failure of his efforts. In his last message, he nevertheless tried to give some motive for hope: 'Fellow citizens! It is with shame that I declare that independence is the only thing we have achieved, at the cost of everything else. But that at least opens the door for us to realise our other aims, in the splendour of glory and liberty.'[1] He had come to realise the failure of his ideals through many bitter disappointments. As he told Heres in 1823: 'It is truly a gigantic task that we have before us, fraught with difficulties, for there is a state of general demoralization, which affects even the most determined. The battle-field is the whole of South America; our enemy, every circumstance; our soldiers represent every faction and every country, and each has his own colour, his own law and his own separate interest. Only Providence can put some order into this chaos with its almighty hand, and until I see it I cannot believe in this miracle.' Five weeks before his death, he summed up for Juan José Flores: 'i) America is ungovernable by us; ii) he who serves a revolution ploughs the sea; iii) the only thing one can do in America is emigrate ... '

Bolívar did what he could, but the sheer size of the enterprise defeated him, as well as the lack of collaboration, which ensured that the political change took place, but very little else. In the five years that he was away from Bogotá, there grew up in Colombia a whole counter-revolutionary structure, against which he was finally impotent, and which ended up by expelling him. The Liberator wrote to José Fernández Madrid on 21 December 1827: 'The truth is that I see no possibility of permanently stabilising this country ... Colombia and the whole of America are lost causes, so far as this present generation is concerned. Do not be deceived by any other ideas, and if necessary tell the truth to the British Ministers, for lies are always found out.' A year before, his heart had bled when he found himself obliged to write to Santander: 'What must I do? And what must Colombia do? To serve my country, am I to destroy the laws we have built up and wreck our dreams of Utopia? Colombia has no alternative but to dissolve the union and confess her own bankruptcy. Yes, things have reached this point, and to my chagrin I must recognise it and say so.'

For many of those who participated in the wars, the only end to be achieved was the separation from Spain. They were apparently indifferent to other social and economic issues, yet Bolívar encountered bitter opposition to his ideas in the course of his career. There was first of all the opposition to his position as leader. Bolívar was repudiated in Venezuela, New Granada and Haiti. A Congress set up in Cariaco in 1817 tried to topple him from the leadership. When he presented his proposals for a constitution in Angostura, the members paid little attention to his suggestions. Neither indignation nor pleading could move them on the issues of land distribution and the abolition of slavery. So far as the constitution itself was concerned, they opted for a return to the abstractions of 1811, despite a clear demonstration of their detachment from reality. The members of the Constituent Assembly at Angostura rejected the proposal for a Moral Power on the grounds that it was 'unworkable', they rejected Bolívar's pleas for social equality and an end to slavery, they turned down his idea of a hereditary Senate and they even opposed his far-sighted suggestions concerning the right of appeal to the Supreme Court. The distinguished jurist Tomás Polanco writes: 'The Liberator's constitutional schema was scientifically and philosophically correct, well-adapted to national circumstances and politically effective. The Congress did not accept it in its entirety, but instead introduced so many changes that the original idea was lost.'[2]

Nor was Bolívar any more successful in the Cúcuta Congress, the first Gran Colombian Parliament. From the beginning, he saw that this body was following a political line which would inevitably lead to the failure of the revolutionary struggle. He told Santander in 1821, ' ... there will soon be so many learned men that they will have to be banished from the Republic of Colombia, as Plato did with the poets in his. These gentlemen think that their will is that of the people ... Sitting cosily by their fireplaces in Bogotá, Tunja and Pamplona, they think that Colombia is full of simple peasant folk. They have never set eyes on the Carib Indians along the Orinoco, or the Apure shepherds, the sailors from Maracaibo, the men who take canoes up the Magdalena, the Patia bandits, the wild men of Pasto, the *guajivo* Indians of Casanare and the wild Indians and negroes who live like animals in the isolated regions. Don't you agree, Santander, that these legislators, who are ignorant rather than evil, and conceited rather than really ambitious, will drag us into anarchy, which will be followed by tyranny, in a word, into disaster? If the *llaneros* do not finish us off, these smooth philosophers will do it.'³ The Venezuelan historian Carlos Felice Cardot has studied the reaction in Caracas to the Cúcuta Constitution.⁴ It was far from being favourable, for the strengthening of the union of Gran Colombia implied the loss of Caracas' traditional privileges as metropolis. The seeds of La Cosiata were already present in the Cúcuta Congress, it was rather like a delayed reaction bomb, which would destroy completely Bolívar's plans.

The same process was visible in other parts of South America. In Bolivia and in Peru, the Liberator's advice was similarly rejected. The financial élites everywhere skilfully neutralised the revolutionary content of his ideas. Sometimes they kept up a revolutionary appearance and rhetoric, but in fact they were very clear as to where their interests lay, and their concessions never went beyond empty promises. The Bogotá, Caracas and Quito élites took advantage of Bolívar's years of absence in the south to obtain control of the machinery of state, or significant sections of it, and turn it to their own use. The dream of revolution and the union of all the countries was abandoned in favour of petty satisfactions, the consolidation of acquired gains and the reinforcement of the old national boundaries. The situation grew increasingly critical in Colombia in the years 1826, 27 and 28. The Republican order was a great disappointment to the mass of the people, for those who had traditionally exercised power were clearly continuing to do so. The internal conflict grew so intense that Bolívar came to feel that the whole basis of political organization should be changed, by means of direct consultation with the mass of the people. He proposed a congress at which all points could be thoroughly aired, especially mistakes originating in the inadequate Cúcuta Constitution, and solutions agreed. A great Colombian historian, Indalecio Liévano Aguirre has described the fate of this proposal: 'Bolívar's determination, which he expressed from Peru, of convening a Grand Constituent Assembly which would allow the people to express freely its point of view, must be seen in the context of the fierce divisions which at that point raged between Colombians. The Liberator's enemies only accepted the idea of the Congress after they had taken the necessary steps to assure themselves in advance of their dominant position in the assembly. While Bolívar was on his way to the capital from Venezuela, the Congress, under pressure from the Executive, the lawyers of the New Granada bourgeoisie and the Venezuelan *mantuano* aristocrats, issued the famous electoral regulations which practically deprived 95% of the population of the vote. According to these regulations, only those people had the right to vote who owned real estate or who exercised a profession 'without being dependent on any other, as is a day labourer or servant'.

The regulations also adopted the system of indirect or tertiary elections, as a way of multiplying the anti-democratic filters, and demanded that district electors and deputies to the Convention fulfil extraordinary conditions with respect to income and property, making it obligatory to have 'a university degree'. The Ocaña Convention failed because the tremendous conflict between the democratic spirit of the people and the demands of the moneyed classes was not aired in the debates of that Assembly, closed as it was to the people by the electoral regulations.'[5]

The incident which pushed Bolívar towards the 'Dictatorship' is well known. Many legends have circulated in South America concerning this bitter and tragic period of Bolívar's life, usually attempting to draw an analogy between this emergency government of Bolívar's in 1828 and the long series of dictatorships and despotisms which the continent has suffered ever since. All sorts of tyrants have attempted to mitigate their crimes by reference to this supposed similarity, which in fact is non-existent. Bolívar's biographer, the Ecuadorian writer Alfonso Rumazo González, notes that in 1828 'the people accepted the dictatorship with evident satisfaction. The authorities in the rest of the country accepted the Bogotá decision. When Bolívar entered the capital his arrival was greeted with enthusiasm and joy.'[6] Bolívar's dictatorship was of the same type, and served the same purpose, as that of the Roman Republic and that of Miranda. It was a legally constituted régime, which voluntarily declared its provisional nature, fixed a term of office, and promised to convene the national assembly on an agreed date, 2 January 1830. Moreover, Bolívar did not have exclusive power: the Council of State often imposed its collective will, even in delicate matters where Bolívar was personally involved.[7] Despite established opinion on the matter, I must emphasise my own view, that in essentials, Bolívar's revolutionary determination did not waver or fail during this short and troubled period. He did not step down on any vital point: on the contrary, he clung to his declared opposition to slavery and his attitude on the Indian question remained constant, as did his commitment to Latin American unity and to administrative honesty, as one can readily prove by reference to the acts and decrees of this period. So far from being the denial of his revolutionary stance, if we look impartially at the Dictatorship, we see it as Bolívar's last attempt to make the revolution work in concrete terms. These last attempts were all in vain. Yet when he was close to death, Bolívar, through Urdaneta, left a message for America which is still valid today. Urdaneta, moved by affection for Bolívar was persuading him to take power by force, and had engineered in Bogotá *pronunciamentos* calling on Bolívar to take over leadership in the capital. Bolívar replied: 'Though tempted to cede to the arguments and persuasions of agents, and the many friends I have in this country, and even letters received from Bogotá, I cannot find it within myself to accept power which has no other basis than the decisions of two town councils. ... I cannot lower myself to the position of a usurper, however much I struggle to overcome my repugnance. Santa María declares that if I do not accept power there will be an upsurge of dreadful anarchy, but what can I do against the steel barrier that separates me from the Presidency? This barrier is legality: I have no legal right to power, and the man who has it has not renounced it: therefore, let us await the elections. When that time comes, either I shall obtain legitimate rights, or there will be a new President. The political perspective will be clearer, and we will know whether our country exists or does not exist. Then, and only then, can I accept executive power, assuming the elections have been legally carried out.'[8]

Gran Colombia did not survive Bolívar's death. Páez, Santander and Flores, as leaders of the old national states, now revived, had the satisfaction of dividing the booty amongst them. All dreams of equality, justice and liberty disappeared. In each of the new, fragmented nations, the social order took on a clearly militarist character, and a 'new' era began, marked by the distribution of *haciendas* to military leaders and the continued existence of slaves, cheated of their freedom. The process can be seen at work in the tragic history of Venezuela in the century following Bolívar's death, a tragedy rendered the more poignant by the fact that that country had been the birth-place of the Liberator, though it should be stressed that none of the South American Republics escaped the bitter consequences of failure. Bolívar had predicted: 'Many tyrants will rise over my grave ... their civil wars will plunge them into bloodshed.' Towards the end of his life, he said: 'This country will enevitably fall into the hands of the undisciplined multitude, only to pass to petty tyrants ... of every race and colour.' This was the story of Venezuela from 1830 onwards, a long tale of disaster. From being the birth place of liberty, it now became its grave. The *caudillos* realised all their aims, helped by greedy politicians and by the prostituted talents of unscrupulous hacks. There was always a group of 'advisers' around the *caudillo*, ready to give a cloak of legal respectability to his whims, while he was in control, or to push him in the required direction when the real masters of the situation gave the sign. It is to the machinations of these advisers, rather than to the sins of the often sincere *caudillo*, that many of Latin America's sufferings should be attributed. Venezuela suffered dreadfully in those first hundred years. Seven dictatorships followed one upon another, for eighty years, producing a monotonous catalogue of tyrannies of every type: *llanero*, Andean, central, from Oriente; learned dictators, illiterate dictators; sometimes one man, sometimes his whole family, sometimes his cronies; pseudo-progressive régimes, reactionary régimes, nationalistic régimes, régimes that sold out to foreign interests; some hideously cruel, others genial. All equally odious, all equally opposed to the concept of freedom, of which Bolívar said: 'Man, when he loses freedom, according to Homer, loses the half of his soul.'

José Antonio Páez initiated this era of counter-revolution in Venezuela. In the Constitution produced by the 1830 Congress, a system of indirect elections was introduced, the electors being restricted according to economic criteria. The continuation of slavery was affirmed and a centro-federal system adopted. Páez made the mistake of protecting José Tadeo Monagas, who initiated a family dictatorship consisting of himself, his brother and his son and an extensive network of relations. They were in power for twelve years from 1847 and in effective control for nearly forty, during which time they cynically ignored the will of the nation, as demonstrated by the famous phrase, 'the Constitution can be used to justify anything'. After the dreadful Federal War of 1859–64, came the rule of Falcón, supposedly for the people, though in fact he took no steps to improve the life of the people. It was a strange dictatorship. His time in office, which ended in 1868, was marked by a lack of progress, instability and anarchy. Antonio Guzmán Blanco was a different type of dictator, a civilised, educated, well-travelled man, though self-willed and proud. He was known as the 'Illustrious American'. He accumulated a large fortune and won popular acclaim, though once again Venezuela's hopes of progress were dashed. He governed directly for fourteen years (1870–77: 1879–84: 1886–88) though his influence was felt for twenty. Joaquín Crespo was a semi-liberal President, a genial man who lasted two terms (1884–86: 1892–98) and attempted to prolong his influence through his protégé Ignacio Andrade. Cipriano Castro's was a supposedly nationalist dictatorship (1899–1908). The height of his folly was to place himself in the hands of the North American Foreign Minister, who as 'Venezuelan plenipotentiary' signed a treaty with his own superior, the North American Secretary of State. His was a dictatorship of high-sounding phrases and bitter disappointments. Juan Vicente Gómez, too, came to power on a wave of hope that once again proved unfounded. Gómez became 'South America's shame', with 38,000 prisoners, some of whom spent more than twenty years in jail. It was an endless and bloody tyranny (1908–35), which sold itself to foreign oil interests. Gunboats from Europe, North America and other South American countries were brought to Venezuela's shores to help keep internal order.

All the South American Republics have dreadful memories of similar régimes. Rosas and Perón in Argentina, Rodríguez Francia, Carlos Antonio López and Stroessner in Paraguay, Melgarejo in Bolivia, Ramón Castilla and Leguía in Peru, Juan José Flores, García Moreno and Veintemilla in Ecuador, Rafael Carrera, Justo Rufino Barrios, Estrada Cabrera and Ubico in Guatemala, Tiburcio Carias in Honduras, Zelaya,

Adolfo Díaz and the Somoza family in Nicaragua, Trujillo in Santo Domingo, Machado and Batista in Cuba, Porfirio Díaz in Mexico, the Haitian Emperors Christophe and Soulouque and the infamous dynasty of the Duvaliers. These governments represent political underdevelopment. They are governments which do not depend on ability, nor knowledge, nor even native wit. All over the continent, these régimes are shored up by the military, so strongly criticised by Bolívar. Tyrants in different countries join together to hold their people in subjection and the noble calling of soldier has been dragged in the mud. Army officers have been occupiers and exploiters of their own people, and at the same time have been ignominiously used as foremen on the *haciendas* of their superiors, with the private soldiers turned into unpaid labourers, given starvation rations by the government.

Another manifestation of the counter-revolution, apart from the dictatorships, was the long series of civil wars which afflicted our Republics, especially Venezuela. During the first hundred years of Venezuela's counter-revolution, no less than 354 violent encounters took place; the pendulum seemed to oscillate between tyranny and fratricidal chaos, from the artificial calm of repression to the frenzy of hatred. Bolívar had understood that the men who made up the independence armies would want the reward of their sacrifice, and it was for this reason that he conceived of the idea of distributing land to the soldiers. The *caudillos* paid no attention to these just measures, but cruelly mocked the aspirations of their followers, forgetting with Machiavellian cynicism the promises they made when they needed support. There was a transformation of society, but only at the top. Counts, marquises and nobles of the colonial era gave way, or more commonly allied themselves, to generals, colonels and lawyers, the new masters of the situation. The demobilised soldiers found themselves unemployed. During their period of service they had grown accustomed to violence and its corollary, looting. They had won respect and fear, as well as substantial material gains. Naturally enough, these individuals, with increased desires and diminished satisfactions, were ready to throw themselves into adventures which at least offered them employment in work they understood, which is why there were always men ready to follow any self-appointed Messiah.

'I fear peace more than war', declared Bolívar to Gual.[8a] 'Believe me, we are on the edge of an abyss, or rather, of a volcano which is about to erupt.' He well understood the reactions of the *llaneros* 'who now have no hope of obtaining the fruits of their feats of arms', and foresaw that they and others would readily become cannon-fodder for the civil wars. It is no exaggeration to say that 1,000,000 lives were lost in the civil wars in Venezuela alone. From 1830 to 1935, there were not five continuous years of peace, and the same is true for other countries. From 1828 to

1855, Mexico was torn by an almost continuous civil war, as were Central America, Argentina and Colombia. Only two countries were saved from these civil wars, for very different reasons: Paraguay and Brazil. In the case of Venezuela, there was an explicitly anti-Bolívar tone to these wars, which revolved around the question of federalism. The social order after 1830 encouraged the exploitation of the people, especially the rural masses; it was a thinly-disguised military régime, with laws which favoured usury and imposed exemplary sentences for rural banditry, the result, clearly, of hunger and desperation. This order reached a crisis in 1859, a crisis which the Valencia Convention, though composed of some very brilliant and sincere men, could do nothing to avert. The most ferocious repression was not sufficient to suffocate protests which arose from a deep and bitter frustration. From 1859 to 1864, with old wounds not yet healed, Venezuela was once more at war. The immediate pretext was unimportant, for as Antonio Leocadio Guzmán confessed: 'If the other side had cried federalism, we should have cried centralism.' Yet it served to point to deep divisions that existed in Venezuelan society. A return to federalism at this point meant a return to the fragmentation of colonial times, and was, therefore, objectively reactionary. Bolívar's centralism was the truly progressive concept. Centralism lent itself to planned development, federalism to a laissez-faire system which diverted energy from certain vital tasks. However, since the order instituted after the success of the independence movement was so manifestly unjust, its opponents mistakenly assumed that it was the centralist system which was at fault. In fact, the federalist movement, by decentralizing the government and multiplying the number of states, simply multiplied the centres of discontent and conspiracy. A new social phenomenon appeared: 'local revolts' aimed at bringing down provincial governments. Within the federation, instability became the rule. There were no less than sixty local disturbances in the first five years of the federation.

Throughout America, moreover, federalism has had even more tragic consequences. In the quarrel about federalism versus centralism, the real issues were ignored and a secondary issue became primary. The burning questions of the poverty of the masses and discrimination against certain sectors of society were ignored, emphasis falling more on superficial political issues. In 1838, federalism caused the break-up of Central America. There was a long battle in Argentina between Buenos Aires and the provinces. In Chile, federalism had collapsed in 1828. In Brazil and Mexico, federal systems were adopted, not without disturbances. Mexico suffered a federal war in 1858–60, in which the liberals, members of the federalist side, opposed the clericalist conservatives, and which extended into the struggle against the French intervention and the unhappy Emperor Maximilian. Brazil's federal structure came into being in 1891 when the Empire became a Republic.

Another symptom of the instability which resulted in America from the counter-revolution was the proliferation of 'Constitutions', each one the product of a deep political crisis and the manifesto of a new beginning, which usually collapsed within a very short space of time. As Jesús de Galíndez has written: 'In 150 years of Independence, we see that the Dominican Republic has had 25 Constitutions, Venezuela 23, Haiti and Ecuador 18, Bolivia 16, Honduras 14, El Salvador, Peru and Nicaragua 12. Some countries had a new Constitution every year at one point, some two in one year. Constitutions were revoked, then restored later. Some Constitutions did not last long enough even to come into operation.'[9]

South America paid for these political errors in blood, as Bolívar had warned: 'The American situation is so extraordinary and so dreadful, that no man should flatter himself that he could keep order there, even in one city.'[10] 'The whole of America is a dreadful picture of bloody disorder. We are living on the edge of a volcano, so demoralized that we abandon all principles of legality ... resorting to the only effective method ... force, used intelligently at the appropriate time and place.' This and other, similar, warnings were valid then for South America, and will continue so, no-one knows for how long, as Bolívar stressed: 'Unless America retraces her steps, accepting her own impotence and ... listening to the voice of order and reason, there can be but little hope of stability for her governments, and a new colonialism will be the inheritance we leave to posterity.'

The political field was not the only one in which retrograde steps followed upon Bolívar's death. In all the fields in which he had preached advanced measures, the same phenomenon can be seen. The situation after his death came to be as bad as, or worse than, before the revolution had ever taken place. One example is Bolívar's attempts to inaugurate a just system of land distribution. Despite the eloquence of his plea to the Angostura Congress to recognise the distribution without delay, that body made so many alterations to the text as to completely alter its nature. They removed certain vital words from Bolívar's ruling on property rights, in which he had boldly exempted the state from obligatory compensation and widened the circumstances under which expropriation could take place, thus leaving traditional property rights almost intact. So far as the actual distribution of land was concerned, instead of its being confined to combattants, most of whom were from the rural peasantry, the category of beneficiaries was widened to include 'not only soldiers, but also employees in the administrative branches of the army, and all those who in any way have served the Republic in these difficult and dangerous times'.[11] Moreover, Bolívar had wanted a rapid and effective distribution, for which reason he had entrusted the task to an ad hoc committee. By a regulation of 31 July 1820, the Congress altered this arrangement to one whereby, instead of actual land, payment was to be in Treasury Bonds. This regulation effectively sabotaged the land distribution programme. Bolívar was in Bogotá when the law was published in Angostura. He demanded the revision of these steps which 'have denied and destroyed the reforming intention of the law, burdening the state with an immense debt, without, however, assuring ... the livelihood of men who defended our country in her worst hours'.[12] Through the Minister, Briceño Méndez, he addressed Gual, desiring him to ask the Congress to put through the necessary correction, referring to the 'adulteration' of his law, on the grounds that it now required the distribution of bonds and the auctioning of lands 'which cannot possibly take place, due to the circumstances in which the country finds itself, and because the profession of arms does not allow its members to absent themselves from their posts, to attend an auction'. Convinced of the grave danger, Bolívar begged Gual, not merely to demand an urgent reform in the law, but also to 'suspend the issue and distribution of the bonds, with a view to preventing their devaluation, which can only ruin our soldiers even further'. He reiterated that the Congress must meanwhile dictate certain measures reassuring the soldiers concerning the fulfilment of these frequently repeated promises of reward. It would be extremely dangerous if they should ever begin to doubt the sincerity of these offers, on which all of them based their hopes. 'The day of peace is approaching, when these soldiers will be discharged; if, when these soldiers return to their homes, they are not sure of ever enjoying their reward, we shall have a repetition of the defections which the Spaniards suffered when they subjugated Venezuela in 1814. I only hope it will not be the sign for a civil war, which threatens us because of the obvious differences between social groups.'

Despite Gual's pleas, the Congress only agreed with great reluctance to suspend the issue of bonds, on 1 September 1821. The expected disaster had already taken place, in that the bonds had been snapped up by speculators, whose interests were protected by a clause safeguarding the rights of owners of bonds other than the immediate recipients. The bonds, moreover, had lost 95% of their value, though as Briceño Méndez pointed out, 'the soldiers who manage to sell them at that price are quite happy. One can be sure that not a single one of the original recipients of the bonds still holds them, all, or nearly all, having passed into other hands, the hands of usurers, and at the extremely low price I have stated. It would not have required much foresight to see that the issue and circulation of mere notes would cause a complete loss of public confidence, for it was creating paper money with no funds to back it ... and giving it into the hands of men who were desperately poor and found themselves forced to sell it for any sum which would relieve their immediate needs.' The idea of extending the distribution to civilians was kept, an idea which, though on the surface just, was in fact tantamount to sabotage of the measure's intentions. Lands were given to bureaucrats who had no interest in agriculture, and the number of applicants increased to an impossible extent. Bolívar again spoke out against this through Briceño Méndez: 'Can one compare the rights of a soldier, who has sacrificed his health, his repose, his blood and everything men hold most dear, to those of a civilian who, remote from danger, runs no risk other than that faced by the general population, and considering the difference in esteem between them, and the considerable salaries which the latter's type of work has always attracted?'

None of these difficulties and objections made Bolívar desist from the task of seeing the land distributed. Despite the unsatisfactory nature of the law as it stood, he did everything in his power to ensure that its provisions were carried out. Thus, in January 1821, he gave General Páez full powers to carry out the agrarian reform in Venezuela. Páez, however, preferred to look after his own interests. Nine months after accepting these powers, he expressed a desire that the magnificent *hacienda* La Trinidad, seized from the Marquis of Casa León, should be transferred to his name. The government gave the order to the Vicepresident: 'In recognition of the services of His Excellency General Páez ... he is assigned ... the aforementioned *hacienda* La Trinidad for its intrinsic value, to be determined by qualified surveyors. Please draw up the appropriate deeds in the name of the government. In payment the following will be accepted: first, the Yagua ranch, for its value, also to be properly determined: second, the total salaries owing to him, which will thus be completely settled: third, future salaries: fourth, the sums he may obtain from the produce of the *hacienda*; in this way, the illustrious leader's desires are met, as well as those of the government, which is gratified to be able to meet his request.'[13]

If the soldiers suffered disappointment and disillusion, much greater was that of the Indians. The decree of May 1820 in favour of the restoration of Indians lands was ignored or, even worse, made the occasion of further frauds. On 12 February 1821, Briceño Méndez, on Bolívar's instructions, signed a document which gives eloquent testimony of these tragic facts: Bolívar had heard many complaints 'in every single one of the villages ... through which he has passed', for not only had the new regulations not been put into operation, but the general situation of the Indian 'far from having been improved by the restoration of their lands and thus the means to support their family, has been made worse by the robbery of their lands, or by their being confined in many areas to barren land and to smaller areas than they had before ... The usual excuse for this iniquitous treatment of the Indians ... is the establishment of a school and payments to the master.' We have seen that Bolívar ratified the decree of 1820 and charged the General Commander of Tunja with personal responsibility for the land distribution programme, urging him to 'always have in mind the improvement of the lot of this section of the population, in the same measure as it has been until now oppressed and degraded'. Bolívar concluded with the hope that he would not hear any further complaints on this score, and emphasised that the cause of the Indians was that of 'natural justice and reason'. This decree followed the path of so many others, being incorporated in a law of 4 October 1821, but thereafter ignored. The pattern was a familiar one: first a purely rhetorical bow in the direction of the general principle, the Indians being declared 'equal in everything to other citizens, and subject to the same laws', then an almost textual transcription of Bolívar's decree, but with an immediate rider which neutralized it almost completely. The lands would be distributed to the Indians 'as soon as circumstances permit'. In fact, when Bolívar returned from Peru at the end of 1826, he found that the Indians had been the victims of barefaced robbery, and when he tried to remedy this, he came up against the selfish interests of the oligarchy, supreme in Colombia since 1821, which won him fresh enemies.

In 1830, the problem of economic injustice and the poverty of the masses still persisted, despite the changes at the top. Revolutionary ideals had fallen victim to the machinations of a few men, some of them of humble origin, who rose to the ranks of privilege and forgot their beginnings. The state was generous with these men. All the most desirable *haciendas* passed into their hands, via innumerable sales, tenancies, transfers of deeds and so on. The *hacienda* La Soledad in Güiria went to General Santiago Mariño; Yaguaraparo to General Juan Bautista Arismendi; El Trapichito to Colonel Cornelio Muñóz; El Rincón in Maracay to Colonel José Lugo; Yoco in Güiria to Colonel Francisco Martínez; *haciendas* in Cumaná and Caracas to General José Francisco Bermúdez. Caracas landowners, anxious to get their hands on the land the state proposed to distribute, published a manifesto in three languages, which they circulated widely, attacking Bolívar. This was in 1819. In 1821, they tried a new weapon, flattery, in their attempts to persuade Bolívar to hand the estates back to them. Bolívar replied coldly and correctly that he was not in a position to interfere with the legal process. If plaintiffs thought they had justice on their side they must have recourse to the law. Many of these rich landowners were also senators, deputies and civil servants, and they managed to destroy the revolution. Soldiers of the Magdalena division addressed a memorial in 1828 to the Ocaña Convention, in which they denounced the farcical events they had witnessed. 'There has been nothing but injustice, neglect and contempt ... Into whose hands have the confiscated lands fallen? Those of wealthy men who bought up deeds for the fifth or sixth part of their value; the government unjustly favoured them, so that when a soldier came forward asking for a certain farm to be assigned to him, it was to find that it had already been assigned to a civilian ... The papers had been sold for the price they would fetch, and thus became a focus for speculation, plotting, usury and corruption ... '[14]

The whole process can be clearly seen in the progress of a decree of Congress of 5 August 1830, revoking Bolívar's orders concerning the confiscation of property. Páez now cynically declared that the confiscations were 'contrary to the rights of a free people'. (The *caudillos* had already grabbed most of the land.) The official commentary on this decree, published in the *Gazeta de Caracas*, implied that Bolívar had been a subversive influence: 'No less worthy of public approval is the decree which we reproduce here, abolishing the confiscation laws, always detestable in the eyes of just men, for they were based on war reprisals and they enshrined in law, as a right of society, a type of robbery which is rightly condemned when perpetrated by an individual. This civilised and humane act with which our representatives open the new era of the regeneration of Venezuela will win to our side the affection, respect and support of all right-thinking men, both within and without the country. With measures such as these, so urgently demanded by justice, we shall be able to restore order, calm and morality, as well as the respect and esteem of other powers, which the subverters of the Republic had succeeded in losing. Once this philanthropic decree has been accepted, the honest landowner can quietly enjoy the *hacienda* he inherited from his fathers, or which he built up with his own hands, and be sure that it will also survive to be the support of his innocent children, free of the fear that some diligent bond holder will discover amongst his ancestors some pro-Spanish taint, and make this the excuse for seizing the *hacienda*.'[15]

It goes without saying that the people mainly affected by this philanthropic measure were those with little influence, such as the widow of General Anzoátegui, who was deprived of the estate on which she and her family depended, to allow it to be restored to a well-known royalist. The *caudillo* Governments, from Páez onwards, were implacable against the peasant agitation which arose in response to this failure of the land programme. Of all the *caudillos*, Páez was the one who grew richest during his period of power. As he himself wrote to Santander: 'My head is filled with the desire to destroy my enemies: if they could be expelled tomorrow from the Republic, my sole ambition would be to organise and increase the properties presented to me by the state ... this country has showered me with honours, it has more than compensated me for my efforts to defend myself and achieve independence.'[16] Bolívar confided to Perú de Lacroix on 12 May 1828: 'Letters from Caracas sadden me, they all mention the poverty in the country and the stagnation in trade and agriculture: only General Páez says nothing of this, undoubtedly because his own affairs are doing well, and he is indifferent to public poverty.'[17] In his will, made in New York on 24 July 1865, Páez declared that when he married in 1809 he 'owned nothing', yet, although he spent his life in the war and politics from 1811 onwards, his fortune came to include: the *hacienda* La Trinidad in Maracay; the Customs House in Puerto Cabello, probably the main building in the town; a house in Maracay and a piece of land with a small house adjacent to it; houses rented out in Valencia; small portions of inherited land in Apure, near the town of Rincón Hondo; the immense cattle farm of San Pablo, probably the biggest in the Republic, spread over a number of provinces and which 'in 1848 was worth a great deal, with 20,000 sheep, 700 mares, 300 mules and around 500 horses'. Páez also rented the *hacienda* Chuao, which belonged to the University. He was proud of having turned it into 'a very valuable property', and detailed the coffee trees, cocoa, cane-sugar that grew there. He also noted without shame: 'I have still to receive from the government the value of the slaves which I owned in La Trinidad and San Pablo'.[18] As a last will and testament, it contrasts very unfavourably with that of Bolívar, as does Santander's.[19]

During the tyrannies, land became more than ever concentrated in very few hands. Political power was the most rapid road to wealth, as it was in other unfortunate countries of Latin America. The Mexican Revolution in the 20th century fought to abolish *latifundios*, and even to this day there are very large estates in some countries. This in turn exaggerated the tendency towards monoculture, preventing industrial development, and thus contributing to the ignorance and physical weakness of the population. The *latifundio* is the typical form of landholding associated with rural exploitation in Latin America. It imposes starvation wages and long hours on a rural population which is tied to the earth, with no means of escape or protest. The tyrant Gómez, in Venezuela, owned approximately 1,250,000 hectares of grazing land and 120,000 hectares of farm land, some in his favourite state of Aragua, some in the neighbouring Carabobo, some in his native Táchira and the remainder in other provinces of Venezuela and Colombia. There is an outstanding example of the same phenomenon in the *hatos del Caura*, an immense *latifundio* which General Joaquín Crespo formed during his period as President. Juan Vicente Gómez bought this *hacienda* from one of Crespo's successors for 80,000 *bolívares* in 1911. In 1926, he sold it to the nation for 16,000,000 *bolívares*.

In many other aspects, the years Bolívar spent in the south were used by his opponents to build up a structure in Gran Colombia which was totally different from Bolívar's ideal. The Cúcuta Congress abolished the old taxes without creating new ones. The financial élite was utterly opposed to paying taxes of any kind, and suggested the easier and more lucrative alternative of heavy loans to the state. As Liévano Aguirre remarks, their preference for this system is easily understood: 'By means of this system, the independence wars became a focus for lucrative speculation. The people paid with their dead, and with their blood, on which no interest is paid. The businessmen, on the other hand, recovered both their initial capital and the accumulated interest.'[20] Even so, financial circles in Bogotá, Antioquia and Cartagena soon tired of supplying cash loans, and they applied subtle pressure on the government to seek loans abroad. There is the sorry tale of the English loan. The financial circles in question supplied the agents who negotiated the loan with England on Colombia's behalf, agents who proceeded to exact a commission for their services. Liévano Aguirre continues: 'As the country was dominated by a powerful oligarchy, the loan ... was used to import English textiles and products, so that within a short time it was back in England, without really having served any function in this country. The access to foreign currency facilitated by the loan, instead of being used for the purchase of capital goods, industrial machinery or agricultural tools, was used for consumer goods which for the most part were competing with home produced goods, that is, the loan was used to satisfy the consumer demands of the privileged minority.' Part of the English money was lost through the collapse of the firm negotiating the loan. Bolívar tried constantly to oppose this type of speculation, an endeavour which provoked attacks on his life, such as the one which took place on 25 September 1828. He also made valiant attempts to reorganize the treasury in Venezuela. He announced to Urdaneta from Caracas in 1827: 'A treasury regulation is about to be ordered which should bring in a fair amount of money. If we can eliminate theft, reduce expenditure and increase income, we can go ahead, and be sure of having money to pay.' Shortly afterwards he told José Gabriel Pérez: 'In the two days I was in Bogotá, I reduced state expenditure by 6,000,000, and some considerable reforms have also been carried out in Venezuela. Public morality has had some severe lessons and some edifying examples.'[21]

All over Latin America, the period after Bolívar saw the systematic surrender of national resources to foreign companies. Juan Vicente Gómez is the supreme example of this policy of *entreguismo* in Venezuela, with his reduction of mining taxes from the levels set by his predecessor, Cipriano Castro. In 1927, the Venezuela Oil Concession, which belonged to the Shell group, earned 3,400,000 dollars on an investment of 10,000,000 dollars. The Lago Petroleum Company, a subsidiary of Standard Oil, on a working capital of 3,500,000 dollars made nearly 8,000,000 dollars. The shares rose almost 600% between 1924 and 1927. In the seven years from 1923 to 1930, the Republic earned 187,000,000 *bolívares* from hydrocarbons. In the same period, it exempted the oil companies from import duties to the sum of 219,000,000 *bolívares*. As the Minister of Development remarked: 'These companies are taking away our petroleum, and the Venezuelan Government is paying them for doing it.'[22] Laws concerning petroleum were made for the convenience of foreign companies. The first specific law on petroleum in Venezuela was in 1920. The only Venezuelans to benefit were the small circle of Gómez's supporters, and even they received very little. The law was modified in 1921, but when it became clear that the foreign companies were not happy with the arrangements, Gómez, as accommodating with foreigners as he was intransigent with his fellow countrymen, called the oil companies together: 'You know about petroleum', he told them. 'You make the laws. We are novices in the business.'[23] The law of 1922 was drawn up by lawyers representing the oil companies, and it was they who introduced modifications in 1925, 1928 and 1935. 'The Venezuelan petroleum laws are the best in the world for the oil companies', Gómez complacently declared in 1930. His régime was bolstered by the oil consortia and by their friends and associates in foreign governments, and the same story could be told of many execrable Latin American régimes, with a few changes of date, and substituting for the word *petrol* the words *gold, copper, silver, tin, iron, bananas, coffee, wood or rubber* as appropriate. The story has been told in novels and in protest songs, but it should serve another purpose, that of a lesson for the future. The Balkanization of the Latin American continent served the ends of foreign exploiters.

If we turn now to the question of slavery, we see the same retrograde steps being taken, in spite of Bolívar's advice, as in other areas. The sad facts are that slavery continued to exist long after Bolívar, that its survival was due to the activities of men who had collaborated with him in the independence movement, and that the only remnant of his teaching was a purely rhetorical nod in the direction of social equality. As with land reform, a combination of empty oratory, delay, and the introduction of unnecessary complications defeated Bolívar's intentions. The Angostura Congress took eleven months before deciding, in January 1820, to remit the question of the abolition of slavery to 'the Colombian House of Representatives, which is to meet at the beginning of next year'.[24] The debate on the subject can be followed in the records of the Congress. Don Fernando Peñalver, though acknowledging the urgency of settling the slavery question, reminded the assembly that agriculture in Venezuela was dependent on slave labour, and asked that Bolívar's request should not be put into effect 'until the Congress has been informed of the regulations determining the use to be made of freedom by those who have never known it'. The issue was passed over to those deputies who had the responsibility for interpreting the Constitution. They were asked to produce a Bill 'as soon as possible'. Four months later, they had still done nothing. Only one deputy, Pumar, attempted to re-introduce the topic. Finally, after another month's delay, the discussion began. In the session of 17 August, 'it gave rise to several disturbances', the Secretary noted. It was postponed several times. In the session on 8 November, 'the bill on the freedom of slaves came up for discussion, and Señor España rose to say that he considered it a matter of much greater urgency to verify the truth or otherwise of a rumour that corpses had been appearing in the river these last few days ... '[25] In the decree which remitted the issue to the House of Representatives, the first article declared that slavery was 'legally abolished'. The second then arranged that 'the situation will continue as at present in all three Departments of the Republic.'[26] It also established the duty of the state to compensate owners whose slaves were called up into the army. Incredibly, it contained the following: 'Out of respect for the laws, customs and habits of other nations, we declare that any slave who has escaped from a foreign country will be imprisoned and returned to his owner.' Those who had aided his escape, and had hidden or protected him, would also be punished. Cleverly, the preamble was full of splendid-sounding sentiments: 'Seeing the state of ignorance and moral degradation of these people, we must make them men before we can make the citizens ... It is also necessary to give them the means of subsistence, along with freedom ... Liberty ... must come slowly, like sight to those who have been blind, so that they are not dazzled by the sudden splendour of the day.'

Bolívar returned to the task at the Cúcuta Congress, pressing home the emotional advantage of the victory of Carabobo, which had been won 'by the army of liberation, whose blood has flowed in the cause of liberty'.[27] The Congress, unable to postpone any longer the inevitable, dictated on July 1821 a complicated 'Law on the freedom of children born to slaves, and the abolition of slavery and the slave trade'.[28] Again they stressed the idea of 'gradual' emancipation, in order not 'to endanger public order nor violate the legitimate rights of slave owners'. Any positive measure in the bill was immediately neutralised by what came after. The first article freed 'children born to slaves after the date of the publication of this law', but the second went on to add that these children must repay their mothers' masters for the cost of their food, clothing and education by 'works and services which they are to perform up to the age of eighteen'. Article five established that 'no slave shall be sold outside the province in which he lives, to avoid the breaking up of families', but it added, 'this prohibition is only valid until the children reach the age of puberty'. It did go so far as to say that slaves introduced into a province in defiance of this law were automatically free.

Mild though this law was, the Congress ensured that it would not be carried out, by entrusting its execution to individuals who had a direct interest in the continued existence of slavery. Nor were these men always survivors from the old order. Sometimes they were the very people who had struggled for freedom, generals, magistrates and deputies. These were the same men who, by means of the treasury bond maneouvre, managed to seize the lands confiscated from their former colonial owners, and now they needed slave labour to run these possessions. Santander spoke up on behalf of these groups in New Granada, but Bolívar resisted his demands: 'The direction of this revolution has been decided, and no-one can stop it now.' To try to turn back was not only unjust and an error, but imprudent, even dangerous. Bolívar recommended to Santander that he persuade his selfish followers of the wisdom of accepting the new order: 'I believe it would be very useful to educate these men, carried away by self-interest, or what they falsely conceive to be in their interests ... '[28a] The Vicepresident, however, had joined common cause with those determined to maintain slavery. On 3 May, the Governor, José Cancino wrote to Santander from Buga: 'My dear General: ... concerning the steps I should take with regard to the slaves ... you stated, quite correctly that to free the slaves would ruin the region of Choco. For this reason, you decided to leave it to my discretion ... remarking that if I did carry out the instructions, it should not be done everywhere. On arriving in the Province I was to rule, I learned that out of 14,000 inhabitants, 9,000 are slaves. I concluded that it would be unwise to free even a single one; however, the reasons I have already told you forced me to do so to some extent, I hope in a way which will avoid any dangerous transition ... Nevertheless, on my arrival at Cauca, I learned of a ban which protects all the slaves without exception ... which will be the ruin of that province and of Choco. I foresee many dangers, which I am anxious to avoid. I have, therefore, tried to come to arrangements with Governor Concha, as you will see from the enclosed document, while awaiting further orders.'[29] A Colombian law, dated 18 February 1825, considered engaging in the slave-trade a crime of piracy, and laid down the death sentence for those found guilty. It should be noticed that not even this law escaped the duplicity to which we have referred. Article 4 made it clear that the law did not apply to the traffic between one Colombian port and another, even if for purposes of sale.

Bolívar's decisions in relation to Indian slaves in Peru were also defeated, as were his representations to the Bolivian Congress. He wanted it to introduce into the Constitution a clause recognising the freedom of the slaves, who would therefore be effectively freed by the publication of that document. The Congress approved the following text: 'All those who until now were slaves are Bolivian citizens and are therefore legally free by the publication of this Constitution; but they may not leave their master's house except in the manner to be laid down by a special law.'[30] When Bolívar was forced to return to Caracas because of the Cosiata rebellion, he attempted to ensure that at least the 1821 law on slaves should be put into operation, demanding that he be informed frequently and personally of the progress made in that direction. It was then that he discovered the complicity of numerous people anxious to see the law fail, and introduced the energetic decree of 28 June 1827 to which we have already referred. A year later, he promulgated a decree in Bogotá giving instructions for the Juntas in charge of the freeing of slaves to act quickly. They were to constitute themselves within one week of the issue of the decree and were to meet regularly, at least once a week. The *jefe político*, or failing him, the first *alcalde*, was to be responsible for seeing that these instructions were carried out.

Bolívar was fully aware of how little he had achieved of his ideals. Exhausted by his military tasks, and by immense labours of administration, he could not struggle alone against the massive conspiracy of those who refused to collaborate in the creation of a just system, and instead tried to combat his measures with all the selfish strength at their disposal. Bolívar saw the manifestations of anarchy, saw how his ideas were attacked at every turn, and realised that it was impossible to construct a new order without a revolution. In July 1826, he wrote in anguish to Santander: 'It is impossible to do anything worthwhile with simple legal reforms, in fact ... we are sick of laws.'[31] What was needed was to liberate and educate the newly freed peoples, strengthen their moral structure and channel in a positive direction the unconscious, anarchic vigour, which in the end could be suicidal, could overflow and destroy the structures of society. 'Legal equality', Bolívar repeated, 'is not enough for the spirit of our people, which wants absolute equality, in public and domestic matters: and afterwards it will want a *pardocracia*, which is its natural tendency ... and the extermination of privilege.' It was clear to him that order and stability could not come from this *pardocracia*, or rule by the *pardo* majority but he pointed out that they were no more likely to come from the *albocracia* or white supremacy which was considered the only acceptable solution in the south, nor from a *nigrocracia*, that 'spectre which terrifies everyone' in Guayaquil in 1830. He spoke at length on the subject to Perú de Lacroix around the time of the Ocaña Congress, referring to 'the state of slavery in which the poor people of Colombia find themselves even now; not only are they beneath the yoke of the *alcaldes* and the parish priest, but also of the three or four wealthy businessmen there are in each parish; in the cities it is the same, except that there are more masters, for one has to include all the clerics, monks and lawyers; liberty and civil guarantees exist only for these men, and for the rich, never for the people, whose slavery is worse than that of the Indians; they were slaves under the Cúcuta Constitution, and they would still be slaves even if we had the most liberal constitution; in Colombia there is an aristocracy of class, of employment and of wealth, equivalent in influence, in pretension and in oppression of the people to the most tyrannous aristocracy of birth and blood in the Old World: ... for although they speak of liberty and civil guarantees, it is only for themselves and not for the people, who they think should continue to be oppressed by them; they also want equality, to rise and become equal with those at present higher, not to be on the same level as those in the lower ranks of society, whom they consider their inferiors.'[32]

In the last years of Colombia, the division of society grew clear: on the one hand, Bolívar and the people, on the other, Santander, Páez, Flores and the oligarchies in Bogotá, Caracas, Quito, Lima, La Paz, Cochabamba and elsewhere. There is evidence of this in a letter from Santander to his follower Azuero, dated 18 January 1828, in which he mentions the 'numerous supporters of Bolívar who have 'frequently threatened our existence'. He feared a confrontation: 'What would be the result? An internal war, which would be won by those who have nothing, who are always the most numerous, and lost by those who have something, as there are so few of us.'[33] We should note the similarity of these words to those used in relation to San Martín's policy in Peru of 'retaining the barriers which divide the different classes in society, in order to preserve the position of the educated classes, which have something to lose'.

The policies of the oligarchies were identical in Buenos Aires, Lima, Bogotá or Mexico City. Torre Tagle, who represented these powerful financial interests in Peru had no hesitation in revealing his motives: 'Citizens of Peru: the tyrant Bolívar and his disgusting followers wish to bring Peru, this proud country, under the tutelage of Colombia ... Bolívar had invited me to open negotiations with the Spaniards, in Peru, in order to gain time, so that he could bring reinforcements, defeat the Spaniards and entrap Peru with his chains. I took advantage of the opportunity to obtain for you an advantageous union with the Spaniards, thus avoiding our ruin.' The Liberator was thus the common enemy of the Spaniards and the Lima reactionaries. Even in Caracas, his compatriots heaped insults on his head, calling him seditious, an imposter, ungrateful, a traitor, a barbarian, a tyrant, a murderer, a coward.[34] In Lima they referred to him as 'the *zambo*', 'Old Simon', 'the tyrant'. After his death, steps were taken to reverse the direction of his anti-slavery legislation. The Valencia Congress replaced the law of the Congress of Cúcuta with another, issued on 30 September 1830, which was hostile to the slaves, in that it raised to twenty-one the age of obligatory service prior to freedom. In return for food, clothing and education, the children of slaves were to give their masters another three of the best years of their lives. There was also a limit of twenty placed on the total number of slaves who could officially be freed in any one year in the whole country. At that rate, a few thousand years would have been necessary to eradicate this social evil from Venezuela. Between 1831 and 1839, only 118 individuals were freed. During Páez's rule, he manipulated article 6 of the law, which was intended to protect young freed slaves. On 27 April 1840, he dictated a decree: 'Whereas, when the freed slaves leave the power of their masters, they will usually lack even the discipline of paternal authority, and are of an age and condition to attract police attention', he ordered that where possible, these young freed men should be attached as apprentices to their former masters, and, ignoring all principles of reason and justice, and even the letter of the law, immediately raised to twenty-five the age of emancipation. (This for a group of people whose average life-expectancy was thirty.) The actual arrangements were cunning: 'When an apprenticeship or contract is dissolved, the Juntas are to ensure that the freed youths, if they have not reached the age of twenty-five, are to enter into similar conditions of contract with another master ... Any apprentice or free servant who leaves the service for which he has contracted without adequate reason, will be restored to that service by the local police ... No person may take into service or apprenticeship any freed youth under the age of twenty-five, except under the conditions explained in this regulation. Contraventions will attract the same penalty laid down for people who employ day labourers who have deserted from other work for which they had contracted.'[35]

Páez boasted about this law in his autobiography, in which he also, incorrectly, related Bolívar's opposition to slavery to a supposed opposition on the part of the Spaniard Rosete. Páez even claimed that he had freed the slaves in Apure, without noting any contradiction between that claim and the 1830 law, or the even more unjust and illegal decree of 1840. Although Venezuela signed a treaty with Great Britain against the slave traffic in 1839, it must be said that within the country slavery continued unabated throughout the first hundred years of independence, though naturally it was forced to adopt numerous forms and suffered continual disturbances. Between 1830 and 1854, slave revolts increased: there were daily escapes, rebellions, acts of violence. José Gregorio Monagas issued his Abolition Law in 1854. By that time the issue had lost a lot of the importance it once had, for while the oligarchies and the dictatorships clung ferociously to their slaves, a change had come over the economic system. Slavery had become an uneconomic method of production, and its abolition began to be proposed as a sound economic move for the owners. They could at least hope to obtain generous compensation for an asset whose value had fallen. According to official estimates, slavery was costing more than it produced, for the wealth produced per head was less than the cost of feeding and maintaining the slaves. Accordingly, the abolition of slavery took place peacefully, amidst general acclamation. Landowners were now assured of a cheap labour force, with fewer costs and fewer headaches. As in all similar cases, the weakest person was the one who suffered. The former slaves were forced to return to their masters because the state made no provision for them. For those not lucky enough to have 'understanding masters', oppression and exploitation increased, for there was now no obligation on the master to feed, clothe or educate his workers. They were paid starvation wages, often not even in cash, but in tokens redeemable only in the *pulpería* or store of the *hacienda*, where the prices were usually twice as high as elsewhere, so that they accumulated debts which tied them to the earth they worked from sunrise to sunset, driven with scourges and whips. The share-cropper system was simply another form of slavery. Legally free, these men were, in fact, slaves through economic circumstances, neglected by the state, exploited by their masters, living without rights, without hygiene, without culture. During the Gómez regime, the fiction of 'domestic service' concealed yet another form of slavery. Army conscripts during the dictatorships were also semi-slaves, in that they could spend ten years in the army working on the leaders' land. Gómez himself gave evidence for the existence of this system in one of his first official speeches.

Turning to Bolívar's other great ideal, that of the unification of Latin America, we find the same destruction after his death that we have already documented in other fields. The *caudillos* were opposed to integration, whether on a national or a continental scale. The *Caudillo de los Llanos*, Páez, was the epitome of these men, whose mental horizon was limited to their own zone of influence, their own private territory, which they could exploit at will. Páez did not threaten to break away from Venezuela, for the geographical position of his region made this impractical. Moreover, he hoped one day to gain control of the whole of Venezuela. In the meantime, he made sure that no one besides himself wielded power in his domain, as can be seen in the destruction in 1816 of a plan for civilian government formed by Doctor Francisco Javier Yanes and some higher officers, amongst them Santander, Serrano, Urdaneta and Serviez.

Gran Colombia never really won the loyalty of its members. Even Bolívar's collaborators did not entirely understand or share his ideas. By a grotesque coincidence, just at the time when the immense Panamá Congress was about to take place, Venezuela was rent apart by the Cosiata conspiracy, in which the Bogotá government was not entirely innocent. Neither Santander nor Páez defended the union, instead they retreated into local pride, happy to see a split develop. Bolívar, however, refused to place the union at risk, and by giving way on what he considered the minor point, preserved unity, to a certain extent at least. In 1827, Bolívar's physical presence was still decisive. The deterioration in the condition of Gran Colombia forced him to accept dictatorial powers, though he did fulfil his promise to convene the Congress, to which in January 1830 he gave his resignation. Death overtook him on the road into exile.

Páez, meanwhile, was drawing nearer and nearer to the idea of Venezuelan secession. He convened his congress on 13 January and it opened in Valencia on 30 April. The Congress of Colombia decided to send a friendly mission from Bogotá to Páez's congress, led by Sucre. However, at the Venezuelan frontier, the authorities, led by Santiago Mariño acting on Páez's instructions, refused to let them through. They therefore met Páez's representatives at Cúcuta, on 18 and 19 April. These were General Santiago Mariño, Monsignor Ignacio Fernández Peña and Martín Tovar. In the records of the meeting, it is made clear that Sucre went straight to the heart of the matter: 'In the event that the Venezuelan Commissioners wished to demonstrate that what had taken place there was a popular movement, and not a military action, as had been thought ... its results should clearly favour the people: no-one in power should bend the people under a yoke as burdensome, or more so, than the one from which they had been released. Although he had been away from Colombia for more than six years, he understood that its ills were not due to what had been called the despotism of the Liberator (for the same number of complaints had been heard during the previous government and in the constitutional period), but to the process of the revolution itself, and the despotism of a military aristocracy which, seizing power everywhere, made the citizens suffer, deprived of all their rights and guarantees. This abuse was so entrenched that not even the immense power of the Dictatorship had managed to budge it. For this reason, with the aim of restoring rights and guarantees completely, he had a proposal which he wished to present to the Venezuelan Commissioners, hoping that, if it met with their approval, they would support it in Venezuela, as he intended to do in the Colombian Congress. The proposal read as follows: "Certain soldiers having disgraced themselves by abusing their powers and influence to trample on the laws, and others being accused or suspected of attempting to change the form of government, it is forbidden to any ... General who has occupied high office in the Republic between 1820 and 1830, to become President or Vicepresident of Colombia, or President or Vicepresident of the Confederation, if it is formed."'[36] Sucre was thus placing the interests of the

Revolution above his own, for his own position would have been affected if the proposal had been accepted. Tovar and Fernández Peña considered Sucre's idea 'just' and were inclined to accept it. General Mariño, however, the last to speak, declared himself 'offended' and urged his companions not to accept the proposal.[37] He also stated that he had no authority to allow the delegation from Bogotá to enter Venezuela in order to inform the Congress there of events in the Colombian Congress. Other conciliatory moves by Sucre were similarly rejected.

Nor was there significantly more enthusiasm for Gran Colombia in New Granada. They were anxious for the break, in order to free themselves from the 'domination' of Venezuela, whom they accused of monopolizing the top and middle positions in the administration and of draining away New Granada's economic resources to subsidize Venezuela.[38] In Ecuador there was also some dissatisfaction, though of a minor sort, with both Venezuela and New Granada, which the Ecuadorians lumped together as 'Colombia', as though deliberately excluding themselves. The white aristocracy of Quito objected to the colour of the skin of the liberation troops, complaining that they had turned the country into 'a Senegalese camp'. They referred sarcastically to a '*nigrocracia*'.

Páez wrote in his autobiography: 'Venezuelan opinion was unanimous in putting me in charge of the situation.'[39] In fact this claim is completely false. Páez manipulated opinion.[39a] Force, which is always more persuasive than principle, was on the side of the separatists. Adversaries, or those suspected of being such, were persecuted and oppressed without mercy. Even the postal system with Bogotá was strictly controlled.[40] Censorship and terror soon convinced the waverers. Sucre and Bolívar died, the former the victim of a cowardly ambush, leaving open the road to dissolution.

It was not only Gran Colombia which fell apart. Bolívar's plans for the unification of the continent also foundered. On 7 October 1824, Santander, the Vicepresident of Colombia, inspired by President Monroe's strictures against the Holy Alliance and the European colonisation of America, hastily arranged for Chancellor Gual to instruct the Colombian representative in Washington to invite the North American government to send a representative to the Panamá Congress.[41] Bolívar did not discover this important fact until 6 April, six months after the order had been given. Santander notified him on 6 February, on acknowledging receipt of the invitation from Lima. Bolívar had not approved this move beforehand, and he refused to sanction it for two reasons, one circumstantial, the other a question of principle. In the first place, he did not want to offend Great Britain, from whom he was expecting vital help, and in the second, he wanted the congress to consist only of Latin American nations. His first warning on the subject is dated 1 April 1825: 'Association with the United States will compromise us vis-à-vis Great Britain ... Please consider the matter carefully, and I shall be interested to hear the results, so that at least one or the other of us may be freed of whatever prejudices we have on the matter.'[42] He repeated the same warning, in even clearer terms, on 8 and 20 May, though he was at that time engaged in travelling around the interior of Peru in an attempt to improve its administration. He was not cultivating a gratuitous antagonism towards the United States, he was simply aware of the cultural and historical differences between the two halves of the continent, and considered it unsuitable to mix the weak, divided nations of the south with the powerful giant of the north. He had expressed his point of view in the Angostura Speech. After praising the United States, considered at that time a model of liberty, he went on to say: 'I must point out, that it has never entered my head to compare two states so different from each other as the English states of North America and the Spanish states of South America.' In 1823, he explained to Bernardo Monteagudo the danger of associating dissimilar nations, when he commented on the problems of asking Great Britain to be the patron of the American league.

On 30 May 1825, he ratified a clear instruction given to Santander ten days previously: 'The North Americans and the Haitians, simply because they are foreigners, are not part of our group. For this reason, I shall never believe that they should be invited into our arrangements for America.' On 21 October, he again stated quite firmly: 'I do not believe the North Americans should come into the Isthmus conference.' He had made his most categorical statement on the matter on 8 October, when he told the Argentinian plenipotentiaries in Potosí 'that he had never been in favour ... of the United States being invited, and that even in private communications he had made his displeasure known to his friends; that such an invitation had surprised him, and that he had written to Santander that if the United States were going to participate, it was almost necessary, or convenient, to avoid the congress taking place, though he was sure this would not be necessary, as the United States would not attend'.[42a]

Santander scarcely replied to Bolívar's communications on the questions, and he did not withdraw the instructions to Salazar, the Colombian representative in Washington. Accompanied by the Mexican and Central American representatives in Washington, Salazar issued a formal invitation to the Panamá Congress to the United States on 2 November 1825. Although the United States government accepted the invitation, their plenipotentaries did not in fact attend, owing to a prolonged controversy in the legislature and the press over the policy of isolationism. Only one of the envoys arrived in Tacubaya, in Mexico, where the Congress had moved after beginning in Panamá. The role of Gual in this matter has been explained by Liévano Aguirre: 'Gual, it is true, followed Vicepresident Santander's instructions in this matter, but not without realising that such drastic alteration to Bolívar's policy could only be justified if it succeeded in transforming the Monroe Doctrine from a unilateral declaration by one of the American governments into a continental agreement, whereby its operation and the occasions on which it would come into use would be decided, not by the United States, but by all the countries of the American hemisphere.'[43]

Despite Bolívar's sympathy for Great Britain, it was not his idea to invite that power to the Panamá Congress. Again, it was an initiative of Santander's. Bolívar was at that time in Lima, and was consulted on the matter after the first steps had in fact been taken. He sent replies to Santander and Revenga on 17 February 1826, giving conditional approval to the idea 'for the moment',[44] taking into account the 'real and immediate' advantages that could accrue from an alliance with Great Britain at that precise moment, when they feared an attack from the sea. Nevertheless, he was uneasy. He had told Monteagudo earlier: 'At first sight, and for a time, it presents certain advantages: but afterwards ... the skeletons appear. Let me explain: it would bring us peace and independence for the present, and some internal guarantees ... this will cost us some part of our national independence, some financial sacrifice and some national humiliation. If England is placed at the head of this league, we will be her slaves.' In the draft of his 17 February reply, he emphasised the importance of the particular moment, and again contrasted the immediate benefits and the long-term disadvantages. Nevertheless, he accepted the fait accompli with a certain optimism: 'In our childhood we need help, when we are grown to men we will know how to defend ourselves. For the moment it is useful to us.'

Santander also took it upon himself on 28 May 1825 to invite the French to send an observer to the Panamá Congress. The invitation was ignored by Charles X, as an ally of Spain. Holland, on the other hand, welcomed the overtures of the Colombian representative in London and attended the Congress, drawn by the interest she felt for her colonies in South America. Bolívar had excluded Brazil from the Congress because of her sympathy with the Holy Alliance, but here again, Santander issued an invitation which was accepted. Bolívar had also excluded Haiti, on the grounds that it was not a Spanish American nation. Santander agreed with this exclusion, but went on absurdly to base the exclusion on racial grounds. He referred to his government's 'reluctance to observe with Haiti the rules of etiquette normally followed amongst civilised nations', and he frustrated the rapprochement attempted by President Boyer's envoy in Colombia. He instructed the Colombian delegates to 'avoid any discussion concerning the recognition of Haitian independence, the sending or receiving of diplomats or the signing of public treaties such as the Republic of Colombia normally signs with other European or American powers'.[45] Santander's conduct was the more repugnant in that the document in question was drawn up by Revenga, who had himself suffered humiliation from colonial racialism, when his university degree was held up for three years because of some gaps in the documentation referring to his *limpieza de sangre* or pure blood. Bolívar had, it is true, invited only six nations, which had formerly belonged to Spanish America. This was not, however, a sign of any lack of affection for Haiti. He rejected completely Santander, Gual and Revenga's prejudiced attitude and declared in 1829: 'A meeting took place between an agent of Haiti and the Minister of State in Bogotá, while I was in Peru. I knew nothing of the meeting until after it was over: at that time, I had no authority in Colombia, for the Constitution and the Congress had taken it from me ... For my part, I cannot refuse to negotiate with the government of Haiti, I owe it too much for that.'[46]

The men who thus invited the United States and European powers to participate in the Panamá Congress were no doubt convinced that they were more open and broad-minded than Bolívar. In fact they were leading the Congress to disaster, for international associations can only be based on mutual interest, which is why Bolívar remarked to Gual and Briceño Méndez that 'a pact with the whole world is in fact meaningless'. The same tactic was being followed here as with the land distribution, or with the slaves. In the case of the former, instead of being restricted to soldiers, the regulations were extended to cover all sorts of public servants, which meant that in the end no-one got the land. In the case of the slaves, they were not freed because it was alleged that first one must solve the problems of education and work for the freed slaves: in other words, the aim was magnified and complicated, in order to prevent its ever being accomplished.

It should be noted that these were not the only points of disagreement between Bolívar and Santander. The latter had resolved to be guided by the local interests to which he owed his support, and this could be seen in his divergence from Bolívar in relation to the dispute between Argentina and Brazil in 1825, a complicated issue, admittedly, which also involved Uruguay, Paraguay, Peru and Bolivia. Bolívar informed Santander of the visit he had received from the plenipotentiaries of the River Plate: 'Alvear and Díaz Vélez came forward to propose, as one of the principal aims of their mission, that I should head an expedition to release Paraguay from French oppression. They say that we are in a very favourable position to carry out this operation, which would bring great advantages to Buenos Aires, most particularly in the war against Brazil. Imagine, then, how great is my embarrassment, being at the head of two states, without being able to decide their wishes or even their best interests. I thus find myself in the painful necessity of refraining from dealing decisively with these missions, or giving my final consent to their requests. I have told them frankly that I shall do for the River Plate whatever my present position allows, and that I shall put all my effort into recommending with all my soul and all my influence, the granting of whatever help or even sacrifices they think necessary from Colombia or Peru to save their country. I hope, my dear General, that you will take note of the principal contents of this letter and will make whatever use of it you think suitable to inform Congress on this matter which is at the same time important, difficult and delicate.' Santander replied with mediocre quibbles to Bolívar's generous proposals for help to the River Plate, sacrificing long-term advantages for short-term gains: 'In accordance with our laws, you must agree that neither you nor I can deploy Colombian troops to help Buenos Aires ... My opinion is that we should not help them, without reflecting on how England' will react ... As for Paraguay, I should think we should not help there either: ... we have no jurisdiction over Paraguay, nor is that province dependent on the Spanish Government ... By virtue of which pact or obligation would we help Buenos Aires in an internal struggle?'[47] This was the culmination of many refusals to join with the Argentinians. 'We have no treaty with the River Plate,' Santander declared. 'The agreement that was drawn up was simply an indication of the bases which were to be established and defined, and besides, it has not been presented here ratified by the Argentine government. These gentlemen approach us now when they need us: when they thought themselves superior to us, they treated us with an impertinent arrogance.' He repeated two months later: 'I have not changed my mind in relation to the help requested by Buenos Aires. We cannot grant it, firstly because there is no pact covering such help and secondly because without the consent of Congress neither you nor I can deploy a single soldier. In any case, the whole principle requires careful thought, so that we do not become needlessly involved in a quarrel.'

The distinguished historian and Bolívar specialist Rufino Blanco Fombona established a parallel between the isolationism of Santander and that of Rivadavia, and pointed up the contrast between these attitudes and Bolívar's generous consideration of the whole of America. He recalled that in 1824, Bolívar, after strenuous efforts, succeeded in obtaining permission from the Colombians to go from there to Peru, whereupon the Vicepresident persuaded the Congress to vote a law forbidding Bolívar's passage from the viceroyalty to any other state of South America. 'The attitude of the government and public opinion in Colombia', he says 'was one of the main obstacles the Liberator encountered ... in his attempts to intervene between the Argentinians and the Brazilians in 1826.'⁴⁸ This opposition to Bolívar's ideas of integration was widespread. Indalecio Liévano Aguirre has made a close study of this question, indeed these considerations are based very largely on his investigations. He writes: 'The New Granada plutocracy, the aristocratic landowners in Venezuela, the merchant and money lending oligarchy in Buenos Aires, the Conservative 'bigwigs' in Chile, the Peruvian aristocracy, the owners of slave labour plantations in Brazil etc., all these groups had a common interest in converting the old colonial administrative areas into sovereign states, in order to seize their own tiny part of political power and be sure that social conflict between those at the top and those at the bottom would be resolved by an Executive, Legislative and Judicial Power formed in their image and likeness.'⁴⁹ If Mosquera's mission to Peru was a success, it was only because the Peruvian government was aware of its need of Colombian help. Even then, reservations were expressed concerning the principle *uti possidetis juris*, and the treaty had to contain the recognition of the duty of mutual military aid, which caused difficulties with Bolívar's subsequent negotiations with Santiago de Chile and Buenos Aires.

In general, Bolívar did not find a warm welcome in Chile for his plans. O'Higgins' government presented various amendments to the Colombian proposals, which had to be accepted, even though they reduced the effectiveness and significance of the treaty. As we have noted in the case of Rivadavia, the treaty which was finally agreed was so weak as to have lost all significance. Santa María's mission to Mexico was a failure at first, but after the fall of Iturbide a treaty was signed with Foreign Minister Lucas Alamán. Liévano Aguirre writes: 'This treaty, signed by Santa María on 19 February 1824, was afterwards repudiated by the Colombian Congress, because Vicepresident Santander, that distinguished statesman, had already signed commercial treaties with the United States and Great Britain, in which he unreservedly granted them *favoured nation status*. Under these circumstances, Colombia could not agree to the system of preferential treatment laid down in the treaty with Alamán, otherwise she would have had to extend similar privileges to the United States and Great Britain.' He adds: 'There is no occasion for surprise, therefore, in the dismay and alarm manifested by the Anglo-Saxon nations, especially the United States, in the face of Bolívar's Hispanoamerican policy, nor their eager support of any scheme to achieve the Balkanisation of what was formerly Spanish America. A political organisation which would divide the huge community of Spanish America into a number of mutually hostile units was the ideal plan for the new imperialists, whose intention was to replace Spain as the metropolis; these imperialists, for the same reasons, supported the native aristocrats in their opposition to the Panamá Congress.'

John Quincy Adams, the North American diplomat, suggested to President Monroe that they should reject the proposal made by England of a joint declaration against the Holy Alliance. The English wanted the declaration to guarantee the ex-Spanish colonies security from attack by an Anglo-Saxon power. Adams insisted that Monroe should make his own declaration, unhampered by the promise which England was endeavouring to extract, with the intention of limiting the power of North America, rather than protecting South America. Thus the Monroe Doctrine appeared in December 1823 in a Message to the Congress, on the pretext of preventing some Russian incursions in the north Pacific: 'The political system of the allied powers is essentially different ... from that of America ... and to the defense of our own, which has been achieved by the loss of so much blood and treasure, and matured by the wisdom of their most enlightened citizens, and under which we have enjoyed unexampled felicity, this whole nation is devoted. We owe it therefore to candour and to the amicable relations existing between the United States and those powers to declare that we should consider any attempt on their part to extend their system to any portion of this hemisphere, as dangerous to our peace and safety.' The real intention of this declaration was to protect North American interests, restraining European ambition. Needless to say, it was not made out of altruism or love of the South American countries. Liévano Aguirre has written on this point: 'For the North American statesmen, the Monroe Doctrine limited itself to announcing the possible intervention of the United States, only in those cases and in those areas of the continent where the North American national interest demanded it. The Secretary of State, Clay, hastened to make this clear, in a note to the North American representative in Mexico, Joel Poinsett: "The United States have not contracted any obligation, nor have they made any promises to the governments of Mexico or South America ... guaranteeing that the North American government will prevent any foreign power attacking the independence or the system of government of these nations ... " (29 March 1826).'

Bolívar thus came up against world powers, in his attempts to integrate South America. Liévano Aguirre continues: 'In Bolívar's thought, the League was a democratic counterpart to the conservative coalition of the Old World; this gave rise to virulent attacks in the press and in the cabinets of Paris, Saint Petersburg and Vienna, and it also led to the English Minister Canning summoning to his office the Colombian representative in London, Sr. Hurtado, to warn him that his Majesty's government did not consider it suitable nor desirable for the new Hispanoamerican Republics to form an alliance based on popular principles, principles which constituted a challenge to the Courts of Europe.'

The North Americans were particularly disturbed, after 1826, by Bolívar's plans for the independence of Cuba and Puerto Rico and the consequent liberation of relatively large numbers of slaves on these islands. There is no doubt that amongst the North American politicians of the day there were many who already had a clear idea of imperialist interests, and realised that Bolívar's efforts constituted a barrier to the effective achievement of their aims. Joel Poinsett in Mexico, Anderson in Bogotá and William Tudor in Lima, though novices, interfered in the internal politics of the countries to which they were accredited, moved, mainly, by anti-British feeling. They formed 'a network of intrigues, the strings of which were manipulated in Washington and in the headquarters of the lodges of the New York rite, intrigues whose aim was to stimulate local feeling and rivalries between the different South American Republics, in order to place obstacles in the way of the formation of the confederations envisaged by Bolívar.'

Unfortunately, many of our politicians fell under the North American spell, and they wandered off the correct path, drawn by a mirage. The facts demonstrate that Bolívar was correct in opposing the presence of the United States at the Panamá Congress. The aim of the Congress, stated as early as 1822 and ratified in the convocation of 1824 was to form 'an assembly of plenipotentiaries from each state, to advise us in times of conflict, to be a means of contact when facing a common danger ... to act as conciliator in our differences'.[50] The instructions given by the North American government to their delegates reveal a completely different aim: 'We reject completely the idea of a body invested with the power to decide disputes between different states, or to decide their conduct in any way.'[51] There was also complete lack of agreement on the question of slavery. It was the fear of seeing this question raised at the Panamá Congress which caused the senators for the southern states to oppose the participation of the United States in the Congress. Colombia, on the other hand, made this one of the six basic points to be decided by the Congress. The United States had previously rejected an agreement drawn up in Bogotá in 1824 against the slave traffic, by Chancellor Gual and the North American representative in Colombia, Richard C. Anderson. It appears that Anderson proposed the agreement on his own initiative, without the consent of his superiors.

The convocation of the Panamá Congress did not meet with an enthusiastic response, despite Bolívar's care in choosing a site in the remote north of Colombia, while he himself was far away in the south. The government of Argentina first of all adopted a confusing and ambiguous attitude, then revealed the extraordinary reasons for her refusal to attend: 'We have shown that the idea of establishing a supreme authority to regulate the most important issues between the different states of the New World is dangerous from every point of view, and it would not be surprising if it should prove to be the seed-bed of destructive wars amongst peoples who have such need of tranquility and peace ... We cannot deny, that there are no doubt points of common interest which should be regulated by a general treaty, to be signed by plenipotantiaries of all the states ... Yet even this, which in other circumstances might seem highly desirable, under present conditions is dangerous ... The influence exerted in the discussions by the Republic of Colombia, or, if she does not exert it, the power given to her to exert it by the present circumstances, would inspire envy and cause even the most rational solutions to be regarded with suspicion.'[52] O'Higgins had been overthrown in Chile. The government which succeeded him, for flimsy reasons, identified with Argentina and declined to send delegates to the Congress. In the case of Peru, Bolívar wanted the Peruvians themselves to assume full responsibility for their external policy, in line with his feeling that nations should come voluntarily to the Congress. As soon as Bolívar stepped back, the Peruvians changed the offers of collaboration which had originally been made by their agent, Vidaurre, and adopted the suspicious attitude of the majority of states. England announced that her representative would take no part in the discussions, and ratified her neutrality in the conflict between South America and Spain. The Emperor of Brazil also emphasized his neutrality on this question.

For all these reasons, the work of the Congress was obviously limited. The treaty of Perpetual Union, League and Confederation signed in Panamá on 15 July 1826, between the Republics of Colombia, Central America, Peru and the United States of Mexico was a weak shadow of Bolívar's aspirations. In the attempt to reconcile divergent views, his ideas had been watered down. For example, his request for the extradition of political criminals was rejected. Even before receiving the news which would confirm his disappointment with the Congress, Bolívar had declared with melancholy realism: 'The Panamá Congress, an institution which would be admirable if it were more effective, is in fact like the Greek madman who tried to direct the ships, seated on rock. Its power is but a shadow, its decrees, advisory, no more.'[53] Hurrying back to Venezuela to deal with the separatist movement led by Páez and Santander, Bolívar met in Guayaquil the Peruvian plenipotentiary Vidaurre, who was returning to Lima from Panamá. Bolívar read the agreements signed, and his disappointment knew no limits. He tried to detain Vidaurre in Guayaquil, to delay the arrival of the documents in Lima, and wrote immediately to Briceño Méndez: 'I have read here the treaties signed in Panamá, and will give you my honest opinion. The agreement on troop contingents, especially on the manner, occasions and quantities in which they should be brought into play, is ineffective and useless ... To say that a serious invasion must be one that involves more than 5,000 men, and to make this a condition of help, is to condemn certain states to occupation ... Moving the assembly to Mexico will bring it under the immediate influence of that power, which is already too dominant, and also under the United States. These and many other reasons, which I shall explain to you personally, oblige me to request that the treaties should not be ratified until I arrive in Bogotá, and can examine them closely with you and others. The Treaty of Union, League and Confederation contains articles whose acceptance would complicate the execution of certain plans which I have made and which I consider useful and of considerable importance. May I therefore insist that the treaties should not be ratified until I arrive. I have told General Santander the same. Please repeat it to him.'

So many failures would have made a lesser man desist from his effort. Bolívar promptly turned to an idea which might prove more feasible, the Confederation of the Andes, involving Colombia, Peru and Bolivia. This was unsuccessful also, but still Bolívar was not persuaded that all hope was lost. Yet the subsequent history of South America has been a story of disintegration. While Colombia was splitting into its component parts, Central America was dividing into five separate Republics. In Venezuela and New Granada, the history of the nineteenth century is the story of disintegration under the slogan of federalism. In 1860, the states of Cauca, Bolívar and Santander declared their separation from the Confederation of New Granada, and formed the States of New Granada. Curiously, it was around this time that ex-President Mosquera almost reached an agreement with the Venezuelan demagogue Guzmán, concerning a possible reconstruction of Gran Colombia. Mosquera's friendship enabled Guzmán to present a proposal to the New Granada Congress. The Colombian Constitution of 1863 contained an article charging the Executive to 'initiate negotiations with the existing governments in Venezuela and Ecuador, with a view to the union of the three areas in one nation'. The idea went no further.

The prevalence of nationalism over the ideal of integration had as its obvious corollary wars between nations. From 1825–28, there was the war between Brazil and the River Plate, from which Uruguay emerged as an independent nation. Less than ten years later, Rosas initiated a long struggle with this recently born state, in an attempt to annexe it. The struggle had two phases: 1836–38 and 1844–52. General Santa Cruz formed the Peruvian-Bolivian Confederation in 1835 by force of arms. In 1836, Chile initiated the war which was to end in 1839 with the destruction of the Confederation. Haiti and the Dominican Republic fought frontier wars between 1844 and 1856. There was the war between the United States and Mexico over the annexation of Texas,

1846–48. In 1864–70, the most dreadful of the inter-American wars, Brazil, Uruguay and Argentina against Paraguay, in which 800,000 died. The war between Chile and Peru and Bolivia broke out again from 1878–83. There were frequent outbreaks of war amongst the Central American states. The Chaco War, 1928–38, bled Paraguay and Bolivia dry.

Several European countries have taken advantage of the split in Latin America to rob and attack our continent with impunity. France intervened in Mexico, placing Maximilian on the throne, 1861–67. They had previously intervened twice in the River Plate, in 1838–41 and 1845–47, and had entered the Mexican port of Veracruz. Spain annexed Santo Domingo in 1861–65 and intervened also in Peru, 1863–67. A number of powers hoped to swallow large chunks of Brazilian territory. England occupied the Falkland Islands in 1833, and also Belize in Central America, and claimed part of Guayana. This country's coasts were attacked at the beginning of the twentieth century by Dutch, French, English and Italian ships. The United States expanded at the expense of Mexico, occupied Cuba, established themselves in Puerto Rico and intervened in Nicaragua, Haiti, the Dominican Republic and Panamá. Roosevelt is not remembered with gratitude by the people of Latin America. From the imbalance between the Latin American states and these powers, it is clear that Bolívar was right, and that is was only by alliance that the South American states could oppose attacks by stronger powers. When England appropriated one sixth of the territory of Venezuela, that country was just emerging from the stage of internal struggle. The British Empire at the time embraced one fifth of the surface of the globe and one quarter of its inhabitants. These attacks, interventions and robberies have sown the seeds of hatred and suspicion. Foreign powers, with their superior technology, have come to exploit our country, using corruption to secure the services of unscrupulous men and financing doubtful enterprises in order to control the men in power.

If we turn to the field of education and culture, we find that Bolívar's efforts here suffered the same collapse after his death as his efforts in the political and economic spheres. In the generation of the revolution, there were men who really attempted to establish the basis of a new moral order. José Rafael Revenga, while in London on behalf of the new Republic, was unjustly imprisoned and then later paid a sum of money for damages. This money he used to buy books and educational material for Colombian schools. Manuel Palacio Fajardo paid out of his own pocket expenses incurred in travelling and living abroad as Colombian representative to several foreign governments. He lived so austerely that the French authorities began to doubt his diplomatic status 'considering the slender means placed at his disposition by his country'.[54] There are other revealing instances of scrupulosity on the part of this generation of politicans and diplomats. General Pedro Briceño Méndez, and Dr. Pedro Gual, made applications to the Congress 'whereby they solicited the necessary previous consent, to accept the snuff-boxes presented to them in the name of his Britannic Majesty by his commercial representative'.[55] One of the outstanding figures of the period was Andrés Bello, who with his pen did more for the liberation of America than many generals. His contribution was especially great in the field of law, where he drew up his *Derecho de Gentes* and his *Código Civil*. The first represented twenty years' work, and was an important manual of diplomacy for the preservation of peace in Latin America. His *Código Civil* was the fruit of thirty years' study and is still in use in Chile, as well as serving as a model for Colombia, Ecuador, Uruguay and Nicaragua and having some influence in Brazil, Argentina and Venezuela. His *Gramática* dealt with one of the most important unifying elements in our continent: the language. It was intended to be used specifically by Latin Americans, and while it recognises that language is a living and dynamic instrument, it also stresses the need to preserve a language from disintegration. Bello was effectively in charge of Chilean external policy from 1832, and had the opportunity to contribute to a policy of continental unity based on legality. He also contributed to the humanisation of war conventions, anticipating in many instances the provisions of the Paris Congress in 1856. Sucre was another of Bolívar's companions who has left behind him a reputation for honesty and integrity. Unfortunately, after Bolívar's death, these qualities disappeared from public life.

The *caudillo* was opposed to education and culture, which he considered incompatible with the values of the *macho*. Páez's diagnosis of 1825 is highly revealing: 'This country needs something different, something to establish order, give proper consideration to those who deserve it and silence the tricksters.'[55a] The last phrase referred to restricting freedom of expression, silencing criticism. According to Gil Fortoul, Páez's reconciliation with the 'doctors' and 'lawyers' only came about with their submission to his will. Other tyrants continued this tradition of hostility to the intelligentsia. Freedom of thought and expression were explicitly guaranteed in all the Constitutions, but were in fact abolished by the majority of the autocratic régimes. There were always journalists and students in the jails, and critics of the régimes were forced into exile. The press suffered censorship and pressures of every kind, as well as the problems caused by the tyrants' refusal to solve or alleviate widespread illiteracy. Universities and other centres of higher education also suffered. After Bolívar's death, the University of Caracas had to struggle to ensure that his provisions for the University were respected, partially at least, by Páez. A great deal was stolen from the property set aside by Bolívar for the future of the institution. For example, the *hacienda* Chuao, which had been intended for the University, was rented out instead to Páez, and finally became the property of Guzmán Blanco. There were constant attacks on the dignity and even the very existence of the institution during the régimes of Joaquín Crespo, Cipriano Castro, the Monagas and Falcón. Juan Vicente Gómez surpassed them all by closing the University for ten years, 1912–22.

Corruption in public life became the norm. Members of governments were able to sell their country, more or less with impunity. Foreign interests never experienced difficulties in finding front men willing to negotiate contracts highly damaging to the national interest. Political life became cruel and bloody, with whole families wiped out in acts of reprisal. Thousands of inhabitants of Táchira, for example, were forced to flee from the cruelty of Gómez. The towns of Pregonero and Queniquea were left completely devastated in 1921. Eustequio Gómez, provincial governor, gave instructions to his henchmen to 'burn, kill and rob', to break down all resistance and impose his rule.[56] Cecilia Pimentel's writing gives an exact and horrifying picture of conditions in Gómez's jails and the atmosphere of his rule of terror.[57] A large number of Latin American novels, combining exact documentary realism with artistic skill, have testified to the horror of these régimes. In general, the tyrants profited by their period in power to accumulate immense fortunes by illicit means. Páez, for example, who in 1809 had nothing, left an immense fortune which is detailed in his will of 1865. Guzmán proudly boasted of his fortune: in 1879, in the Bank of London alone, he had 10,000,000 *pesos*, and he owned an immense number of houses in Caracas. Juan Vicente Gómez owned thousands of properties; in his will the sum of real estate was worth more than 200,000,000 *bolívares*. This corruption had in fact already begun during Bolívar's lifetime, as Revenga took the trouble to point out: 'Some offices have been turned into commercial premises, such is the shameful traffic in bills and notes, and no creditor goes there but is overwhelmed by the commission requested from him for securing payment.'[58] The same corruption was evident in relation to army pay, for pensions were paid in many cases to individuals who had no connection with the army, or who had only taken up the sword to protect their property. Fiscal controls were almost non-existent and certainly ineffective. The officials were corrupt, and attempted merely to give an appearance of legality to their machinations, and avoid detection. Revenga, in his report, while not mentioning names, gives concrete details where possible: 'It is not unusual to see an official staking up to 30 or 40 ounces of gold on one hand of cards; some of them have retired prosperously after only a few months; and there are minor officials who have entered the service empty-handed and accumulated more than 50,000 *pesos* in less than a year.'

Voting became a farce in the years following Bolivar's death. Coups were frequent, and the role of the people limited to the acceptance of the fait accompli. Tyrants had themselves elected or re-elected at will, and sometimes governed through puppets. Figures were manipulated in the elections, the most crude kind of pressures were applied to voters who turned up at the booths, and the acclamation of the crowd became the most popular piece in the repertory of political theatre. Naturally, in these circumstances, intellectual life stagnated. Latin America derived her cultural life from Europe, a prey to pessimistic and decadent currents, such as positivism and determinism, which had originated in very different societies. Science and technology were non-existent. These circumstances made our countries open to foreign penetration, which acted in its own interest, not in ours.

In all this, there was no sign of gratitude towards Bolívar, no recognition of his contribution to the dignifying of Latin America. In February 1831, the Governor of Maracaibo wrote to the Minister of the Interior under Páez: 'Last night, the English captain Riton arrived in this city in the corvette Rosa, from the island of Jamaica, which he left on the 16th of the current month. He brings news of the confirmation of the death of General Bolívar, in the town of Soledad, in the province of Cartagena: of which occurrence there can no longer be any doubt, since all the messages and reports are unanimous. An event of such importance, and which must necessarily bring great benefit to the cause of liberty and the good of the people, is one which I hasten to communicate to the government through you. I am sending a special messenger for this sole purpose. Bolívar, the evil genius, the torch of discord ... the oppressor of his people, has ceased to exist and to promote evils which always fell upon the shoulders of his countrymen. His death, which under other circumstances, in the period of errors, might have caused grief and sorrow to the people of Colombia, must today undoubtedly be the occasion of great joy, for it is a sign of peace and reconciliation for all. What a fateful outcome for his followers, and what a lesson in the eyes of the world, which must see the protection given to us from on high in the shape of this event. I share your joy in this announcement, and offer my esteem and respect. I remain, Sir, your obedient servant, Juan Antonio Gómez.' Joaquín Gabaldón Márquez makes the following comment: 'We might have expected ... to find at least one line in this letter expressing some noble sentiment in relation to the recent death. But no. When we begin to read the words "His death, which in no other circumstances ... ", we expect a last minute recognition of the Liberator. But no. Grief or sorrow on the part of the Colombians would only have been possible in the "period of errors".'59

168

Bolívar's reputation has suffered at the hands of unscrupulous historians, who have exerted themselves to present him as a precursor of the tyrants. His intellectual gifts have been denigrated by cunning reference to his 'vast' range of thought, with the suggestion that he discussed all sorts of subjects but was master of none; sentences have been quoted out of context, to enlist Bolívar on the side of the most disparate philosophies. Where his reputation has not been actively damaged, he has been relegated to the museum, to adorn empty, vulgar and rhetorical speeches. Yet America is ready to receive Bolívar's message unadulterated. The foremost intellectual figures of America have always recognised his importance, Rodó, Martí and Sarmiento paid tribute to his powers, as did the great Spaniard Miguel de Unamuno. Two of Latin America's greatest writers, Pablo Neruda and Miguel Angel Asturias, have immortalised Bolívar's memory:

Everything we have comes from your extinguished life,
your inheritance was rivers, plains, bell towers,
your inheritance is our daily bread, father ...
Captain, combattant, wherever a mouth
calls out for liberty, wherever an ear listens,
wherever a red soldier wounds a brown head,
wherever a laurel of books blossoms, wherever a new
flag is adorned with the blood of our noble dawn,
Bolívar, captain, your face is seen ...
Liberator, a world of peace was born in your arms.
peace, bread, wheat were born from your blood;
from our young blood, which came from your blood,
will grow peace, bread and wheat for the world we will make.[60]

I believe in Liberty, the Mother of America,
creator of pleasant seas on earth,
and in Bolívar, her son, our Lord,
who was born in Venezuela, suffered
under Spanish power, was resisted,
died on Chimborazo,
and descended with the light of the world into hell,
he rose again to the sound of Colombia,
he touched the Eternal with his hands
and is standing on the right hand of God.
Do not judge us, Bolívar, until the last day,
for we believe in the communion of men
who take communion with the people, that only the people
can free mankind, we proclaim

war to the death and without quarter on tyrants,
we believe in the resurrection of heroes
and the enduring life of those who like You,
Liberator, do not die, but close their eyes and continue to watch.[61]

Chapter V References

(1) This quotation and those following occur in *Obras completas* in the following order: II, 1275; I, 845; II, 959, 233; I, 1440.

(2) Preface to *El Libertador y la Constitución de Angostura de 1819*, p.27.

(3) *Obras completas*, I, 566.

(4) *Mérida y la Revolución de 1826 o 'La Cosiata'* (Mérida, 1963).

(5) *Razones socioeconómicas de la conspiración de setiembre contra el Libertador* (Caracas, 1968), pp.33–36.

(6) *Bolívar*, p.347.

(7) Amongst many pieces of evidence, see: To Briceño Méndez, November 1828. 'Concerning the convening of the national representative body, which I offered in my organic decree, and which it seems did not find favour with the majority, so tired are they of congresses, the Council of State is at work at this moment to determine how and when it should be convened: and though I wished to have the electoral regulations drawn up, the Council of State did not approve this measure.' To General Urdaneta, November 1829: 'With reference to the negotiations undertaken with the French and English governments, I feel we have already become too deeply involved and the situation is dangerous ... We should not, then, take any other steps, but leave the Congress to do its duty, as it thinks best. To do otherwise is to usurp its functions and compromise ourselves excessively.' To General Pedro Alcántara Herrán: 'I have ordered that the War Ministry be offered to you again and suggested that Cuervo be given a different post by the Council. You will hear if they accept this.' To Estanislao Vergara: 'My final decision is that the Council must do or undo whatever it thinks best ... All this and whatever else turns up must be decided by the Council, to whom I refer everything, absolutely everything, for I am resolved to give no more orders.' *Obras completas*, II, 506, 825–829.

(8) This quotation and those following occur in *Obras completas* in the following order: II, 915; I, 1324; II, 959, 1141.

(8a) *Obras completas*, I, 560.

(9) *Iberoamérica. Su evolución política, socioeconómica, cultural e internacional* (New York, 1954), p.197.

(10) This quotation and those following occur in *Obras completas* in the following order: II, 933, 684, 733.

(11) *Materiales para el estudio de la cuestión agraria*, p.264.

(12) This quotation and those following occur in O'Leary, *Memorias*, XVIII, 393–395.

(13) This quotation and those following occur in *Materiales para el estudio de la cuestion agraria* in the following order: pp.316, 283, 284, 309.

(14) Blanco & Azpurúa, XII, 135–137.

(15) *Materiales para el estudio de la cuestión agraria*, p.536.

(16) C. Felice Cardot, *Venezolanos de ayer y de hoy* (Caracas, 1971), p.132.

(17) Perú de Lacroix, p.241.

(18) *El Universal*, Caracas, Suplemento 'Estampas', No. 731, 8 de octubre de 1967.

(19) For Bolívar's will see: *Obras completas*, II, 987. For Santander's: *Archivo del General F. de P. Santander*, (24 vols. Bogotá, 1913–32), XXIV, pp.347ff.

(20) *Razones socioeconómicas de la conspiración de setiembre contra el Libertador*, p.9.

(21) *Obras completas*, II, 64, 116.

(22) R. Betancourt, *Venezuela: política y petróleo* (Mexico-Buenos Aires, 1956), p.54.

(23) Information given to the journalist Clarence Horn by the managers of the firms. *Fortune*, New York, March 1939.

(24) *Correo del Orinoco*, Angostura, No. 51, 5 de febrero de 1820 (Paris, 1939).

(25) R. Cortázar & L. A. Cuervo, *Congreso de Angostura. Libro de actas* (Bogotá, 1921), pp.21, 102, 120, 163, 220.

(26) This quotation and those following occur in *Correo del Orinoco*, No. 51.

(27) *Obras completas*, I, 576.

(28) *Cuerpo de Leyes de la República de Colombia, 1821–27.* (Caracas, 1961), p.31.

(28a) *Obras completas*, I, 444.

(29) Santander, *Archivo*, IV, 245.

(30) *Documentos referentes a la creación de Bolivia*, II, 346.

(31) This quotation and those following occur in *Obras completas* in the following order: I, 1291, 1076; II, 957.

(32) Perú de Lacroix, p.310.

(33) This quotation and those following occur in I. Liévano Aguirre, *Bolívar* (Bogotá, 1950), pp.298–325.

(34) Blanco & Azpurúa, VI, 648.

(35) *Gazeta de Venezuela*, Caracas, Ano X, No. 485, 3 de mayo de 1840.

(36) Blanco & Azpurúa, XIV, 174–179.

(37) Páez, *Autobiografía*, II, 56.

(38) Blanco and Azpurúa provide a summary of the arguments presented by New Granada: 'Look at the immense military salaries, which at the moment are paid almost entirely out of our depleted resources. More than two-thirds of the money goes to Venezuelans ... Look at the Prefectures ... the provincial governorships ... army command ... official bodies: in New Granada, nearly all the posts are occupied by Venezuelans, yet there are no citizens of New Granada employed in Venezuela, in fact Páez has been very careful to send all of them back to this country. Only miserly sums of money have come into New Granada from Venezuela, since the time of the union, whereas large sums have been transferred from the coffers of New Granada to help Venezuela, quite apart from the fact that New Granada meets almost the entire cost of central government. For nearly all the officials and employees of the

central government come to have their salaries made up in Bogotá, out of New Granada's money, though it would never occur to one of our citizens to go and ask for his pay in Venezuela ... If we ignore the prestige and moral force of belonging to the union, the Republic of New Granada would be happier, freer and richer if separate from Venezuela and governed by her own sons. Then Venezuelan domination of all the higher civilian and military posts would cease, for it has certainly not ... made for the happiness of the people of New Granada.' *Documentos para la historia de la vida pública del Libertador*, XIV, 173.

(39)   *Autobiografía*, II, 16.

(39a)   There is a revealing letter from his private secretary, Antonio Carmona, to Rufino González: 'Valencia, 17 November 1829. Dear Rufino: I cannot write a long letter, though I have a great deal to tell you, for we do not have time even to scratch our head in this office, working day and night, often into the small hours, to despatch the mail and the envoys going out to Oriente, Apure, Occidente, Maracaibo and everywhere else: Don Carlos and the General want them all to carry written copies from here of the declaration to be made in the Town Councils, the village assemblies and here, there and everywhere: for the records have to show ... that there was not a single corner of the Republic that did not want three things, viz. rejection of the union with New Granada, The General for Head of State, down with don Simón. Everyone is to demand this, otherwise he is an enemy and ... Enrique Domínguez has been entrusted with propaganda in the valleys ... He is carrying the declarations in his belt ... he should be passing through Victoria. If he finds there that he has to go to Caracas before carrying on to Calabozo, it will only be for a short visit, which you should use to consult him: he has all the instructions and will tell you what you have to do. Obey him as if he were the General himself, or don Carlos or the Doctor. If he does not go to Caracas, see the letters to Iribarren and Alfonso: then set to work. *Separation for Venezuela. Repudiation of Bolívar. Páez for leader.* Just follow these lines. No time to write more for the present. Your dearest friend, A.C. November 24: Domínguez is not now going to Caracas. He has to hurry to Calabozo and Apure, so he has gone via Güigüe.' Blanco and Azpurúa, *Documentos para la historia de la vida pública del Libertador*, XIII, 707.

Francisco A. Labastida has shown how the 'unanimous' opinion in favour of Páez was obtained: quite unconsciously, he wrote to Páez on February 1830 concerning the methods used by the military head of the Escuque region: 'Even the Popular Assemblies he made the plaything of his insolence, for he wanted the citizens to sign a copy, not of what they had really discussed and decided in their meetings, but of papers which he had drawn up in his own house, and he threatened those who refused to obey. Your Excellency, can this really be called liberty? Can a people really be free which, when it assembles together, finds in the main square a cavalry squadron lined up with a company of riflemen? If the papers Sr. Segarra wanted us to sign had dealt with real complaints ... his insistence would have been acceptable: but to ask us to sign a string of insults and abuse concerning General Bolívar did not seem acceptable, for we feel we can repudiate his authority and still treat him with courtesy.' A. Mijares, 'La evolución política de Venezuela,' *Venezuela Independiente* (Caracas, 1962), p.81.

(40) From Barinas, the Governor informed the Secretary of State in the Ministry of the Interior, on 2 March 1830: 'Today the General Commander sent me the order from the ministry dated 21 of last month, concerning the requirement that the mail from Bogotá should come to this General Headquarters without anyone being allowed to open it ... ' *Archivo General de la Nación*, Caracas, Gobierno de la República, Secretaría del Interior y Justicia, Sección General, Vol. V, Folio 269.

(41) O'Leary, *Memorias*, XXII, 514.

(42) This quotation and those following occur in *Obras completas* in the following order: I, 1075–76; II, 1138; I, 1108, 1211.

(42a) Restelli, Ernesto, *La gestión diplomática del General de Alvear en el Alto Perú* (Buenos Aires, 1927), p.126.

(43) *Bolivarismo y Monroísmo*, p.84.

(44) This quotation and those following occur in *Obras completas* in the following order: I, 1265–68, 791.

(45) O'Leary, *Memorias*, XXIV, 283.

(46) This quotation and those following occur in *Obras completas* in the following order: II, 742; I, 1421, 1190.

(47) This quotation and those following occur in O'Leary *Memorias*, III, 239, 210, 230.

(48) *Bolívar, pintado por sí mismo* (Caracas, 1959), pp.217–220.

(49) This quotation and those following in *Bolivarismo y Monroísmo* in the following order: pp.11, 25, 32, 40, 53, 56.

(50) Bolívar, *Obras completas*, I, 1012.

(51) J. M. Yepes, *Del Congreso de Panamá a la Conferencia de Caracas* (Caracas, 1955), I, 62.

(52) P. A. Zubieta, *Congresos de Panamá y Tacubaya* (Bogotá, 1912), p.31.

(53) *Obras completas*, I, 1407, 1431.

(54) Parra Pérez, *Una misión diplomática venezolana ante Napoleón en 1813*, p.73.

(55) *Codificación Nacional de todas las leyes de Colombia* (Bogotá, 1925), III, 330.

(55a) Bolívar, *Obras completas*, I, 1287.

(56) *Boletín del Archivo Histórico de Miraflores*, Caracas, No. 14, p.209.

(57) *Bajo la tiranía, 1919–35* (Caracas, 1970).

(58) Blanco and Azpurúa, XI, 285.

(59) *El Bolívar de Madariaga y otros Bolívares* (Caracas, 1960), p.171.

(60) Literal version by the translator of Pablo Neruda, 'Un canto para Bolívar,' Tercera Residencia, *Obras completas* (Buenos Aires, 1956), p.262.

(61) Literal version by the translator of Miguel Angel Asturias, 'Credo,' *Obras completas* (Madrid, 1968).

VI Present and future

A re-appraisal of the personality and historical significance of Simón Bolívar is now due, to combat false or distorted versions of the truth, whether of the type which confine Bolívar to the museum by stressing his importance in the past, or the more cynical use of his example by tyrants and despots. More recently, revolutionary attitudes, based on a copy of foreign models rather than a genuinely Latin American experience, have also sought justification in Bolívar's career, emphasising those aspects of his thought or activity which suit their case, though their concentration on material advance to the neglect of the spirit and of freedom could not be further from Bolívar's ideals. After many years of being monopolised by conservative thinkers, Bolívar has now become the hero of the far left. Neither group has been helpful in promoting the ideology of the real Bolívar. Another powerful movement, with vast financial resources, which has enlisted the help of Bolívar's reputation is the Pan-American movement, again pursuing objectives far removed from those of Bolívar. Useful as it is to compare situations removed from each other in time and space, one must beware of merely engendering confusion by failing to make necessary distinctions. While the Pan-American movement, directed from Washington, has undoubtedly had certain positive results, other consequences have arguably been unfortunate. Whatever one's analysis of its successes and errors, or the balance between altruism and imperialist greed, in this movement, the objective historian must always demonstrate that its aims were not those of Bolívar.

Thanks to the initiative of the Secretary of State, James G. Blaine, the first Inter-American Conference was held in Washington in 1889–90. It was inconceivable that this Conference should follow Bolívar's ideals, for his interests did not coincide with those of the United States, whose ambition it was to fill the vacancy left by Spain. The United States policy was defined from the beginning of the nineteenth century: the classic method of 'divide and conquer' was at the centre of their diplomatic aims. The task was not a difficult one, as we have seen, for the national oligarchies in each country refused to participate in the integration Bolívar counselled, preferring to collaborate with the aims of their neighbour to the north. Naturally, the divergence between Bolívar's ideals and those of the United States diplomats was not evident in the speech with which Blaine closed the deliberations of the Conference, for it was confined to generalisations concerning peace and prosperity with which no reasonable man could quarrel. It is interesting to note, however, that Blaine did recognise the differences between the United States and the Republics of South America, for he referred to 'the dedication ... *of two great continents* to peace and that prosperity which can only be founded on peace'. Naturally, the Conference achieved little, since apart from agreements on trade and communications, which were basically serving the ends of United States expansion, the main emphasis fell on a negative point — the avoidance of armed conflict: 'We maintain that this new Magna Carta which has abolished war, replacing it with arbitration between the American Republics, is the first and most important fruit of the Inter-American Conference.' The Conference resulted in the creation of the Commercial Office of the American Republics, which in 1910 adopted the less pragmatic title of Pan-American Union. The ideology of this organism, published in its propaganda leaflets, is crystal clear to anyone who reads these pamphlets with an unbiased eye. There was an attempt to relate its activities to those of Bolívar: 'Although the Panamá Congress failed to achieve Bolívar's objectives, it constituted a first step in the direction of continental unity and the creation of the Inter-American System.'[1] In fact the objectives of the system, far from encouraging the unity of the American states on a basis of equity and justice, were clearly vulgar and utilitarian: certain creations, such as the Inter-American Railway and the Pan-American Highway, while relatively beneficial to all concerned, were chiefly so to the imperial power. An exception should be made for the Pan-American Sanitation Office, established in 1902 to coordinate the struggle against yellow fever and malaria, and whose work was clearly humane. It is the oldest established international entity in the world, and its achievements are to be praised.

Between 1890 and 1954, there were ten great conferences of American governments, at which no name was evoked more frequently than that of Bolívar. Yet in these ten encounters, the divided nations of South America, partly because of external pressure and partly because of factors for which they themselves were responsible, failed to speak with a united voice. In the history of Pan-Americanism, the United States have always been the dominating force, and at times they have not even tempered their brusque Anglo-Saxon approach to spare their neighbours' humiliation. Any 'aid' which has come to the countries of South America from the well-stocked coffers of the United States has exacted its price of submission and political support. The Good Neighbour Policy of Franklin D. Roosevelt and Kennedy's Alliance for Progress were partial and short-lived attempts to repair the damage. Yet the mechanisms of exploitation have not diminished, on the contrary, they have increased. The penetration of North American capital into South America has not ceased for a single moment. The alienation produced by this situation is a tangible fact. What is required is a true policy of cooperation, free from the humiliating connotations of 'aid'. The Organisation of American States, restructured and given this title in 1948, could be the point of contact between the states of North America and those of the centre and south. No-one would wish to deny that our relative geographical situation invites cooperation, but it must be based on justice and mutual interest.

At the same time, Latin America must reach out towards the other nations of the earth — again a lesson that we might have learned from Bolívar. He argued in 1814: 'The ambition of the European nations carries the yoke of slavery to every part of the globe: these parts of the globe should try to develop a balance between themselves and Europe, to destroy the latter's domination. I call this world-balance, and it should enter into the calculations of American policy.'[2] Substitute for 'European nations' in the first sentence the words 'imperialist powers of any kind' and the lesson is still valid today for the countries of the Third World.

The American states have at their disposal today numerous organisms and bodies which, with the necessary alterations, could serve the ends indicated by Bolívar. The General Assembly and the Permanent Council of the Organisation of American States, together with the Meeting of Consultation of Ministers of Foreign Affairs could organise contacts between the two continents, if both were internally united. There are the Inter-American Economic and Social Council and the Inter-American Council for Education, Science and Culture. For more particular tasks there are such bodies as the Inter-American Juridical Committee, the Inter-American Commission on Human Rights, the Pan-American Health Organisation, the Inter-American Commission of Women, the Inter-American Children's Institute, the Special Consultative Committee on Security, the Inter-American Indian Institute, the Pan-American Institute of History and Geography, the Inter-American Institute of Agricultural Sciences, the Inter-American Statistical Institute, the Inter-American Nuclear Energy Commission and the Inter-American Defence Board.

Several useful initiatives have been taken. The treaties signed between the Bolivarian countries in 1911, concerning copyright and equivalance of academic titles and the 'Andrés Bello' cultural Agreement of 1970, as well as numerous agreements on grants for study, exchange of books, scientific information, artists, teachers and so on are useful measures which could be extended. Associations of workers, students, teachers and other professionals, and the existence of entities such as the Union of Latin American Universities, the Latin American Social Sciences Faculty and the Latin American Social Sciences Research Council, all tend towards the integration which will be our strength. The Latin American Free Trade Association, the Andean Group, the Central American Common Market, the plans for the Caribbean area and the Economic Commission for Latin America represent a step forward for small countries with scarce resources, in the struggle for development.

To achieve development without the sacrifice of freedom and equality is the greatest challenge facing our countries in this century. It is not an impossible task, for our continent has vast natural resources. The solution of the caudillo or dictator is now superannuated, and the whole individualist concept must give way to more collective forms of organisation. Militarism is an inevitable corollary of underdevelopment, which must be overcome through what is now called *conscientización* (awakening the consciousness of the need for social change) amongst the military, making of it the organ responsible for ensuring the stability and order required by a constitutional, democratic and representative régime. We must have an acceptable process for the election of our rulers, and a method for replacing them in an atmosphere of peace and tranquility. The working class, through its trade union organisations, must assume its responsibilities. Political parties, too, must play their part in the democratic process, so that the needs of the majority and the minority, the party in power and the opposition, are met. Capital must function within a framework of equity, limiting its desires in the interests of the creation of an atmosphere of liberty conducive to development. As Bolívar told Santander, referring to the opponents of his anti-slavery measures: 'I think it would be useful to educate these men, blinded by their own interest, though their true interest should show them the way ... I think they should be told ... what they ought to know.'[3]

All the structures which in the last hundred years have permitted different forms of neo-colonialism in South America must be changed. The goal of integration should be publicised and discussed in the schools and in the media. In the teaching of history, less emphasis should be placed on petty nationalism. It is of no use breaking the present structure of oppression if these are to be replaced by new forms of colonialism. Our journalists, novelists, poets, playwrights, musicians and painters can help to destroy the old mentality and prepare the development of the new. We have been waiting for the revolution in South America for 150 years, and can wait no longer. Within a democratic system we can, and must, advance towards the ideals expressed by Bolívar: justice, freedom, equality, unity and development. It is true that democratic régimes are thin on the ground in Latin America. Those which exist should be strengthened. There are many today who for reasons of their own proclaim the death of democracy, yet as the Universal Declaration of Human Rights shows, democratic values are still cherished by the majority of mankind. This does not apply simply to the exercise of the right to vote. Democracy is in the content of a system, not in the external forms, and it involves not only the sovereignty of the people and the guarantee of civil liberties, but the achievement of justice and equality. It is the only system which contains within it the mechanism for its own correction, and therein lies its principal advantage.

In the present situation, where other continents, too, are struggling to raise other people to the dignity of free men, Latin America has an important and responsible role to play. In this task, she can do no better than be guided by Bolívar, whose thought has been vindicated by history. He did not preach hatred or death, he accepted the use of violence only when it was strictly necessary. He is the true representative of the Latin American spirit.

Chapter VI References

(1) *El sistema interamericano. Su evolución y función actual* (Washington, 1963), pp.2–4.
(2) *Gazeta de Caracas, No. XXX,* 6 de enero de 1814.
(3) *Obras completas,* I, 444.

Select Bibliography

Works cited in the text and in footnotes.

(A fuller bibliography may be found in the Spanish edition: *Bolívar: un continente y un destino* (Caracas, 1972).

América y el Libertador (Publicaciones de la Secretaría General de la X Conferencia Interamericana, Caracas, 1953).

Archivo General de la Nación, Caracas, Gobierno de la República, Secretaría del Interior y Justicia, Sección General, Folio 269.

Asturias, Miguel Angel, 'Credo,' *Obras completas*, (Madrid, 1968).

Bello, Andrés, 'Derecho Internacional II; *Obras completas*, XI (Caracas, 1959).

Bernal Medina, Rafael, *Ruta de Bolívar* (Calí, 1961).

Betancourt, Rómulo, *Venezuela, política y petróleo* (Mexico-Buenos Aires, 1956).

Bierck, Harold A., *Vida pública de don Pedro Gual* (Caracas, 1948).

Biggs, James, *Historia del intento de don Francisco de Miranda para efectuar una revolución en Sur América* (Caracas, 1950).

Blanco, José Félix & Ramón Azpurúa, *Documentos para la historia de la vida pública del Libertador* (14 vols. Caracas, 1875–78).

Blanco Fombona, Rufino, *Bolívar, pintado por sí mismo* (Caracas, 1959).

Boletín del Archivo Histórico de Miraflores Caracas, No. 14.

Bolívar y su época (Publicaciones de la Secretaría General de la X Conferencia Interamericana, 2 vols. Caracas, 1953).

Bolívar, Simón, *Cartas del Libertador*, XII (Caracas, 1959).

— *Decretos del Libertador* (3 vols. Caracas, 1959).

— *Documentos referentes a la creación de Bolivia* (2 vols. Caracas, 1924).

— *Escritos del Libertador* (In process of publication since 1967 by the Sociedad Bolivariana de Venezuela, Caracas).

— *Itinerario documental de Simón Bolívar* (Caracas, 1970).

— *Obras completas* (Compiled with notes by V. Lecuna, with collaboration of E. Barret de Nazaris, 2 vols. Havana, 1947).

Briceño Iragorry, Mario, *Introducción y defensa de nuestra historia* (Caracas, 1952).

Codificación Nacional de todas las leyes de Colombia, III, 1827–28 (Bogotá, 1925).

Constitución Federal de Venezuela, 1811 (Reproducción facsimilar de la edición de 1812, CORPA, Caracas, 1961).

Correo del Orinoco, Angostura, 1818–21 (Academia Nacional de la Historia, Paris, 1939).

Cortázar, Roberto & Luis Augusto Cuervo, *Congreso de Angostura. Libro de actas.* (Bogotá, 1921).

Cuerpo de Leyes de la República de Colombia (Consejo de Desarrollo Científico y Humanístico, Universidad Central de Venezuela, Caracas, 1961).

Díaz Sánchez, Ramón, *El caraqueño* (Caracas, 1970).

Documentos relativos a la insurrección de Juan Francisco de León (Instituto Panamericano de Geografía e Historia, No. 1, Caracas, 1949).

El libertador y la Constitución de Angostura (Publicaciones del Banco Hipotecario de Crédito Urbano, Caracas, 1970).

El sistema interamericano. Su evolución y función actual (Secretaría de la OEA, Washington, 1963).

Encina, Francisco A., *Bolívar y la Independencia de la América Española. La Primera República de Venezuela. Bosquejo psicológico de Bolívar* (Santiago de Chile, 1958).

Febres Cordero, Julio, 'Arcaísmos institucionales e influencias románticas en el Libertador,' *Boletín Histórico*, Fundación John Boulton, Caracas, No. 26, 1971.

Felice Cardot, C., *Mérida y la Revolución de 1826 o 'La Cosiata'* (Mérida, 1963).

— 'Rebeliones, motines y movimientos de masas en el siglo xviii venezolano, 1750–81,' *El movimiento emancipador de Hispanoamérica*, II (Academia Nacional de la Historia, Caracas, 1961).

— *Venezolanos de ayer y de hoy* (Caracas, 1971).

Fortune, New York, March 1939.

Gabaldón Márquez, Joaquín, *El Bolívar de Madariaga y otros Bolívares* (Caracas, 1960).

Galíndez, Jesús de, *Iberoamérica. Su evolución política, socioeconómica, cultural e internacional* (New York, 1954).

Gandía, Enrique de, *Bolívar y la libertad* (Buenos Aires, 1957).

Gazeta de Caracas, No. XXX, 6 de enero de 1814 (Vol. IV, 1813–14 Academia Nacional de la Historia, Paris, 1939).

Gazeta de Venezuela, Caracas, Año X, No. 485, 3 de mayo de 1840.

Gil Fortoul, J., *Historia Constitucional de Venezuela* (3 vols. Caracas, 1942).

Griffin, Charles C., *Los temas sociales y económicos en la época de la Independencia* (Caracas, 1962).

Guerrero, Luis Beltrán, 'Bolívar, historiador del futuro,' *Candideces*, Quinta serie, Caracas, 1967.

Humboldt, Alexander von, *Viaje a las regiones equinocciales del Nuevo*

Continente (5 vols. Caracas, 1941–42).

Larrazábal, Felipe, *Vida de Bolívar* (New York, 1883).

Lecuna, Vicente (ed.) *Cartas de Santander* (3 vols. Caracas, 1942).

— *Catálogo de errores y calumnias en la historia de Bolívar* (2 vols. New York, 1956).

Liévano Aguirre, Indalecio, *Bolívar* (Bogotá, 1950).

— *Bolivarismo y Monroísmo* (Bogotá, 1969).

— *Razones socioeconómicas de la conspiración de setiembre contra el Libertador* (Caracas, 1968).

López, Casto Fulgencio, *Juan Bautista Picornell y la conspiración de Gual y España* (Caracas-Madrid, 1955).

Mancini, Jules, *Bolívar y la emancipación de las colonias españolas* (Paris-Mexico, 1914).

Manning, William R., *The Independence of the Latin American Nations* (2 vols. Oxford University Press, 1925).

Materiales para el estudio de la cuestión agraria en Venezuela (Consejo de Desarrollo Científico y Humanístico, Universidad Central de Venezuela, Caracas, 1964).

Mendoza, Cristóbal L., 'Discurso en el Sesquicentenario de la Batalla de Carabobo,' *Boletín de la Academia Nacional de la Historia*, Caracas, No. 214, abril–junio 1971.

— *Las primeras misiones diplomáticas de Venezuela* (2 vols. Caracas, 1962).

— Preface to *Escritos del Libertador VIII.*

Mijares, Augusto, *El Libertador* (Caracas, 1964).

— 'La evolución política de Venezuela,' *Venezuela Independiente* (Caracas, 1962).

Miranda, Francisco de, *Archivo* (15 vols. Caracas, 1929–38).

Mitre, Bartolomé, *Historia de San Martín y la emancipación sudamericana* (4 vols. Buenos Aires, 1957).

Neruda, Pablo, 'Un canto para Bolívar,' Tercera Residencia, *Obras completas* (Buenos Aires, 1956), p.262.

Nucete Sardi, José, *Aventura y tragedia de don Francisco de Miranda* (Venezuela, 1964).

O'Leary, Daniel Florencio, *Memorias* (33 vols. Caracas, 1879–87).

— *Narración* (3 vols. Caracas, 1952).

Oviedo y Baños, José de, *Historia de la conquista y población de la Provincia de Venezuela* (New York, 1940).

Páez, José Antonio, *Autobiografía* (2 vols. Caracas, 1946).

Palacio Fajardo, Manuel, *Bosquejo de la revolución en la América española* (Caracas, 1953).

Parra Pérez, C., *Bayona y la política de Napoleón en América* (Caracas, 1939).

— *Historia de la Primera República de Venezuela* (2 vols. Caracas, 1959).

— *Una misión diplomática venezolana ante Napoleón en 1813* (Caracas, 1953).

Pereyra, Carlos, *Breve historia de América* (Santiago de Chile, 1938).

Pérez Vila, Manuel, *La formación intelectual del Libertador* (Caracas, 1971).

Perú de Lacroix, Luis, *Diario de Bucaramanga* (Caracas, 1935).

Pi Sunyer, C., *El General Juan Robertson, un prócer de la Independencia* (Caracas, 1971).

Pimentel, Cecilia, *Bajo la tiranía, 1919–35.* (Caracas, 1970).

Polanco A., Tomás, Preface to *El Libertador y la Constitución de Angostura de 1819.*

Prieto F., Luis Beltrán, *El magisterio americano de Bolívar* (Caracas, 1968).

Registro Oficial, No. 54, Bogotá, 1829.

Restelli, Ernesto, *La gestión diplomática del General de Alvear en el Alto Perú* (Buenos Aires, 1927).

Rodríguez, Simón, *El libertador del mediodía de América y sus compañeros de armas defendidos por un amigo de la causa social* (Caracas, 1971).

Rodríguez Villa, A., *El teniente general don Pablo Morillo* (2 vols. Madrid, 1920).

Rumazo González, Alfonso, *Bolívar* (Caracas-Madrid, 1955).

Salcedo Bastardo, José Luis, *Visión y revisión de Bolívar* (Buenos Aires, 1966).

Santander, F. de P., *Archivo* (24 vols. Bogotá, 1913–32).

Silva Otero, Aristides, *La diplomacia hispanoamericanista de la Gran Colombia* (Caracas, 1967).

Suárez, Ramón Darío, *Genealogía del Libertador* (Mérida, 1970).

Textos oficiales de la Primera República de Venezuela (2 vols. Biblioteca de la Academia Nacional de la Historia, nos. 1 & 2, Caracas, 1959).

'Transcripción del expediente original de la Real Audiencia de Caracas sobre domicilio tutelar del menor Don Simón de Bolívar, originado por la fuga de éste de la casa de su tutor,' *Boletín de la Academia Nacional de la Historia*, Caracas, No. 149, enero–marzo 1955.

Ugalde, Pedro, 'Presencia y magisterio de Miranda en la revolución chilena,' *Cultura Universitaria*, Universidad Central de Venezuela, Caracas, XVII–XVIII, 1950.

El Universal, Caracas, Suplemento 'Estampas', No. 731, 8 de octubre de 1967.

Verna, Paul, *Pétion y Bolívar* (Caracas, 1969).

Yepes, J. M., *Del Congreso de Panamá a la Conferencia de Caracas* (2 vols. Caracas, 1955).

Zubieta, P. A., *Congresos de Panamá y Tacubaya* (Bogotá, 1912).

Index of names

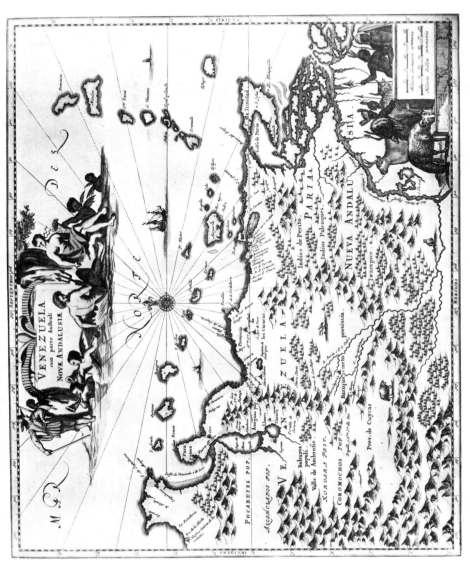

Map 1 : Venezuela

Map 2: Central and South America

MEXICO AND C. AMERICA

SOUTH AMERICA

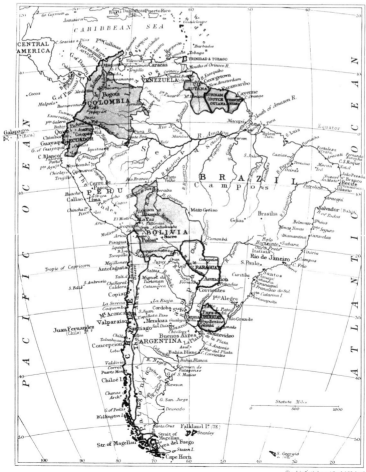